DERICK THOMSON AND THE GAELIC REVIVAL

For Christopher

DERICK THOMSON AND THE GAELIC REVIVAL

PETRA JOHANA PONCAROVÁ

EDINBURGH
University Press

Edinburgh University Press is one of the leading university presses in the UK. We publish academic books and journals in our selected subject areas across the humanities and social sciences, combining cutting-edge scholarship with high editorial and production values to produce academic works of lasting importance. For more information visit our website: edinburghuniversitypress.com

© Petra Johana Poncarová, 2024, 2025

Edinburgh University Press Ltd
13 Infirmary Street
Edinburgh EH1 1LT

First published in hardback by Edinburgh University Press 2024

Typeset in 10/12 ITC New Baskerville by
Cheshire Typesetting Ltd, Cuddington, Cheshire

A CIP record for this book is available from the British Library

ISBN 978 1 3995 0119 4 (hardback)
ISBN 978 1 3995 0120 0 (paperback)
ISBN 978 1 3995 0121 7 (webready PDF)
ISBN 978 1 3995 0122 4 (epub)

The right of Petra Johana Poncarová to be identified as author of this work has been asserted in accordance with the Copyright, Designs and Patents Act 1988 and the Copyright and Related Rights Regulations 2003 (SI No. 2498).

Contents

Position Statement and Acknowledgements		vi
Note		ix
1	Introduction	1
2	Thomson's Thought and Work in Context	16
3	*Gairm*	62
4	Scholarship, Activism and Translations	106
5	Gaelic Revitalisation in Thomson's Poetry and Short Stories	131
6	Thomson's Legacy	171
Bibliography		179
Index		189

Position Statement and Acknowledgements

My involvement with Gaelic started with a general interest in Scotland that led me to modern Scottish Gaelic literature, which I first encountered in the bilingual anthology *Nua-Bhàrdachd Ghàidhlig/Modern Gaelic Poetry* (1976). It was the works of the five poets included that motivated me to learn the language, so that I could access their writing in the original.

As a person brought up in the Czech Republic speaking Czech, my compulsory education featured a great deal of positive discussion of the Czech national revival, which occurred during the late eighteenth and the nineteenth century and connected efforts to revitalise Czech language and create a Czech culture with the endeavour to obtain political emancipation from the Habsburg Empire. This background made me sensitive to and instinctively supportive of other revivalist efforts that are still ongoing. My place of birth in North Bohemia brings with it strong connections to displaced people, their language and the material traces of their existence – the vanished and erased German-speaking neighbours, the connected linguistic and cultural loss, and their imprints in the form of ruined towns and villages overgrown with woods that mark the Sudetenland and its borders. These phenomena likely prepared the ground for my interest in the Clearances, and their literary reflections.

Many of my friends and colleagues are deeply involved in the Gaelic movement, and in my own manner, I have become part of it too. However, as I remain based in Central Europe, I have retained the position of an outsider, which brings about both practical hindrances and a sense of disconnection, but also the advantage of a different perspective and a certain freedom. My account of Derick Thomson, although I have tried to make it balanced, is not and cannot be completely detached, and the decision to undertake this book also had a personal and revivalist motivation, to provide grounds for due appreciation of Thomson as one of the makers of the modern Gaelic world who conceptualised it in such a way that it would be open and welcoming to people with no familial ties to Gaelic Scotland.

This monograph is based on my previous research on Thomson, which has resulted in a number of publications – some appeared in Scotland, some on the Continent, some in English and some in Gaelic – including essays, book chapters, the Scotnote study guide *The Gaelic Poetry of Derick Thomson* and my PhD dissertation on Thomson's political poetry, which

I defended at Charles University in Prague in 2020. All these are listed in the bibliography and, when relevant, I refer to these previously published results in footnotes. My aim was to integrate all these findings into a coherent presentation of Thomson's involvement with the Gaelic revival, and to complement it with completely new perspectives, findings, and arguments. It is my hope that this monograph will contribute to a wider appreciation of Thomson's diverse and inspiring legacy and raise his profile both in Scotland and abroad.

My whole interest in Scottish Gaelic literature probably would not have led to a career, were it not for Martin Procházka, supervisor and dear friend, whose backing and faith in my work made it possible for me to focus on Gaelic literature in Prague and to lay the grounds for Gaelic Studies as a field at Charles University and in the Czech Republic.

Christopher Whyte, whose friendship came as Derick Thomson's precious posthumous gift, shared with me his personal memories of Thomson and critical insight into his works. His introductions put me in touch with a number of people who have helped me in various projects related to Thomson, including Ian MacDonald and Ronald Renton, whose advice, practical assistance and generosity have been of great importance.

For many years, the help and friendship of Murray Pittock has been instrumental in our efforts to promote Scottish studies in Prague, and his resolute support and kind encouragement have been crucial for my own work and development too.

During my stays at the Gaelic college Sabhal Mòr Ostaig, I had the chance to learn about Gaelic language and culture from Meg Bateman, Màiri Sìne Chaimbeul, Iain Urchardan, Cairistìona Primrose and the late Tormod Caimbeul, and I am grateful for their kindness and all that they have shared with me. Cairistìona Cairn and Greg MacThòmais, librarians of Sabhal Mòr Ostaig, provided me with a safe haven for many happy research stays, and their enthusiasm and readiness to help is a blessing. Caoimhín Ó Donnaile, Iain Howieson, Doug Fraser, Iain MacInnes, John Boa and other friends made me feel welcome in Scotland and in different ways helped me on my way towards Gaelic.

Colleagues from the Department of Anglophone Literatures and Cultures have my gratitude for valuable advice when I was preparing the proposal for this book, and also for their friendship and the atmosphere of support and camaraderie: Mirka Horová, Klára Kolinská, Václav Kyllar, James Little, Radvan Markus, Ondřej Pilný, Justin Quinn and Daniela Theinová.

Ronald Black, Michel Byrne, Rob Dunbar, William Gillies, Peter Mackay, Wilson McLeod, Donald Meek and other Gaelic scholars have inspired me by their own work, and I appreciate their generous help, feedback and advice regarding my own enterprises, which motivated me to do better.

The existence of the database *Gairm Air-loidhne* (DASG, University of Glasgow) made finishing this book much easier and helped me to discover new materials. I acknowledge a grateful debt to all members of the team involved in its creation.

Aniela Korzeniowska and Izabela Szymańska, founders and organisers of the bi-annual conference Scotland in Europe, gave me the opportunity to present my first paper on Scottish literature and publish the first essay. At these conferences I had the chance to make the acquaintance of Derrick McClure and the late Margery Palmer McCulloch, whose friendship, support and advice have been formative and precious.

The possibility to be involved in the Scottish Revival Network, led by Scott Lyall and Michael Shaw, helped me to clarify my thoughts and gave me the possibility to connect with colleagues in the field and learn from them.

The staff of Edinburgh University Press have been unfailingly supportive, and I am grateful for their patience and commitment to the book.

The completion of this book would not have been possible without the practical help, emotional support and intellectual companionship of Martin Světlík.

Note

Translations

When quoting from Gaelic documents, the original version is given first and the English translation follows. Unless stated otherwise, all the translations from Gaelic documents are my own. Official translated titles of poems, articles, volumes, etc., are given in round brackets, titles provided by myself in square brackets.

Personal names

For personal names, the Gaelic version of the name is included in round brackets on the first occurrence, to establish the connection, and later the English version is used throughout the text.

Abbreviations

All abbreviations are introduced in the text and at the first mention the full name is given. These are some of the most frequently used:

An Comunn Gaidhealach: ACG
Scottish National Party: SNP
Highlands and Islands Development Board: HIDB

References to *Gairm* editorials

When references are made to editorials from the magazine *Gairm*, they include the number of the issue and the year of publication (*Gairm* 1: 1952). In these cases, footnotes are omitted, as the editorials were usually one page and are thus reliably identified.

Spelling

Since this is not a study in the development of Gaelic orthography, the Gaelic quotations were aligned with the standardised Gaelic spelling, which Thomson was happy to support and adopt when it was introduced, to achieve consistency.

CHAPTER ONE

Introduction

In the essay 'The Role of the Writer in a Minority Culture', published as part of the *Transactions of the Gaelic Society of Inverness* in 1966, Derick Thomson (Ruaraidh MacThòmais) notes that in 'reviving, or renewing, or developing the life of a minority culture' the writer's role is a crucially important one, and sketches what authors can do to contribute to the survival and flourishing of lesser-used languages and minoritised cultures.[1] He stresses that the 'writing in the minority language must not be too inward-looking, too introspective with regard to its own society, as this underlines the sense of isolation in the public', and argues that employing the language for more general purposes has the potential to enhance the prestige of the minority society and increase its competitiveness with the majority.[2] He also claims that 'much can be done to foster writing by providing media for publication and a more widespread interest' in literature, which goal can be accomplished both by societies and organisations and by small groups and even individuals, and emphasises the 'usefulness of encouraging journalism', underlining its twin psychological and propagandist value.[3]

Thomson further proposes that 'in a situation such as the Scottish Gaelic one, it would be most useful to have a reasonably close liaison between the scholar and the writer, if the work of rehabilitation is to go ahead smoothly and quickly'.[4] He advises and warns that this imaginary writer should 'cultivate a tougher skin, and should not be afraid of speaking his mind, even if by so doing he drives himself into some sort of voluntary exile'.[5] To fulfil the role, the writer should endeavour 'to increase the flexibility and the range of writing in the language, to provide a minimum bulk of such writing, to express the ethos of his society but also to interpret the outside world to it, and to satirise it periodically'.[6]

With his typical readiness to follow his own advice and give a lead, Thomson's career and involvement with the Gaelic revitalisation efforts in the second half of the twentieth century are an exemplification of the essay's proposal, including the twinning of the role of the writer and

[1] Derick Thomson, 'The Role of the Writer in a Minority Culture', *Transactions of the Gaelic Society of Inverness* XLIV (1964–6).
[2] Thomson, 'The Role of the Writer', 266–7.
[3] Thomson, 'The Role of the Writer', 271.
[4] Thomson, 'The Role of the Writer', 265.
[5] Thomson, 'The Role of the Writer', 270.
[6] Thomson, 'The Role of the Writer', 271.

the academic. The Gaelic scholar John MacInnes (Iain MacAonghuis) recalled in 1972 that he initially lived under the impression that Derick Thomson and Ruaraidh MacThòmais were two separate individuals:

> About a quarter of a century ago two interesting figures appeared on the Gaelic scene. One was Derick Thomson, a young scholar of Aberdeen and Cambridge; the other Ruaraidh MacThòmais, a new Gaelic poet. I still recall my astonishment on realizing they both inhabited the same body: that of the present Professor of Celtic Languages and Literature in the University of Glasgow.[7]

The recollection is both amusing and illustrative, for when one looks over a summary of Thomson's work, it would be easy to imagine even more people being responsible for it. Donald E. Meek (Dòmhnall Eachann Meek), a fellow expert on Gaelic literature and culture, gave an account of his various roles in a eulogy delivered at Thomson's funeral in 2012 and described him as a 'scholar, teacher, Professor, language planner, poet, businessman, editor, politician, propagandist, chairman of boards and trusts in abundance'.[8] Scholar and editor Ronald Black (Raghnall MacilleDhuibh) hailed Thomson as 'the father of modern Gaelic publishing',[9] and John MacInnes described him as a person who 'has done more for Gaelic than any other individual in the entire history of our people', acknowledging that it is a large claim, but 'one that can be made confidently and without exaggeration'.[10]

Thomson's legacy does indeed stand out by its sheer volume, but it equally impresses by its diversity, consistent high standards, open critical approach and inclusive European outlook. His career spanned almost sixty years, arguably reaching its peak in the three decades of the 1950s to the 1970s but continuing well into the 2000s. Most of the activities he undertook during his long and productive life were aimed at the preservation and further development of Scottish Gaelic as a viable, versatile language able to take on the modern world, and the promotion of Scottish political independence. This study aims to describe his work in the Gaelic movement comprehensively and in detail, and to evaluate its impact at the time and its continuing legacy.

In his recent monumental monograph *Gaelic in Scotland*, Wilson McLeod notes that in the period between 1872 and 2020, the number of Gaelic users in Scotland decreased by more than four-fifths, and the language steadily weakened as a means of daily communication. He also points out

---

[7] John MacInnes, 'Review of *An Rathad Cian*', *Scottish International* (January 1972), 36.
[8] Donald Meek, 'Appreciation of Professor Derick S. Thomson: funeral oration, as delivered', *Passages from Tiree* [Donald Meek's personal blog], 5 April 2013, <http://meekwrite.blogspot.cz/2013/04/appreciation-of-professor-derick-s.html> Accessed 15 April 2023.
[9] Ronald Black, 'Introduction', *An Tuil* (Edinburgh: Polygon, 1999), xl.
[10] John MacInnes, 'The Poetry of Derick Thomson: An Introduction', *Bàrdachd le Ruaraidh MacThòmais* [audio CD with booklet] (Perth: Scotsoun & Artistes, 2002), 2.

that in recent decades, 'the position of Gaelic has become increasingly contradictory, with this ongoing decline in the total number of Gaelic speakers and the intensity of Gaelic use coexisting with a dynamic of revitalisation, heightened recognition and increased public status'.[11] As this book tries to illustrate, the life and work of Derick Thomson were part of these contradictory and dynamic processes in the Gaelic world in the twentieth century, and he exerted an important influence on them.

Research on Thomson: state of affairs

While there is no shortage of appreciative comments that acknowledge the magnitude and impact of Thomson's work, as the quotes included in the previous passage illustrate, there have been surprisingly few attempts to determine what exactly he did, how, to what end and what were his theoretical outlooks, and until relatively recently, conspicuously little critical attention has been paid to all aspects of Thomson's career.[12]

As McLeod notes, 'there are very few detailed studies of specific historical issues or events relating to Gaelic policy or movements, and most of these relate to the nineteenth and early twentieth centuries rather than the more recent period',[13] and a reader or researcher who comes to the Gaelic world from the outside will be surprised to discover the non-existence of modern monographs on some of the most important authors, and the deficit in critical biographies and editions of primary texts. The scarcity of research on Thomson as an author, scholar and activist reflects the state of affairs in both these fields. McLeod also refers to 'the lack of institutional and community memory in relation to the work of previous generations of Gaelic activists and organisations', especially in contrast with Ireland, the Basque Country and other countries, communities and regions where lesser-used and minoritised languages are present.[14] The paucity of engagement and critical appreciation of Thomson's legacy is part of this general trend but may have other causes still.

During Thomson's lifetime, most responses to his work took the form of reviews of his poetry collections that appeared in various Scottish magazines. The majority of academic works published so far deal with his poetry as well, and there have been essays and book chapters with both chronological and thematic orientation.[15] The prevailing framework has been the

---

[11] Wilson McLeod, *Gaelic in Scotland: Policies, Movements, Ideologies* (Edinburgh: Edinburgh University Press, 2020), 5.
[12] The bibliography of works on Thomson, included in this volume on pp. 181–4, attempts to be as comprehensive as possible.
[13] McLeod, *Gaelic in Scotland*, 4.
[14] McLeod, *Gaelic in Scotland*, 54–5.
[15] These general works include: Iain Crichton Smith, 'The Poetry of Derick Thomson', *Towards the Human* (Edinburgh: Macdonald Publishers, 1986); Ian MacDonald, 'The Poetry of Derick Thomson', *Alba Litteraria: A History of Scottish Literature*, ed. Marco Fazzini

poetry of place, a concept deeply rooted in the Gaelic poetic tradition, and both popular and critical attention was paid especially to Thomson's Lewis verse, where he explores his complex relationship to his native island and its culture; and to a lesser extent, to his writing about Glasgow, the city where he spent most of his life.[16] Other studies have explored the theme of religion in his poetry,[17] the topic of Gaelic language and its situation,[18] the focus on sensuous perception[19] and his work with symbols.[20] In terms of comparative studies, Thomson has been explored together with fellow Scottish Gaelic writers Sorley MacLean (Somhairle MacGill-Eain)[21] and Aonghas MacNeacail,[22] and alongside the Irish poet Máirtín Ó Direáin,[23] again with a focus on home and exile.

Little attention has been devoted to other aspects of Thomson's career, as scholar, editor, translator, journalist, prose writer and organiser. Three essays so far discuss Thomson's journalism and the quarterly *Gairm* (1952–2002) which he co-founded and edited for fifty years,[24] one explores

(Venezie Maestre: Amos Edizioni, 2005); Christopher Whyte, 'Derick Thomson: the Recent Poetry', *Aiste* 1 (2007); Ian MacDonald, 'Derick Thomson: Poet and Scholar', *Scottish Language* 37 (2018). The thematic works are listed below.

[16] For instance, listed in chronological order: Michelle Macleod, *Cianalas Redefined*, doctoral dissertation (University of Aberdeen, 1999); Michelle Macleod and Moray Watson, 'Ruaraidh MacThòmais: the Glasgow Verse', *Glasgow: Baile Mòr nan Gàidheal/City of the Gaels*, ed. Sheila M. Kidd (Glaschu: Roinn na Ceiltis, Oilthigh Ghlaschu, 2007); Niall O'Gallagher, 'Sùil eile air bàrdachd "Ghlaschu-ach" Ruaraidh MhicThòmais', *Aiste* 3 (2009–10); Petra Johana Poncarová, *From the Woods of Raasay to Glasgow Streets: Poetry of Place in the Works of Sorley MacLean and Derick Thomson*, MA dissertation (Charles University, 2014); Petra Johana Poncarová, 'Derick Thomson's *An Rathad Cian* (The Far Road, 1970): Modern Gaelic Poetry of Place Between Introspection and Politics', *The Poetics of Place and Space in Scottish Literature*, ed. Monika Szuba and Julian Wolfreys (Palgrave Macmillan, 2019).

[17] Petra Johana Poncarová, '"Eadar Canaan is Garrabost" (Between Canaan and Garrabost): Religion in Derick Thomson's Lewis Poetry', *Studies in Scottish Literature* 46:1 (2020). Also included in the collection *The Ghost at the Feast: Religion in Scottish Literary Criticism* (ed. Patrick Scott, 2020).

[18] Petra Johana Poncarová, '"Nuair a Dh'fhalbhas a' Ghàidhlig" (When Gaelic Goes): Gaelic in the Poetry of Derick Thomson', *Scottish Culture: Dialogue and Self-Expression*, ed. Aniela Korzeniowska and Izabela Szymańska (Warsaw: Semper, 2016).

[19] Iain Crichton Smith, 'A Sensuous Perception: An Aspect of Derick Thomson's Poetry', *Feill-Sgrìbhinn do Ruaraidh MacThòmais – Scottish Gaelic Studies* XVII (1996).

[20] Christopher Whyte, 'Derick Thomson: Reluctant Symbolist', *Chapman* 38 (1984).

[21] Christopher Whyte, 'The Gaelic Renaissance: Sorley MacLean and Derick Thomson', *British Poetry from the 1950s to the 1990s*, ed. Gary Day and Brian Docherty (London: Macmillan, 1997); Ronald Black, 'Sorley MacLean, Derick Thomson, and the Women Most Dangerous to Men', *The Bottle Imp* 21 (July 2017).

[22] Michel Byrne, 'Monsters and Goddesses: Culture Re-energised in the Poetry of Ruaraidh MacThòmais and Aonghas MacNeacail', *The Edinburgh History of Scottish Literature, Vol. 3*.

[23] Michelle Macleod and Mícheál Mac Craith, 'Home and Exile: A Comparison of the Poetry of Máirtín Ó Direáin and Ruaraidh MacThòmais', *New Hibernia Review* 5:2 (Summer 2001).

[24] Ian Grimble, 'The Poet and Scholar as Journalist', *Scottish Gaelic Studies* XVII (1996), 159–71; Ronald Black, '*Gairm*: An Aois Òir', *Aiste* 2 (2008); Petra Johana Poncarová, 'Ruaraidh MacThòmais is *Gairm*', *Rannsachadh na Gàidhlig 9: Cànan is Cultar*, ed. Meg

his Gaelic short stories,²⁵ one his scholarly work focused on the Ossian controversy²⁶ and one his engagement with Ireland.²⁷ A Scotnote Study Guide devoted to Thomson's Gaelic poetry appeared in 2020, also in response to the inclusion of Thomson's poetry in the school-leaving exams in Scotland.²⁸ The Derick Thomson website, at the moment in Gaelic only, was launched in 2016.²⁹ For Thomson's publications in *Gairm*, the database *Gairm Air-loidhne* [Gairm Online] is now an indispensable resource, together with the accompanying publication *Gairm: Ùghdar is Dealbh, Rosg is Rann, 1952–2002* (2022).³⁰

The most productive critics writing on Thomson have been, alphabetically, Ronald Black, Ian MacDonald (Iain MacDhòmhnaill), John MacInnes, Michelle Macleod (Michelle NicLeòid), Iain Crichton Smith (Iain Mac a' Ghobhainn) and Christopher Whyte (Crìsdean MacIlleBhàin), as the bibliography of resources on Thomson included in this study demonstrates, with my own work following up on theirs in recent years. Whyte's engagement with Thomson is most diverse, as it comprises reviews of his poetry collections from the time of their first publication, two extensive interviews about his life and work, academic essays and book chapters that discuss his poetry both thematically and chronologically, and passages devoted to Thomson in the monograph *Modern Scottish Poetry* (2004).³¹

When one compares this state of affairs, for instance, with the amenities available to researchers and readers who wish to engage with the work of Sorley MacLean, that include critical editions of his complete poetical output and some of his correspondence, several essay collections, a

---

Bateman and Riseard Cox (Slèite: Clò Ostaig, 2019). According to entries in *Gairm Airloidhne*, a continuation of Black's article, '*Gairm*: An Aois Òir (2)', is currently being prepared for publication.

²⁵ Petra Johana Poncarová, 'Old Women, Dreams, and Reversed Revivals: Derick Thomson's Gaelic Short Stories', *Scottish Literary Review* 13: 2 (2021).

²⁶ Petra Johana Poncarová, 'Derick Thomson and the Ossian Controversy', *Anglica* 29: 3 (2020).

²⁷ Petra Johana Poncarová, 'Derick Thomson and Ireland', *Litteraria Pragensia* 33:65 (July 2023).

²⁸ Petra Johana Poncarová, *The Gaelic Poetry of Derick Thomson* (Scotnote Study Guide. Glasgow: Association for Scottish Literary Studies, 2020).

²⁹ *Ruaraidh MacThòmais/Derick Thomson* <https://ruaraidhmacthomais.wordpress.com/> Accessed 15 April 2023.

³⁰ *Gairm Index* <https://dasg.ac.uk/gairm/> Accessed 15 April 2023. *Gairm: Ùghdar is Dealbh, Rosg is Rann, 1952–2002*, ed. Tòmas MacAilpein and Roibeard Ó Maolalaigh (Glaschu: Clò Oilthigh Ghlaschu, 2022).

³¹ Whyte had close personal and professional links to Thomson, as his own career as a Gaelic poet and translator into Gaelic is connected with *Gairm*, which published his translations from a number of European languages in the 1980s and his own poetry in the 1990s. Gairm Publications also brought out his first collection, *Uirsgeul* (1991). For a discussion of these, see Chapter 3. In 1991, he completed a PhD on the poetry of William Livingstone (Uilleam MacDhunlèibhe) under Thomson's supervision at the University of Glasgow (theses.gla.ac.uk/3982).

scholarly monograph and a dedicated bilingual website with a number of open-access resources, the want of critical engagement with Thomson, who is often mentioned together with MacLean as the other major twentieth-century Gaelic poet, becomes all the more striking.

In terms of public commemoration, MacLean is also much more visibly present in Scotland. In his native island of Raasay, his poetry is featured on tourist information boards and a memorial cairn in his honour is located near the cleared village of Hallaig, which inspired his most famous eponymous poem. He is one of twelve poets honoured by a bust in Edinburgh Park, South Gyle, copies of which were also gifted to the Scottish National Portrait Gallery.[32] Thomson, on the other hand, has no such public prominence, with the exception of the bust located on the premises of the Scottish Poetry Library in Edinburgh.[33] In 2018, The Gaelic Books Council (Comhairle nan Leabhraichean) decided to name their annual prize for the best new book of Gaelic poetry after Thomson, creating the 'Duais Ruaraidh MhicThòmais' (Derick Thomson Award), taking a promising step in this direction.

One of the possible reasons for this comparative lack of engagement and visibility is that Thomson's death occurred only in 2012, and that some temporal distance might still be needed for a serious and measured evaluation of his achievement. In comparison with MacLean, whose imposing poetry and striking personality perhaps lend themselves more easily to romanticised images and a more straightforward identification with the landscape of the Hebrides, and who, after thirteen years in Edinburgh, spent a substantial part of his life in Plockton and in Braes, Skye, Thomson's poetry and personality, quieter and more reticent, combined with the fact that he did not return to live in the Gaelic-speaking areas and was based mostly in Glasgow, are less prone to such appropriations. Whyte has fittingly described this difference in terms of dynamic range, noting Thomson's preference for *pianissimo* and *mezzo piano*, with occasional employment of *mezzo forte*, with MacLean quite often going for a *fortissimo* and further, and observing that the latter's utterance has a 'public, bardic strain, where Thomson is more introspective, exhibiting a richer and more highly developed sensuality and an almost Proustian awareness of earliest impressions, with the associated ability to achieve regeneration by recalling them'.[34]

It is also likely that Thomson's high standards and self-acknowledged tendency to elitism,[35] the critical outlook expressed in a number of articles

---

[32] Ian Wall, *Twelve Poets at Edinburgh Park* (Edinburgh: Scottish National Galleries, 2005).
[33] 'A Tour of the Scottish Poetry Library in Gaelic', *Scottish Poetry Library*, 22 March 2021 <https://www.scottishpoetrylibrary.org.uk/2021/03/spl-tour-gaelic/> Accessed 15 April 2023.
[34] Whyte, *Modern Scottish Poetry*, 157.
[35] In the chapter 'Gaelic in Scotland: Assessment and Prognosis', Thomson admits the 'frankly elitist attitude'. *Minority Languages Today*, ed. E. Haugen, D. J. McClure and D. Thomson (Edinburgh: Edinburgh University Press, 1981), 18.

and *Gairm* editorials, and the commitment to provide Gaelic culture with satirical and critical impulses, as formulated in 'The Role of the Writer', indeed led to something approaching the voluntary exile he knowingly mentioned in the same essay, which, in a relatively small and close-knit cultural environment may continue to manifest itself by the reluctance to engage with this legacy so far.

Aims and structure

This study strives to redress the absence of a full-length monograph devoted to Thomson's work and focuses on his involvement with the Gaelic revitalisation efforts, as it is a framework that allows the inclusion of a discussion of most of his initiatives in the realms of creative writing, scholarship, journalism, editorial work and organisational activities. As it is the first academic monograph on the subject, this broad focus has been favoured over more specific thematic delineations, and hopefully such specialised studies are going to emerge in the not-too-distant future too. It attempts to balance relevance for Gaelic and Scottish context with accessibility and interest for international readership and to bring in a broader perspective by referring to developments in other countries and regions and general works on linguistic and cultural revival.

As a whole, this book seeks to prosaically describe Thomson's contributions to the Gaelic revitalisation efforts, and to abstract his vision and theoretical views from his writing. It also identifies his inspirations and influences, both in Scotland and internationally. Apart from the relevance of this project for the general rehabilitation of Thomson to his place in Gaelic culture and Scottish culture in general, it is also topical as an exploration of revivalist and political engagement in the works of a person who left a significant mark on Gaelic Scotland, at the time when the position of Gaelic in Scotland and Scotland's political future, in the British Isles and in Europe, are of momentous importance and will likely continue to develop dramatically in the near future. By exploring Thomson's thought and career, it also manages to map some aspects of Scottish history, politics and culture in the second half of the twentieth century from the perspective of the Gaelic world, trace certain trends in Gaelic revitalisation and in research into Gaelic and lesser-used languages, and outline how European and global developments were reflected in Scotland.

This study builds on various works of Gaelic scholarship. It had the good fortune to emerge right after McLeod's incisive *Gaelic in Scotland* had been published. The monograph provides a much-needed general and detailed overview of the development of Gaelic from 1872 and is employed here as a background to the discussion of Thomson's role in the movement and his contributions. It also refers to a number of studies of Gaelic literature, Scottish history, culture and politics, and it attempts to broaden the outlook by drawing in works of scholarship from other contexts, including works that engage with Ireland and Irish revival and theoretical expositions on language revival and nationalism.

This introductory chapter concludes with a biography of Thomson, which summarises the main events of his life and career, as such an overview is currently not available in print or online, and in keeping with the commitment to readership not acquainted with the Gaelic world and its main players. A timeline that brings together the milestones of Thomson's career and the most important events in the history of the Gaelic language and of Scotland is included at the end.

Chapter 2 introduces Thomson's work and thought in context. It sketches the history of Gaelic in Scotland and of the Scottish independence movement, and the interplay between the two. It abstracts and summarises Thomson's opinions on Gaelic in Scotland, as formulated in the essay 'The Role of the Writer in a Minority Culture' (1966), in the collection *Gàidhlig ann an Albainn/Gaelic in Scotland* (1976), which he edited and contributed to, and in the pamphlet *Why Gaelic Matters* (1981). The chapter also introduces several figures with special relevance to Thomson, including Ruaraidh Erskine of Mar (Richard Stuart Erskine)[36] and Hugh MacDiarmid (Christopher Murray Grieve). Finally, it explores Thomson's engagement with other lesser-used and minoritised languages and literatures, especially his sustained interest in Ireland and Wales.

Chapter 3 is devoted to a detailed account of the quarterly *Gairm* and its role in the Gaelic revitalisation in the second half of the twentieth century. It examines the two agendas of *Gairm* that were present during the history of the magazine in changing degrees: the aim to provide diverse and appealing reading material in Gaelic that would attract a broad popular readership, and the more elitist focus on supporting modern literature and journalism that would follow the latest international trends. Thomson, as a co-founder, editor for fifty years and author of most of the editorials, shaped the direction of the quarterly and through it the development of Gaelic literature, most importantly modern poetry and short fiction, and contributed to the expansion of various formats of discussing current affairs in Gaelic. The chapter concludes with a detailed analysis of Thomson's own contributions to the magazine, including creative work, essays on various topics, travelogues and reviews.

Chapter 4 considers Thomson's scholarly output in relation to the Gaelic revival, especially his two lifelong research interests: the Ossianic publications by James Macpherson (Seumas Mac a' Phearsain) and the related controversies, and the works of the eighteenth-century Gaelic poet Alexander MacDonald (Alasdair Mac Mhaighstir Alasdair). Thomson's publications reveal the significant political dimension of both topics and

---

[36] The spelling of Erskine's name differs in sources between 'Mar' and 'Marr'. I decided to adopt the version 'Mar', in keeping with Thomson's usage in the entry for the *Oxford Dictionary of National Biography*.

their relationship to the position of Gaelic in Scotland and in Europe. The chapter explores the two seminal results of his scholarly work, the monograph *An Introduction to Gaelic Poetry* (1974) and *The Companion to Gaelic Scotland* (1983), which he edited. It also examines his engagement with translation into Gaelic as a vital part of the revitalisation process, his own activities as a translator and his organisational work, including the foundation of The Gaelic Books Council.

Chapter 5 traces the topic of Gaelic language and revitalisation efforts chronologically through Thomson's seven poetry collections, offering detailed commentary on famous poems, such as 'An Tobar' (The Well) and 'Cisteachan-laighe' (Coffins), and also on lesser-known relevant works, paying special attention to the early nationalist verse from *An Dealbh Briste* (The Broken Picture) and to the last three collections that have so far been subject to little critical analysis. It uncovers references to the situation of Gaelic in his short stories, including the scathing satirical portrayal of some strands in the Gaelic revival in 'Foghar, 1976' [Autumn, 1976] and subtle commentary in 'Tea Feasgair' [Evening Tea], a story which reveals remarkable links to Thomson's poetry.

The final chapter, Chapter 6, summarises Thomson's legacy in relation to the Gaelic revitalisation efforts and the future developments of areas in which he was active and of issues he was invested in, including the Gaelic periodical press after *Gairm* and the SNP's attitudes to Gaelic. Possible directions for further research into Thomson's life and work are outlined at the end.

Derick Thomson: a biography

Derick Smith Thomson came from a family of Gaelic-speaking intellectuals, teachers and ministers from the Isle of Lewis in the Outer Hebrides.[37] His father, James Thomson (Seumas MacThòmais, 1888–1971), who was born and brought up in Tong near Stornoway, studied at Aberdeen University and after military service worked as the head of the Gaelic department at Nicolson Institute, the secondary school in Stornoway which caters for pupils from the whole island. In 1922, he became the headmaster of the primary school in Bayble (Pabail), a village in the Point (An Rubha) district of Lewis, east of Stornoway, a post he held until 1953.[38]

James Thomson was himself a renowned poet, the first ever to receive the Bardic Crown at the National Mòd, an annual festival of Gaelic arts, in 1923

---

[37] For help with gathering and checking genealogical information concerning Derick Thomson's family in census records, I am greatly indebted to Dr Caoimhín Ó Donnaíle, An Teanga, Skye, lecturer in computer science and genealogy at Sabhal Mòr Ostaig.
[38] T. M. Murchison, 'James Thomson', *The Companion to Gaelic Scotland*, ed. Derick S. Thomson (Gairm: 1994), 288–9.

in Inverness.[39] In 1953, a selection of his poetry was published in a volume entitled *Fasgnadh* (Winnowing).[40] He co-edited a collection of Lewis verse *Eilean Fraoich* (1938), collaborated on a play *The Spirit of the Tartan* with Arthur Geddes and preached Gaelic sermons in the Church of Scotland where he was an Elder.[41] He was involved in promoting Gaelic in education, especially in secondary schools, and compiled an anthology of Gaelic poetry, *An Dìleab: Gaelic Verse for Advanced Divisions and Intermediate Classes* (1934), for school use. An active member of An Comunn Gàidhealach [ACG], the Highland Association, he served as editor of its magazine *An Gàidheal* (The Gael) between 1958 and 1962.[42] James Thomson's work thus encompasses various fields of Gaelic revitalisation, from engaging in community activities and bringing the language into the public sphere to writing, publishing and editing, and the same breadth and diversity will be later seen in the activities of his son.

Derick Thomson's mother, Christina 'Tina' Smith (Tìneag Aonghais Alasdair, 1888–1968), was born in Keose, beside Loch Erisort in the Lochs. For one year, she studied Celtic at Glasgow University together with her sister Malcolmina. She became a schoolteacher and taught in the Leurbost primary school. According to Thomson, she had a great interest in traditional Gaelic poetry, especially William Ross (Uilleam Ros) and Duncan Ban Macintyre (Donnchadh Bàn Mac an t-Saoir), and a large repertoire of Gaelic song,[43] and his own regard for eighteenth-century poetry and his detailed knowledge of traditional song may be at least in part attributed to these early influences.

James and Christina were married on 18 August 1916 at the Imperial Hotel in Aberdeen, when James was already serving in the army during the First World War. Their first son, named James like the father, was born on 3 June 1917, while James Sr. was still stationed in France. After the war, the family settled in Lewis. Derick Thomson was born on 5 August

---

[39] 'Programme of the Seventieth National Mod | Winners of Previous Competitions | Crowned Bards', An Comunn Gaidhealach (1973), 111 <https://digital.nls.uk/125945837> Accessed 15 April 2023.

[40] Derick Thomson and Finlay J. MacDonald published some verse by James Thomson in *Gairm*, for example in *Gairm* 4 (1953): 'Tha 'm Fraoch fo Bhlàth' [The Heather is Blooming] and 'Cuimhne Mo Shamhraidh' [A Memory of My Summer]; and 'Tailmrich na h-Ùine' [Footsteps of Time] in *Gairm* 6 (1953). The review of *Fasgnadh* by Iain A. MacDhòmhnaill appeared in the same issue of *Gairm*, as part of the section 'An Sgeilp Leabhraichean' [The Bookshelf], 183–5. James Thomson also contributed a number of articles to the quarterly, on topics such as the history of fishing in Lewis to *Gairm* 1–3 (1952–3) and Gaelic education to *Gairm* 22–3 (1957–8).

[41] Derick Thomson, 'A Man Reared in Lewis', *As I Remember: Ten Scottish Authors Recall How Writing Began for Them*, ed. M. Lindsay (London: Robert Hale, 1979), 125.

[42] Donald MacAulay, 'Introduction', *Derick Thomson: The Far Road and Other Poems*, Lines Review 39 (December 1971): 3; Derick Thomson, 'An Gàidheal', *The Companion to Gaelic Scotland* (1993), 115.

[43] Derick Thomson, 'Poets in Conversation', *Taking You Home*, ed. Andrew Mitchell (Glendaruel: Argyll Publishing, 2006), 91.

1921 in Stornoway and grew up in Upper Bayble. The household was fully bilingual,[44] and according to Thomson's recollections, his first language was English and he became equally fluent in Gaelic and English from about the age of five.[45] As McLeod notes with reference to earlier works of scholarship, in the second half of the twentieth century the native intelligentsia played an important role in minority rights movements that emerged in a number of countries in the aftermath of the Second World War,[46] and Thomson can be seen as one of the representatives of this trend in Scotland, with an upbringing in a Gaelic-speaking home in Lewis followed by a prestigious university education.

Thomson's parents were members of the Church of Scotland.[47] James Thomson held the position of an Elder and combined this role with his Gaelic activities.[48] Derick Thomson naturally got acquainted with the more radical Evangelical denominations in Lewis too, including the Free Church, and later explored his complex relationship to the religious landscape of the island of his upbringing in a number of poems and discussed the topic extensively in essays and interviews.[49]

Thomson gained his first education at Bayble primary school and continued at the Nicolson Institute in Stornoway. It was during his years at the Nicolson that his interest in Scottish nationalism started, and the 1935 General Election when a nationalist candidate, Alexander MacEwen, the first leader of the then newly formed Scottish National Party, ran for the Western Isles, was especially formative.[50] In autumn 1939, Thomson entered Aberdeen University, where he enrolled for English Literature and Celtic. At the university, his nationalist stance developed further through reading, both pamphlets and Scottish literature, and personal encounters with prominent SNP activists such as Bruce Watson, David Murison and especially Douglas Young (1913–73), classicist, poet and translator into Scots from a number of languages, who also had a keen interest in Gaelic. In the 1940s, Young was the leader of the SNP.

Thomson's studies were interrupted by the Second World War. As he partly

---

[44] 'My father and mother habitually spoke in Gaelic to each other, but frequently enough spoke English to each other also, without any sense of strain. They had decided to make English my first language, though Gaelic had been my elder brother's. I think this was a carefully worked-out policy, for we were in the midst of an almost totally Gaelic environment, and they reckoned Gaelic would come easily.' Thomson, 'A Man Reared in Lewis', 124.

[45] Derick Thomson, 'Poets in Conversation', 91. The constant switching between the two languages, unmotivated by deficiency in either of them, has been a frequent feature among fluent Gaelic speakers of Lewis.

[46] McLeod, *Gaelic in Scotland*, 142.

[47] Thomson, 'A Man Reared in Lewis', 125.

[48] Derick Thomson, 'A Man Reared in Lewis', 125.

[49] I discuss Thomson's writing on the subject in '"Eadar Canaan is Garrabost" (Between Canaan and Garrabost): Religion in Derick Thomson's Lewis Poetry'.

[50] Thomson, 'A Man Reared in Lewis', 134.

shared the opinion, common among Scottish Nationalists at that time, that the war was 'someone else's quarrel' and an 'intrusion on the Scottish realities', he was not keen to volunteer.[51] In a mischievous nationalist gesture, he listed English among his foreign languages and England among his foreign travels during an interview for officer training, which unsurprisingly did not lead to an offer, but he was nonetheless trained at camps in Bradford and Cranwell. From 1942 to 1945, he served with the Royal Air Force, stationed in Rodel in Harris and in Point in Lewis,[52] and according to his own recollections spent his free time reading about Celtic studies and Scottish literature and politics, which 'left little time for radar theory'.[53]

In 1945, Thomson returned to Aberdeen, graduated in 1947 with First Class Honours, and went on to study at the University of Cambridge, where he embarked on Section B of the Archaeology and Anthropology tripos (Anglo-Saxon, Norse and Celtic) and obtained a First-class degree. This doctoral programme was, as Meek points out, established by the pioneering scholars Hector Munro Chadwick and Nora Kershaw Chadwick, who wished to encourage bridge-building and interdisciplinary approaches to the Celtic and Germanic strands in early British cultural history, and Thomson's later career shows how he benefited from such a broadly conceived interdisciplinary degree.[54] His monograph *The Gaelic Sources of Macpherson's 'Ossian'*, which appeared in 1952, was substantially the content of the tripos thesis submitted at Cambridge.[55]

After graduation, he took the post of Assistant in Celtic at the University of Edinburgh in 1948. He also worked as a collector of Gaelic folklore for what was to become the School of Scottish Studies and he travelled to a number of places to interview tradition bearers.[56] His stay in Edinburgh proved rather short, as he was offered another job at the University of Glasgow in 1949, which he accepted – a newly established lectureship in Welsh. To improve his command of the language, Thomson spent the first half of 1950 at the University College of North Wales, Bangor.[57] During his stay, he would naturally become acquainted with the efforts to promote the Welsh language, and Welsh revitalisation policies and initiatives continued to inspire him throughout his life, as discussed in Chapter 2 and Chapter 3.

[51] Thomson mentioned this in the interviews with Whyte (259–60). He also noted that there was a general unwillingness among Scottish Nationalists to fight in the British army, as they considered conscription a violation of freedom of the Scottish people. 'Some Recollections', *Spirits of the Age: Scottish Self Portraits*, ed. P. Henderson Scott (Edinburgh: The Saltire Society, 2005), 58.
[52] Thomson, 'Some Recollections', 58.
[53] Thomson, 'A Man Reared in Lewis', 134.
[54] Meek, 'Appreciation of Professor Derick S. Thomson: funeral oration, as delivered', <http://meekwrite.blogspot.cz/2013/04/appreciation-of-professor-derick-s.html>.
[55] Thomson, 'Preface', *The Gaelic Sources of Macpherson's 'Ossian'* (Edinburgh and London: Oliver & Boyd, 1952; published for the University of Aberdeen), v.
[56] Thomson, 'Some Recollections', 61.
[57] Thomson, 'Some Recollections', 60.

The most substantial academic outcome of his interest in Welsh language and literature was the edition of *Branwen Uerch Lyr* (Branwen the Daughter of Llyr, 1961), the second of four branches of the Mabinogi, which he prepared for the Dublin Institute for Advanced Studies.

Thomson's first poetry collection, *An Dealbh Briste* (The Broken Picture), appeared in 1951, published by Serif Books in Edinburgh. In the same year, he approached Finlay J. MacDonald (Fionnlagh Iain MacDhòmhnaill), then involved in the Gaelic department of the BBC, with the suggestion to establish a Gaelic quarterly, and the result was the magazine *Gairm*. In 1958, the magazine was complemented by Gairm Publications, which went on to produce a wide range of books, including poetry and short story collections, dictionaries, textbooks and children's literature, and operated until the 1990s.[58]

In 1952, Thomson married Carol Galbraith (Carol Nic a' Bhreatannaich, 1930–2017)[59] from Kintyre and over time, six children were born into the marriage, one daughter and five sons.[60] In 1956, he was appointed Reader in Celtic and became the head of the Celtic department at the University of Aberdeen, where he spent seven years.[61] After the death of Angus Matheson (Aonghas MacMhathain) in 1962, Thomson became Chair of Celtic at the University of Glasgow and remained in the position for nearly thirty years, until his retirement in 1991. He served as the chairman of the Gaelic Book Council from its foundation in 1968 until 1991, while Ian MacDonald worked as its director.

Politics began to play a more important role in Thomson's life in the 1960s, and he was active especially in the Pollokshields area of Glasgow.[62] SNP politicians Winnie Ewing and Billy Wolfe asked him to stand for the party as a candidate, but Thomson refused, believing he would make a more productive contribution to Scotland as an academic.[63] When the SNP adopted a Gaelic Policy in 1978, Thomson was one of the main instigators, chairing the committee which prepared the document, and the topic

---

[58] A list of all the volumes published by Gairm Publications up to 1977 was included in the anniversary issue, *Gairm* 100, 311–15.

[59] Carol Nic a' Bhreatannaich was born in Campbeltown in Argyllshire. She became involved in Gaelic music and joined a local choir when she was six years old. She graduated with an MA degree from the University of Glasgow and then gained a qualification for teaching in primary schools and for teaching maths in secondary schools at Jordanhill College in Glasgow. In 1951, she won a gold medal at the Mòd in Edinburgh. She continued to be active as a musician and dancer and also wrote poetry in Gaelic and mainly in Scots. 'Carol Nic a' Bhreatannaich', BBC Alba *Bliadhna nan Òran* <http://www.bbc.co.uk/alba/oran/people/carol_nic_a__bhreatannaich/> Accessed 15 April 2023.

[60] Ranald Thomson (1963–2001) predeceased his parents. Donald Thomson (born 1954) died in 2018.

[61] The editorial for *Gairm* 17 (1956) points out that the editors part ways, and while Finlay J. MacDonald stays in Glasgow, Derick Thomson departs for Aberdeen.

[62] Thomson, 'Some Recollections', 62.

[63] Thomson, 'Some Recollections', 62.

received substantial coverage in *Gairm*, as discussed in Chapter 3. Three collections of verse appeared in the 1960s and 1970s: *Eadar Samhradh is Foghar* (Between Summer and Autumn, 1967), *An Rathad Cian* (The Far Road, 1970) and *Saorsa agus an Iolaire* (Freedom and the Eagle, 1977), all produced by Gairm. Thomson's two major scholarly publications, *An Introduction to Gaelic Poetry* and *The Companion to Gaelic Scotland* (edited), also came out during this period.

After his retirement, Thomson continued to be active as the editor of *Gairm* until 2002, and published three more volumes of verse: *Smeur an Dòchais/Bramble of Hope* was brought out by Canongate in 1991, *Meall Garbh/ The Rugged Mountain* by Gairm Publications in 1995 and *Sùil air Fàire/ Surveying the Horizon* by Acair in 2007. In the 1990s and 2000s, he also took on further academic and organisational commitments, including the collection of European poetry translated into Gaelic, *Bàrdachd na Roinn-Eòrpa an Gàidhlig* (1990), and the conference *Gaelic and Scots in Harmony*, which resulted in a publication of the same name (1991).

In recognition of his activities, Thomson garnered numerous awards: in 1974, he was the first recipient of the Ossian Prize, which was founded in the same year by F.S.V. Foundation in Hamburg for individuals who conducted outstanding work in the context of minoritised cultures, and the Oliver Brown Award in 1984. He held honorary degrees from the University of Wales (1987), Aberdeen University (1994) and the University of Glasgow (2007). He was elected a Fellow of the Royal Society in Edinburgh in 1977 and of the British Academy in 1992. He died on 21 March 2012 in Glasgow, at the age of ninety, and was buried at the Glasgow Linn Cemetery.

In the year of Thomson's birth, the census listed 158,779 Gaelic speakers in Scotland. The census conducted in 2011, a year before his death, listed the figure of 57,602, revealing a decrease of almost two-thirds. This sharp drop was accompanied, as McLeod notes, by the gradual development of Gaelic education, media and publishing, and the embodiment of Gaelic in various official structures.[64] This book seeks to examine how Derick Thomson responded to these phenomena and how he contributed to the preservation and further development of the Gaelic language in Scotland and beyond.

---

[64] McLeod, *Gaelic in Scotland*, 1, 5.

Timeline[65]

1921: birth of Derick Thomson
1921: census, 158,779 Gaelic speakers
1923: first Gaelic radio broadcast
1931: census, 136,135 Gaelic speakers
1934: foundation of the SNP
1945: SNP gains its first seat at Westminster (Robert McIntyre)
1951: publication of *An Dealbh Briste*
1951: census, 95,447 Gaelic speakers
1952: publication of the first issue of *Gairm*
1956: foundation of the Chair of Celtic, University of Glasgow
1961: census, 80,978 Gaelic speakers
1967: publication of *Eadar Samhradh is Foghar*
1968: foundation of The Gaelic Books Council
1970: publication of *An Rathad Cian*
1970: Donald Stewart becomes *SNP* MP for Western Isles
1970: discovery of the Forties oilfield
1971: census, 88,892 Gaelic speakers
1974: publication of *An Introduction to Gaelic Poetry*
1977: publication of *Saorsa agus an Iolaire*
1979: unsuccessful devolution referendum
1981: census, 82,620 Gaelic speakers
1982: publication of *Creachadh na Clàrsaich*
1983: publication of *The Companion to Gaelic Scotland*
1991: census, 65,978 Gaelic speakers
1991: publication of *Smeur an Dòchais*
1993: beginning of government-funded Gaelic TV broadcasts
1995: publication of *Meall Garbh*
1997: successful devolution referendum
1999: return of the Scottish parliament
2001: census, 58,652 Gaelic speakers
2002: publication of the last issue of *Gairm*
2007: publication of *Sùil air Fàire*
2011: census, 57,602 Gaelic speakers
2012: death of Derick Thomson
2014: unsuccessful Scottish independence referendum

---

[65] Census figures quoted according to Donald MacAulay, *The Celtic Languages* (Cambridge: Cambridge University Press, 1992). 2011 census figures come from table KS206SC. The same figures are given by McLeod, *Gaelic in Scotland*, 20. The chronology included in *The Companion to Gaelic Scotland* (1993 edition, 309–11), most likely compiled by Thomson himself, was consulted and several items included in this timeline.

CHAPTER TWO

Thomson's Thought and Work in Context

This chapter presents various contexts for Derick Thomson's thought and work. It provides a brief overview of the history of Gaelic in Scotland and of Scottish nationalism, and some general observations on the topic of linguistic and cultural revival. It also summarises Thomson's double commitment to revitalisation of Gaelic and Scottish political independence and outlines his involvement with the SNP. As Thomson never wrote any definitive treatise on his vision of the Gaelic revival, the chapter brings together opinions he expressed in essays, book chapters and pamphlets on the subject. It mentions Thomson's relationship to Ruaraidh Erskine of Mar and Hugh MacDiarmid, and finally his engagement with revivalist initiatives in Wales and Ireland.

Gaelic in Scotland

Several resources that outline the history of Gaelic in Scotland are now available: apart from McLeod's recent *Gaelic in Scotland*, which provides a general introduction and focuses on movements and policies between 1872 and 2020, the reader can also consult *The Edinburgh Companion to the Gaelic Language* (2010), edited by Moray Watson and Michelle Macleod, Kenneth MacKinnon's older study *Gaelic: A Past & Future Prospect* (1991) and Thomson's own overviews included in *Gàidhlig ann an Albainn/Gaelic in Scotland* and in *Why Gaelic Matters*. The following passage, which is based on these sources, presents a summary of selected important events and tendencies in the history of the language for the sake of convenience.

Scottish Gaelic (Gàidhlig) belongs to the Celtic branch of the Indo-European language family and is closely related to Irish (Gaeilge) and Manx (Gaelg) and more distantly to Welsh (Cymraeg), Cornish (Kernewek) and Breton (Brezhoneg). Regarding the emergence of Gaelic in the territory of today's Scotland, Gilbert Márkus, in his monograph *Conceiving a Nation: Scotland to AD 900*, seeks to rectify a widespread narrative of Gaelic migration from Ireland to Scotland, on the basis of recent archaeological evidence:

> If there had been a significant migration of Gaels from Ireland to Scotland *c.* AD 500, as traditional accounts would have it, one would

expect the migrants to have brought with them a fair amount of their material culture as well as their language. But if there was no major migration, however, there was certainly longstanding and regular contact between Ireland and the west of Scotland. The North Channel of the Irish Sea had been for centuries a highway for the movement of people and goods, and so for cultural exchange.[1]

He argues that the presence of Gaelic-speaking people in western Scotland should be understood in this context and suggests that 'rather than ask how Gaelic got from Ireland to Scotland (the question that Bede's narrative was designed to answer) we might do better to imagine Ireland and western Scotland as a single linguistic zone in which Gaelic evolved'.[2]

McLeod summarises the challenging and complex history of Gaelic in Scotland in the following manner:

Gaelic slowly emerged as the dominant language of Scotland in the central Middle Ages but following language shift it became confined to the northwest of the country. In the subsequent centuries Gaelic became stigmatised as a language of poverty, backwardness and even barbarism. Since the middle of the eighteenth century, against the background of severe economic and social disruption, language shift from Gaelic to English in the traditional Gaelic area gathered pace, so that the position of Gaelic as a community vernacular is now weaker than ever before.[3]

In the first millennium, as McLeod notes, Scotland was a 'multi-ethnic, multilingual land', characterised by identities and affinities that were often fluid.[4] Gaelic became the language of the Kingdom of Alba, the first unified monarchy in Scotland, which emerged in the ninth century, and was most influential in the eleventh century, while the royal government of Scotland started to turn towards Scots (known as Anglian or Inglis), a West Germanic language closely related to English, and Gaelic began to recede gradually to the north and west.[5]

As early as the thirteenth century, there are records of Gaelic resistance to the royal government of Scotland, when the Gaelic-Norse rulers of a powerful and largely independent island lordship including the Hebrides and the Isle of Man, the Lords of the Isles, strove to assert their independence

---

[1] Gilbert Márkus, *Conceiving a Nation: Scotland to AD 900* (Edinburgh: Edinburgh University Press, 2017), 78.
[2] Márkus, *Conceiving a Nation*, 78–9.
[3] McLeod, *Gaelic in Scotland*, 6.
[4] McLeod, *Gaelic in Scotland*, 6.
[5] Thomson, 'Gaelic in Scotland: The Background', *Gàidhlig ann an Albainn/Gaelic in Scotland*, 3–4.

from the Scottish crown.⁶ From the late 1300s, there is also evidence of negative attitudes towards the people of the Highlands and Islands on the part of the inhabitants of the Lowlands, and of the perception of the region as alien and underdeveloped.⁷ The Highlands and Islands have thus been seen as a separate entity in Scotland and marginalised and othered on these grounds.

The sixteenth century saw the disintegration of Gaelic society based on the clan system and on the authority and patronage of the vanished Lords of the Isles.⁸ As McLeod observes, 'anti-Gaelic prejudices intensified in the later sixteenth century, when the Reformation transformed Lowland Scotland into a bastion of reformed Protestantism'.⁹ After the Union of the Crowns in 1603, when James VI of Scotland ascended the English throne as James I, anti-Highland policy grew in severity, taking a distinct shape in the Statutes of Iona (1609), a set of laws aimed at obliterating the overall distinctiveness of the region and the related political threats, which required Highland chiefs to send their heirs to be educated in the Lowlands. According to McLeod, 'in the late sixteenth and seventeenth centuries the government in Scotland had expressed an aggressive policy of linguistic assimilation – if not extirpation – in relation to the Gaelic language' but there has been no official ban on Gaelic at any point.¹⁰ In 1688, James VII/II, the last Catholic monarch of Scotland, England and Ireland, was deposed in the so-called 'Glorious Revolution' and his descendants made several attempts to regain the throne. The Union of the Parliaments of Scotland and England in 1707 meant that power shifted even more to England, as Scotland lost its own governing body.

During the seventeenth and eighteenth centuries, the exiled Stuarts sought and received support in Ireland and in Gaelic-speaking areas of Scotland after they had lost the throne to William of Orange, and a series of rebellions in Great Britain and Ireland occurred between 1688 and 1746 with the aim of restoring the Stuarts to the throne. Although many Gaels actually fought for the Hanoverians and the Highlands and Islands were by no means universally Catholic, the region became firmly linked with the Roman faith and the military threat of the Jacobite risings, and its population was styled as primitive and treacherous.

When the 1745 rising led by Charles Edward Stuart, grandson of James VII/II, was defeated at Culloden in 1746, the repercussions targeted Gaelic-speaking areas and increased the cultural and social crisis and the existing rift, although use of the Gaelic language was never actually

---

[6] Ian Grimble, 'Introduction', *The Future of the Highlands*, ed. Derick S. Thomson and Ian Grimble (London: Routledge & Kegan Paul, 1968), 9.
[7] McLeod, *Gaelic in Scotland*, 10.
[8] Grimble, 'Introduction', *The Future of the Highlands*, 11.
[9] McLeod, *Gaelic in Scotland*, 11.
[10] McLeod, *Gaelic in Scotland*, 30.

prohibited.[11] James Macpherson's Ossianic publications, emerging in the 1760s, in the aftermath of these events, fundamentally influenced the image of Gaelic Scotland and Gaelic language both internally and internationally, and provided a major impulse in the development of European Romanticism.

During the second half of the eighteenth century and into the nineteenth century, the environment and culture of Gaelic Scotland were influenced by rapid industrialisation of the Lowlands, which were attracting a migrant workforce, and also by population removals in the Highlands and Islands motivated by landowners' desire to employ land for more profitable purposes, mostly sheep grazing and hunting. These events, generally known as the Highland Clearances, occurred mostly between 1780 and 1860.[12] The Highlands and Islands thus lost a significant part of their Gaelic-speaking inhabitants to emigration both to the Lowlands and overseas, in some cases no doubt motivated by private ambition and initiative but often forced overtly by removals and covertly by lack of opportunities. This led to the creation of Gaelic diasporas in Canada, Australia and other parts of the world. In Cape Breton, Nova Scotia, Gaelic is still spoken in some communities and is the subject of local revivalist initiatives.

The above-mentioned developments in the nineteenth century resulted in a depopulation of the region and a substantial weakening of the position of the Gaelic language, and created a society which was largely impoverished and hindered by internal conflicts, external pressures and imposed policies. These developments, in combination with existing prejudice, resulted in what Silke Stroh describes as 'the double marginality of the Gàidhealtachd, both within Scotland and within Britain'.[13] However, the era also presented new possibilities related to the British imperial enterprise, creating a complex dynamic between the Highlands and Islands and the United Kingdom that involved both oppression and opportunity, especially in relation to the military, as recruits from the Highlands and Islands joined the British Army in great numbers and the staple image of the brave and loyal Highland soldier emerged,[14] competing with the older notion of the culturally alien and politically unreliable Highland population. Scottish and also Highland involvement in the slave trade is gradually being mapped by researchers.[15]

---

[11] McLeod, *Gaelic in Scotland*, 12.
[12] See, for instance, Eric Richards, *The Highland Clearances* (Edinburgh: Birlinn, 2008).
[13] Silke Stroh, *Uneasy Subjects: Postcolonialism and Scottish Gaelic Poetry* (Amsterdam: Rodopi, 2009), 12.
[14] See McLeod, *Gaelic in Scotland*, 12.
[15] See, for instance, Kate Phillips, *Bought and Sold: Slavery, Scotland and Jamaica* (Edinburgh: Luath Press, 2022); David Alston, *Slaves and Highlanders: Silenced Histories of Scotland and the Caribbean* (Edinburgh: Edinburgh University Press, 2021); Tom M. Devine (ed.), *Recovering Scotland's Slavery Past: The Caribbean Connection* (Edinburgh: Edinburgh University Press, 2015).

The period from the late eighteenth century also witnessed the start of the first wave of Gaelic revivalist activity, and a more favourable view of the Gaelic language started to emerge within Scotland. As McLeod notes, 'this era saw significant controversy concerning the role of Gaelic in the state education system, newly established by the *Education (Scotland) Act 1872*, widespread agitation for land rights in the Gaelic-speaking areas, and the foundation of the first modern Gaelic organisation, An Comunn Gàidhealach'.[16] Glasgow established itself as a Gaelic centre in the Lowlands, 'Baile mòr nan Gàidheal' [the big city of the Gaels], and this urban context, although it did not provide the same opportunities for the daily use of the language in the community, gave rise to a number of initiatives facilitated by the city environment. Gaelic publishing grew in connection with the expanding markets that emerged in Glasgow, Inverness and other parts of the country.[17]

The impact of the First World War on the Gaelic-speaking population of Scotland was devastating: as MacKinnon points out, drawing on the results of the 1921 census, 'the Gaelic population bore a disproportionate share of war casualties and dislocation'.[18] The sinking of *HMY Iolaire*, when more than two hundred returning servicemen drowned on 1 January 1919 within sight of Lewis, became one of the symbols of these losses. Immediately after the war, some positive developments in relation to Gaelic occurred too, including, as McLeod notes, 'issues involving the implementation of the *Education (Scotland) Act 1918*, which brought about a somewhat increased role for Gaelic in the education system'.[19] The roots of these changes can be observed even before the war, including the activities of W. J. Watson, a native Gaelic speaker who took the chair of Celtic at the University of Edinburgh in 1914 and was involved in the foundation of the Scottish Gaelic Texts Society.[20]

The twentieth century saw the gradual rise of interest in Gaelic, first as an academic subject and with emphasis on Celtic philology, and later with shifting focus to the contemporary living language, literature and traditional music. Especially from the second half of the twentieth century, growing provision for Gaelic in the education system and in the media and greater visibility and a gradual diversification of the Gaelic movement can be observed. At the same time, negative attitudes to the language persist,

---

[16] McLeod, *Gaelic in Scotland*, 2.
[17] Michelle Macleod, 'Language in Society: 1800 to the Modern Day', *The Edinburgh Companion to the Gaelic Language*, ed. Michelle Macleod and Moray Watson (Edinburgh: Edinburgh University Press, 2010), 27–9.
[18] Kenneth MacKinnon, 'A Century on the Census: Gaelic in Twentieth-Century Focus', *Gaelic and Scots in Harmony: Proceedings of the Second International Conference on the Languages of Scotland*, ed. Derick Thomson (Glasgow: Department of Celtic, University of Glasgow, 1990), 166.
[19] McLeod, *Gaelic in Scotland*, 2.
[20] Thomson, 'Gaelic in Scotland: The Background', 6–7.

ranging from new variations on the centuries-old prejudice of Gaelic being backward and alien to Scotland to ostensibly pragmatic complaints about the allegedly excessive costs of keeping the language alive.

In 2001, the UK ratified the European Charter for Regional or Minority Languages, with respect to Gaelic and Scots in Scotland. The *Gaelic Language (Scotland) Act* was passed in 2005 by the Scottish Parliament, which was reopened in 1999, and led to the foundation of Bòrd na Gàidhlig [The Gaelic Board], the official development body charged with preparing the national Gaelic language plan. A designated Gaelic TV channel, BBC Alba, started to broadcast in 2008. As the timeline included at the end of Chapter 1 illustrates, the numbers of Gaelic speakers according to the census steadily dropped, and this decline coincided with the gradual rise of recognition, support and opportunities related to the language, creating tensions and challenges which form the background of Thomson's career and activities.

Scottish nationalism

The medieval Wars of Independence and famous victories over the English armies, the Declaration of Arbroath which asserted Scottish freedom in a letter addressed to Pope John XXII, the Union of the Crowns in 1603 and the Union of the Parliaments in 1707, the Jacobite rebellions: all these events constitute important elements in the discourse of Scottish independence, but this overview focuses on more recent political developments and the activities of people who perceived Scotland as an independent nation which should have control over its own territory.

In the second half of the nineteenth century, the 'home rule' movement, demanding a devolved assembly, started to gain support in both Ireland and Scotland. In 1885, two institutions were established to manage the country's interests within the United Kingdom: the post of Secretary for Scotland and the Scottish Office. Before the outbreak of the First World War, the concept of universal 'home rule' was promoted by the Liberal government, which proposed that Scottish home rule would follow after the same arrangement in Ireland, turning the United Kingdom into a federal system. Negotiations about the Scottish Home Rule bill were however put aside due to the immediate concerns of the First World War.

After the war, the political situation was much changed. In 1922, Ireland, with the exception of the six counties, became a free state and a civil war over the Anglo-Irish Treaty followed. As Murray Pittock points out, it is rather surprising how little Scottish nationalists were affected by the developments in Ireland in between 1916 and 1921, apart from artists of nationalist persuasion such as Hugh MacDiarmid and Neil M. Gunn who wrote about Patrick Pearse for the *Scots Independent*.[21] The response among

---

[21] Murray Pittock, *The Invention of Scotland: The Stuart Myth and the Scottish Identity* (London: Routledge, 2014), 145.

Gaelic activists was palpably more excited, and especially Ruaraidh Erskine of Mar was much involved with representatives of Irish nationalism, including contacts with Pearse.[22]

In the 1920s, nationalist activity in Scotland was divided into three major groups: the 'old Home Rulers', the Scots National League and the Scottish Nationalist Movement.[23] The Glasgow University Scottish Nationalist Association, headed by the lawyer John MacCormick, provided the needed impulse for their merging, and the new National Party of Scotland (NPS) was inaugurated on 23 June 1928 in Stirling – both the location and the exact date were chosen to refer to the Battle of Bannockburn, a famous victory of Robert the Bruce over the English in the First War of Independence in 1314.

In 1931, the party had about eight thousand members.[24] In 1934, the Scottish National Party (SNP) came into being through a merger of the NPS and the Scottish Party, which was more oriented towards cultural nationalism.[25] Among the members were also several advocates of Gaelic, but language revival was by no means the primary agenda of the new party. Champions of Gaelic language and culture tended to work within these movements and promote their goals, rather than founding separate initiatives.[26]

The SNP continued to grow gradually throughout the late 1930s and attracted more voters. This reached its peak in the success of Robert McIntyre, who won the Motherwell by-election in 1945 and thus became the SNP's first Member of Parliament. At this time, cultural nationalists were still influential in the SNP: author and adventurer Robert Bontine Cunninghame Graham held the post of its first president until his death in 1936 and novelist Neil M. Gunn served as vice-chair in 1942.[27] However, their influence was gradually receding, as the party sought to adopt a more narrowly political nationalist agenda, and some supporters, including author Eric Linklater, were disappointed to see the party turn away from their historically oriented views towards a modern and more narrowly political programme.[28] A similar development can be observed in Wales, where Plaid Cymru similarly transformed into a social democratic party

---

[22] For Erskine's Irish connections, see Patrick Witt, 'Connections across the North Channel: Ruaraidh Erskine and Irish Influence in Scottish Discontent, 1906–1920', no page number; Gerard Cairns, *No Language! No Nation! The Life and Times of the Honourable Ruaraidh Erskine of Marr* (Perth: Rymour Books, 2021).

[23] F. R. Hart and J. B. Pick, 'Politics and Society between the Wars', *Neil M. Gunn: A Highland Life* (London: John Murray, 1981), 108.

[24] Pittock, *The Invention of Scotland*, 148.

[25] The Scottish Party was formed in 1932 by a group of members of the Unionist Party who favoured the establishment of a Dominion Scottish Parliament within the British Empire.

[26] Patrick Witt, 'Irish Story'; McLeod, *Gaelic in Scotland*, 114–15.

[27] Pittock, *The Invention of Scotland*, 148.

[28] Pittock, *The Invention of Scotland*, 146.

after 1945, while its founders included such pronounced cultural nationalists and advocates of Welsh as Saunders Lewis.[29]

The new SNP, which after the Second World War evolved into a centrist, middle-class party, was rather suspicious of the tradition of cultural nationalism it had inherited from its predecessors.[30] Symbolical acts, such as the stealing of William Wallace's sword from Stirling on 8 November 1936, were seen as bad publicity and a hindrance to the party's attempts to make a decisive impression on the electorate and obtain home rule. A petition demanding home rule for Scotland organised by the Scottish Covenant Association in 1949 attracted over two million signatories but still did not receive much attention from the major political parties.

During the 1950s, the SNP continued to receive rather small electoral support, but started to grow more rapidly in the 1960s and 1970s. With the Empire no longer unbreakable, after many former colonies in Asia, Africa and the Caribbean achieved independence in the decades after the Second World War and the Suez Crisis, the idea of Britishness as a whole was becoming less convincing.[31] Election results started to show Scottish people's discontent with their position in the UK. The Westminster government was perceived as failing, and the attempts to stop the growth of nationalism by addressing social and economic issues by 'the old policy of throwing money at Scottish problems', as Richard Finlay puts it, no longer worked.[32]

One of the SNP's first major achievements was the victory of Winnie Ewing[33] in the by-election in Hamilton in 1967. In that year, the party had about sixty thousand members.[34] While in 1970, it gained only one seat, for the Western Isles, four years later, eleven MPs for the SNP were returned to Westminster, making the general election an unprecedented success.[35] In the 1970s, the independence cause was naturally fuelled by the discovery of North Sea oil (Forties field in 1970, Brent field in 1971) and concerns over control of it and the use of the profits from its extraction. An economic case for independence was put forward, epitomised by the slogan 'It's

---

[29] Pittock, *The Invention of Scotland*, 146.
[30] Pittock, *The Invention of Scotland*, 146.
[31] Neal Ascherson, 'When Was Britain?' *Litteraria Pragensia: Scotland in Europe* 19:38 (December 2009), 3.
[32] Richard Finlay, 'Changing Cultures: The History of Scotland since 1918', *The Edinburgh History of Scottish Literature Vol. 3. Modern Transformations: New Identities*, ed. Ian Brown (Edinburgh: Edinburgh University Press, 2007), 5.
[33] Winnie Ewing (1929–2023) was a Scottish politician and lawyer. She served as President of the Scottish National Party 1987–2005 and presided over the opening of the Scottish Parliament in 1999. Apart from being a member of the British House of Commons and later the Scottish Parliament, she was also a long-serving member of the European Parliament and promoted Scottish interests and independence in Strasbourg and Brussels.
[34] Pittock, *The Invention of Scotland*, 157.
[35] Ian MacDonald, 'The Poetry of Derick Thomson', 653.

Scotland's Oil!'. In the General Election in October 1974, the SNP was the second party in Scotland.[36]

As Neal Ascherson puts it, the fast rise of the SNP in the 1970s persuaded the Labour government that 'constitutional change was necessary, if only to take the wind out of nationalist sails', and a quasi-federal system of devolution was devised which allowed Scotland and Wales elected assemblies and a certain degree of internal autonomy.[37] In 1978, the Scottish and Welsh law about regional parliaments was passed in the House of Commons, with the condition that more than 40 per cent of those registered to vote supported the establishment of these devolved bodies in a referendum.

On 26 January 1979, a Yes campaign for possible Scottish devolution commenced, but was hindered by the unwillingness of the SNP and Labour to cooperate. In the referendum, the supporters of Yes won tightly, but did not manage to overcome the 40 per cent limit, although more than 50 per cent of those who actually voted opted Yes, and the referendum failed. As Pittock argues, the reasons behind the failure were the SNP's inability to capitalise on the support it was able to generate, and its focus on issue politics, such as oil and civil disobedience, and economics, rather than on underlying greater causes, and its neglect of questions of cultural and national identity.[38] In the General Election of 1979, a Conservative government was returned under Margaret Thatcher's leadership and the SNP vote collapsed.

The next breakthrough for the party occurred in 1988, when Margo MacDonald[39] won the by-election in Glasgow Govan. The next year, the Scottish Constitutional Convention, an organisation connecting churches, local authorities and the trade unions, started to campaign for a Scottish Parliament, yet it took another nine years before their efforts were rewarded. After the Labour landslide in September 1997, a referendum on a Scottish Parliament with tax-raising powers was held and the country voted in its favour. Following the *Scotland Act 1998*, the Scottish Parliament was reconvened on 12 May 1999, and five years later, it moved into its own new building at Holyrood.

While, in 2007, the SNP only formed a minority government, in 2011, the party won a majority in the Scottish Parliament. In consequence of the success, the SNP leader Alex Salmond announced that a referendum on independence would be organised in five years' time. The referendum, held on 18 September 2014, ended in a close victory for the Better

---

[36] Pittock, *The Invention of Scotland*, 158.
[37] Ascherson, 'When Was Britain?', 7.
[38] Pittock, *The Invention of Scotland*, 158.
[39] Margo MacDonald (1943–2014) was a Scottish politician, teacher and broadcaster. She was elected MP for the Scottish National Party for Glasgow Govan in 1973. She served as Deputy Leader of the SNP from 1974 to 1979 and as an Independent Member of the Scottish Parliament (MSP) for Lothian from 1999 until 2014.

Together campaign. However, the number of SNP members continued to grow even after the failed referendum, making the party the third-biggest in the UK. Under the leadership of Salmond's successor, Nicola Sturgeon, the SNP enjoyed a landslide victory in the May 2015 UK General Election, gaining fifty-six out of fifty-nine constituencies.

The EU referendum of 2016 revealed a major division between England and Scotland, and the ensuing Brexit negotiations drove the two countries still further apart. After the victory of the Conservatives under Boris Johnson in the General Election in December 2019 and another SNP landslide in Scotland, the party started to campaign for a second independence referendum in 2020, and the campaign for full independence has continued despite the hiatus caused by the 2020–1 Covid-19 pandemic.

Gaelic revival and Scottish nationalism

In the late eighteenth and nineteenth centuries, a wave of linguistic and cultural revivals occurred in many parts of Europe. As Joep Leerssen notes, in terms of the relationship between the nation and language and culture in this period, the thought of German pre-Romantic and Romantic philosophers, such as Johann Gottfried Herder and William von Humboldt, was greatly influential, and most of the European national revivalist movements at that time can be more or less directly traced to Herder's thought.[40]

In Herder's theory, formulated most famously in *Treatise on the Origin of Language* (1772), the nation coincides with language, and individual languages therefore constitute distinct fixed communities whose particular way of thinking is determined by the respective language. Herder promoted the idea that languages are precious in themselves, as they contain the tradition, history, religion and customs of their people, claimed that linguistic variety allows for a diversity of thought, and perceived immersion in one's own history and culture as the only path to real freedom. Herder also stressed the role of culture and language in the formation of nationality and authentic group experience, but also paid close attention to civilisation and will, as people need to choose to speak their own language and discover their own history. An important moment in Herder's theory is the idea of the moral equality of cultures, providing a vital point of departure for the promotion of minoritised languages and cultures. While the ideas of cultural diversity and uniqueness of each language, and, in turn, nationality, are naturally appealing from the perspective of activists defending small languages and nations against absorption into bigger units, they also imply a substantial degree of language determinism.

Vladimír Macura notes in his study of Czech national revival in the

---

[40] Joep Leerssen, *National Thought in Europe* (Amsterdam: Amsterdam University Press, 2010), 97.

nineteenth century that some of its proponents saw language as the basis for the notion of nation and homeland, and in their activities, language was not used as a vehicle for an expression of culture which already existed, rather it was a means of creating culture:

> The world of the Czech is not, in the revivalist understanding, signified by the language means – it is produced by them, for the reality of Czech culture is at the beginning stored mainly in the language, and the use of the language itself creates the culture. The basic concepts of the revivalist ideology, especially the notion of the nation and the homeland, are derived from language. Jungmann defined the concept of the nation in relation to the language, and he decidedly identified the notion of the homeland with the notion of the nation: 'without love for the patriotic language, it is impossible to think about love for the homeland, i.e. for the nation'.[41]

In comparison with the majority of European revivals, the case of Scotland is quite exceptional. While both Gaelic and Scots were involved in the Scottish revival at the fin-de-siècle,[42] no national and linguistic revival comparable to some developments in Continental Europe occurred in Scotland in the nineteenth century.

As Ascherson puts it, 'the construction of Scottish national identity has been in some ways exceptional', and 'Scottish national awareness diverges from Central European models in its lack of emphasis on biological-ethnic and language factors'.[43] In its prevalently non-linguistic orientation, Scottish nationalism also differs markedly from nineteenth- and twentieth-century Welsh and Irish nationalism. According to James G. Kellas, 'Scottish nationalism is based on political and economic demands rather than on cultural or linguistic ones',[44] and McLeod makes a similar point when he notes that 'issues of language and culture have never been prominent in Scottish national movements, in marked contrast to most other European countries', adding that in 'conventional understandings, Scottish national distinctiveness and autonomy inhered primarily in the national institutions that were retained following the Union of 1707'.[45]

Moreover, while in the Welsh and Irish context and in a number of Continental countries which went through a period of national revival in the

---

[41] Vladimír Macura, *Znamení zrodu* [The Sign of Inception] (Prague: H+H, 1995), 53. All quotes from Macura used in this study have been translated by me, as there is no authoritative English version of the text available. Josef Jungmann (1773–1857) was a leading figure of the Czech national revival.

[42] Michael Shaw, *The Fin-de-Siècle Scottish Revival: Romance, Decadence and Celtic Identity* (Edinburgh: Edinburgh University Press, 2020), 21–2.

[43] Neal Ascherson, 'When Was Britain?', 3.

[44] James G. Kellas, 'Politics, Highland (twentieth century)', *The Companion to Gaelic Scotland*, 239.

[45] McLeod, *Gaelic in Scotland*, 42.

nineteenth century, only one candidate for the position of the national language could be readily seized upon and employed as one of the cornerstones of the effort, the more complex linguistic landscape of Scotland prevented such an easy identification with one language and the associated cultural tradition. In Ireland, the general use of Irish was also significantly more common and evenly distributed until much later than that of Gaelic in Scotland. As Alan Titley suggests, the Gaelic-speaking areas in Scotland, unlike the Irish Gaeltacht, were 'never seen in any widespread way as being a treasure-house of [national] cultural revival or a repository of aphoristic wisdom'.[46]

This linguistic diversity and the problematic situation of the two most likely candidates for a 'national' language, Scots and Gaelic, has prevented a full-scale adoption of either of them as a major component of the nationalist campaign. To use Anthony D. Smith's classification, Scottish nationalism has been mostly construed as a civic one, with only certain groups and movements favouring a cultural nationalism based either on Gaelic or Scots and the associated culture.[47]

While it is difficult to claim Gaelic as *the* national language of Scotland, at the same time, as McLeod notes, 'Gaelic clearly has a significant national resonance in Scotland and cannot plausibly be regarded merely as a regional language or the language of a discrete cultural minority.'[48] In recent decades, it has attained more general popularity and a more significant place in public life, in relation to the growing sense of Scottish cultural distinctiveness and the demands for self-government, but McLeod cautions that the 'connection between these phenomena is anything but straightforward, and the relationship between Gaelic and Scottish nationhood and nationalism is complex and in some ways contradictory'.[49]

The position of Gaelic-speaking areas in Scotland is thus doubly challenging, and involves two power centres and wider structures which can be the source of active hostile policies, or mere neglect and indifference, and against which they can define themselves: Scotland as a whole and the UK. However, there has never been a Gaelic separatist movement, calling for the establishment of a sovereign state that would follow the outlines of Gaelic-speaking areas, although Erskine of Mar entertained such an idea for a time.[50]

[46] Alan Titley, 'The Ravelling of Narratives: Irish and Scottish Gaelic Life Stories Compared', *Nailing Theses: Selected Essays* (Belfast: Lagan Press, 2011), 405, quoted in McLeod, *Gaelic in Scotland*, 13.
[47] Anthony D. Smith, *Nationalism and Modernism* (London: Routledge, 1998) and *The Nation in History: Historiographical Debates about Ethnicity and Nationalism* (UPNE, 2000).
[48] McLeod, *Gaelic in Scotland*, 3.
[49] McLeod, *Gaelic in Scotland*, 36. He also points out that some Gaelic speakers have been unionists and supporters of the monarchy, which has also been more favourable to Scotland and to Gaelic than the executive powers at Westminster (43).
[50] See McLeod, *Gaelic in Scotland*, 41.

In a number of ways, the Gaelic revival in the twentieth century resembles the revivals in Continental Europe which occurred in the nineteenth century, for instance in terms of the position of the language and the aims of the movement, but of course it occurred within a very dissimilar social and historical context and in a different environment as far as communication technologies and media are concerned.

Thomson, Gaelic and the SNP

As Donald Meek aptly points out, Thomson was 'totally committed to the cause of Scotland, even when it was unfashionable to be committed to Scotland'.[51] He adhered to this persuasion throughout his life and had the satisfaction of observing the gradual transformation of Scottish nationalism from a marginal political movement to a major and respectable force in Scottish, UK and European politics. In 1999, he witnessed the return of the parliament to Edinburgh, which led to the expectation of a full independence referendum in the future, and he commented on these issues extensively, as discussed in Chapter 3.

Thomson combined support of Scottish independence with commitment to the revitalisation of Gaelic, and in his view, the relationship was that of interdependence and mutual benefit. The two concerns were much entwined in his thought and activities from early on: Gaelic constituted a vital component of Scottish distinctiveness, and a politically independent Scotland would provide a safe framework for Gaelic to survive – and not only Gaelic but Scots and other languages and cultures too. In contrast to the prevailing tendency not to connect Scottish nationalism with a specific linguistic and cultural agenda, Thomson was convinced that a successful campaign for an independent Scotland must not focus solely on economics and social issues. In the words of Crichton Smith, Thomson saw 'the salvation of his own culture as dependent on an independent Scotland',[52] and believed that 'for the Highlander to survive as a real human being' there must be a way of making Scotland into an independent state.[53] In relation to Scotland, Thomson's nationalism is a civic one, inclusive and multicultural, imagining the independent state that would nurture its various cultures and languages, although Gaelic and Scots, as languages with the oldest historical links to Scotland, should be accredited special status.

In terms of political affiliation, Thomson remained faithful to the SNP throughout his life, supported the efforts to separate Scotland from the United Kingdom, and did not suggest the foundation of a new party which

---

[51] Meek, 'Appreciation of Professor Derick S. Thomson: funeral oration, as delivered', <http://meekwrite.blogspot.cz/2013/04/appreciation-of-professor-derick-s.html>.
[52] Crichton Smith, 'The Poetry of Derick Thomson', 141.
[53] Crichton Smith, 'The Poetry of Derick Thomson', 142–3.

would focus on Gaelic Scotland only. Meek recalls Thomson's steady commitment to the SNP:

> One of the 'golden moments' with Derick, which I can remember vividly and with enormous pleasure, was when I went to lunch with him in the Staff Club on the day that Margo MacDonald won the Govan By-election. He was elated, full of joy, as if the future of Scotland was assured – and for him it was assured. He was an optimist from beginning to end, and, although some of us, like myself, simply could not match his boundless energy and his long-haul capability, he did instil into us a very real commitment to what we regarded as important – and, of course, what he regarded as important. With Scottish Nationalists triumphantly in power in twenty-first century Scotland, I often think of Derick, and the pleasure he must have derived from seeing such a remarkable change. Not that he would have regarded it as 'remarkable'. He saw it coming, of course. He told me thirty years ago.[54]

In 1974, Thomson published an article entitled 'Tìr na Gàidhlig ann a Linn na h-Ola' [The Land of Gaelic in the Age of Oil], in which he discusses the situation of Gaelic in Scotland in the context of the changes brought about by the discoveries of North Sea oil fields. In it, he proposes a number of practical steps and policies on how to respond to the situation with regard to Gaelic, and comments on its importance on the national level, in line with the growing support for independence.

> Tha fios agam gu bheil mòran dhaoine air Ghalldachd an-diugh a tha ag iarraidh a' Ghàidhlig a ghleidheil. Tha stàit-sheirbheisich ann an Taigh an Naoimh Anndrais an Dùn Èideann a tha deònach cuideachadh leinn; Goill a dh'iarradh tuilleadh Gàidhlig nar sgoiltean (agus seall an taice làidir a tha maighstirean-sgoile Gallda a' toirt don Ghàidhlig an Steòrnabhagh agus air an Òban); luchd-sgrìobhaidh agus luchd-sgrùdaidh a tha a' cur fàilte air an litreachas ùr againn. Tha dùil agam gur h-ann nas motha bhios an gean seo a' fàs mar a bhios modhan riaghlaidh ag atharrachadh ann an Albainn.[55]

> *I know that there are nowadays many people in the Lowlands who want to preserve Gaelic. The civil servants at St Andrew's House in Edinburgh are eager to help us, Lowlanders who want more Gaelic in schools (see the strong help Lowland schoolteachers are giving to Gaelic in Stornoway and in Oban), writers and critics who are welcoming our new literature. I hope that this mood is going to grow together with the change of rule in Scotland.*

In 1976, Thomson edited and contributed to the volume *Gàidhlig ann an Albainn/Gaelic in Scotland*, which also conveys this hopeful atmosphere and

---

[54] Meek, 'Appreciation of Professor Derick S. Thomson', <http://meekwrite.blogspot.cz/2013/04/appreciation-of-professor-derick-s.html>.
[55] 'Tìr na Gàidhlig ann a Linn na h-Ola', *Gairm* 87 (1974), 209.

readiness to make progress. The publication is discussed in more detail later in this chapter.

In 1978, the SNP adopted a Gaelic Policy for the first time, and Thomson chaired the working group that prepared the document and published it in full in *Gairm* 104 (1978).[56] The policy opens with a brief history of Gaelic in Scotland and presents a summary of its current state. An overview of specific proposed recommendations starts with the acknowledgement of the presence of other minorities in Scotland, naming in particular people with Jewish, Polish, Pakistani, Indian, Sikh and Chinese background, who should be supported in retaining and developing their cultures and languages in Scotland. It suggests that for historical reasons, three languages should be recognised as official – Gaelic, Scots and English – and used in official contexts in a reasonable and equal manner. The policy makes it clear that it does not propose to turn Scotland all-Gaelic or all-Scots, but that both languages should enjoy a special status.

The rest of the document focuses on Gaelic. It recommends that districts and areas should have the possibility of choosing a Gaelic status, and proposes specific steps to be adopted on the level of state government and public affairs; education; local government, civil service and justice; business and trade; and arts and the media. Finally, it lists what needs to be achieved in terms of language development before these steps can be taken, such as creating new terminology and a formal register of Gaelic suitable for public affairs, setting up specialised units focusing on Gaelic and translation attached to different institutions and bodies, founding a Gaelic Academy that would supervise the coinage and employment of new vocabulary and steer language planning in terms of orthography and usage, and finally establishing a Gaelic Secretariat that would implement the proposed policies. The policy is concluded by the expression of hope that the proposals would redress language inequality and ultimately be of benefit to Scotland as a whole and all its people, not only to Gaelic users.[57]

The failed independence referendum of 1979 was a major blow in terms of putting these proposals into practice, but it did not dissuade Thomson from support of both independence and the SNP. In the article 'Gaelic in Scotland: Assessment and Prognosis' (1981), Thomson wrote that only a Scottish Nationalist government could be expected to adopt efficient Gaelic policies, since 'no other political party has committed itself significantly in this area', and the full realisation of Gaelic potential is unlikely to be achieved without a political revolution of a particular kind.[58] While for Thomson, the link between the struggle for Scottish independence

---

[56] According to *Gairm*, the working group consisted of Murchadh Fearghastan, Iain MacAonghais, Fearghas MacFhionnlaigh, Iain MacLeòid and Ruaraidh MacLeòid.

[57] A summary based on the Gaelic version of the policy, as published in *Gairm* 104 (1978), 301–11.

[58] Thomson, 'Gaelic in Scotland: Assessment and Prognosis', 20.

and the revitalisation of Gaelic was essential for the success of both, the SNP was by no means a party that would make Gaelic one of its priorities. As McLeod notes, 'from the late 1940s to the late 1960s the SNP had paid very little attention to Gaelic, but it began to address the language issue more frequently from the late 1960s onwards', but in spite of this change, it still played only a minimal role in the debates leading up to the 1979 referendum.[59]

Although the concern with the Gaelic language is omnipresent in his work, Thomson was not a linguistic essentialist: he considered the language a unique part of Scottish identity which should be embraced and promoted, but he also made it clear the country could exist without Gaelic, although the loss of the language would reduce its diversity and also impoverish it economically. In a number of works, Thomson seems to be driving at a similar point to the one Gwyn Williams makes in *When Was Wales?* in relation to the whole country: 'Wales is an artefact the Welsh produce. If they want to.'[60] Neal Ascherson, who quotes Williams in his *Stone Voices*, develops this thought further: 'Perhaps they no longer want to. [. . .] if they continued to lose their sense of history, then no more artefacts would be produced.'[61] Thomson's worries are of a similar nature: he is aware of the fact that Gaelic Scotland and Scotland as a whole are continually performed and created. If people let go of Gaelic, a significant part of their history and culture, a very different Scotland could emerge without it.

Gaelic and individual commitment

In his study *Language, Education and Social Processes in a Gaelic Community*, Kenneth MacKinnon proposes four models to explain the language shift away from Gaelic. One of them is the 'social morale model', which focuses on the relationship of individual users and communities to the language and on the loss of confidence and lack of commitment.[62] As McLeod notes while surveying the Gaelic revitalisation efforts since the late nineteenth century, one of the key factors that stands out is the failure to achieve critical mass: 'not enough people were directly engaged in Gaelic language organisations and movements, and not enough people were quietly supportive of their efforts', as a result of which 'politicians and policy-makers rarely felt significant pressure to introduce or improve provision for Gaelic'.[63]

---

[59] McLeod, *Gaelic in Scotland*, 145, 176.
[60] Gwyn Williams, *When Was Wales?: A History of the Welsh* (London: Penguin Books, 1985), 304.
[61] Neal Ascherson, *Stone Voices: The Search for Scotland* (London: Granta Books, 2003), 37.
[62] Kenneth MacKinnon, *Language, Education and Social Processes in a Gaelic Community* (London: Routledge & Kegan Paul, 1977). McLeod summarises the models in *Gaelic in Scotland*, 17–18.
[63] McLeod, *Gaelic in Scotland*, 331.

In many of his works, as will be shown in the following chapters, Thomson is persistently concerned with social morale and individual and communal commitment, as the areas where users of Gaelic can do most to reverse the negative trends, and criticised what he perceived as laxity, a tendency to complain and nitpick while refraining from any effort or from suggesting a better alternative, and a lack of enterprise and initiative.

Thomson does not downplay the long-term corrosive impact of historical injustices and harmful policies, but stresses the responsibility of Gaelic users to keep the language and culture alive and the necessity to act, rather than nursing grievances and a feeling of despondency. He urges individuals and communities to elect such representatives and such a government that would make it their responsibility to take better care of the Gaelic language and culture, and strive to make reparations for the intentional damage and neglect of the past.

In relation to people with no familial ties to Gaelic Scotland, Thomson comes closest to what Anthony D. Smith delineates as cultural or linguistic nationalism: he promoted the idea that full socialisation in the host language and culture should gain people not born or brought up with them full acceptance into the community. His thought thus exhibits features of voluntarism. In 'Gaelic in Scotland: Assessment and Prognosis', he presents the following view of Gaelic identity:

> The Gaelic identity is less than secure. Besides the historical reasons for this, and the social or quasi-social reasons, alongside the wholesale intrusion of non-Gaelic influences on the whole of the Gaelic community, it seems to me that there are other, internal, factors that fragment the Gaelic identity. It tends to become parochialised, so that Skye or Lewis or Uist becomes the unit or the touchstone and some very wasteful rivalry develops. Sometimes it shows evidence of class distortion: Gaelic must be equated with folk culture, and so by a rough approximation with a so-called working class. It seems to me more healthy to look on Gaelic as a feature of our national life, and one potentially to be shared by all manner of men and occupations.[64]

The editorial to *Gairm* 3 (1953), co-written by Thomson and Finlay J. MacDonald, goes even further, and after a reference to the smallness of the Gaelic world, rife with regional rivalries, it proclaims: 'Buinnidh *Gairm* do Ghàidheil an t-saoghail' [*Gairm* belongs to the Gaels of the world], and the more the better. Gaelic in Thomson's vision becomes open to all who are committed enough to learn it and to do something for it, irrespective of their place of origin and genetic make-up, and no matter whether they wish to write modern poetry in Gaelic, analyse international politics or are drawn to the language by an interest in folklore and place names, as

---

[64] Thomson, 'Gaelic in Scotland: Assessment and Prognosis', 18.

discussed in more detail in Chapter 3 on the subject of second-language contributors to *Gairm*.

When Thomson seems to approach ethnocentric positions, such as in one section of the long poem 'Meall Garbh' and in some *Gairm* editorials which include harsh critiques of the English and their cultural and economic crimes against Scotland, for instance in the editorial to *Gairm* 83 (1973), the point seems to be, given the overall context of his thought, not to stir up ethnic hatred but rather to denunciate the United Kingdom as a power structure, reject Tory policies and make a statement on behalf of a minority that has been neglected by the state and subjected to hostile policies, and is thus vulnerable to cultural and economic colonisation.

Gaelic and folk culture

Traditional culture, folklore and especially music have played a prominent role in the Gaelic world, also in terms of research, and came to be perceived as one of the main attractions of the language and a vital source of energy for the revitalisation efforts. As McLeod notes, the folk music revival in the 1950s, which promoted the ideas of collecting songs and folklore and preserving heritage, had a strong influence on the Gaelic movement.[65]

In *Gàidhlig ann an Albainn/Gaelic in Scotland*, when commenting on the underdevelopment of Gaelic publishing, Thomson mentions an attitude he likely encountered among some users of Gaelic: that books are not needed, as Gaelic has its folklore and music. He rejects these views as narrow-minded, and argues that while folklore should prosper and develop, it should not dominate Gaelic culture as a whole.[66]

Thomson himself engaged with traditional culture and even contributed to what was to become the School of Scottish Studies as a collector of material and by a number of Gaelic folk songs in his own renditions.[67] His interest in the tradition is well-attested in interviews but he did not rely on folk culture as the basis of Gaelic revitalisation. His efforts tended to focus on the issues of the present and the future, such as finding vocabulary for modern subjects and situations, and publishing new books appealing to children and young people, rather than going back to old songs and etymology.[68] There are traces of looking for a golden age in some of Thomson's poems, with references to the times when Gaelic was the official language of the royal court, for instance 'Cuimhne' (Memory) in *Smeur an Dòchais*, but his priority was keeping the language alive in the twentieth century and flexible enough to handle contemporary issues. The aim of

---

[65] McLeod, *Gaelic in Scotland*, 139.
[66] Thomson, 'Leabhraichean, Litreachas, Foillseachadh', 79.
[67] These recordings of Thomson's singing are freely available through the open-access online archive *Tobar an Dualchais/Kist o Riches* (Thomson's ID as a contributor is 1092).
[68] MacThòmais, 'Tìr na Gàidhlig ann a Linn na h-Ola', 210.

Thomson's pragmatic approach was not resurrecting the ancient past but producing new culture which emerges from using the language in the new situations and contexts.

Another idea which could seem rather controversial from the point of view of some activists was Thomson's refusal to believe that the best way to support Gaelic was to move to one of the remaining communities where the language is still used to some extent in everyday life. He refuted the notion that 'only by living in a strong Gaelic community can a poet be a spokesman of the Gaelic community' and denounced it as 'palpable nonsense'.[69] His own decision was to be based in Glasgow and he never went back to live permanently in his native Lewis. The pronounced intellectualism of his activities, exacting demands and preference for high culture could, not surprisingly, lead to collisions with those who failed to meet his standards or with those who worked for Gaelic in a more limited context and with a less cosmopolitan agenda. This refusal to become 'a voice of the region', to come and live in a traditionally Gaelic-speaking area and engage in local issues on a daily basis, may be one of the reasons why Thomson's legacy has not been celebrated as widely as that of Sorley MacLean, as discussed in Chapter 1.

Nationalism and internationalism

Thomson placed great emphasis on the necessity to communicate with Europe, draw inspiration from the cultures and literatures of other nations and regions, and to fight provincialism and narrow-mindedness, to which Gaelic Scotland in his view understandably tended as a result of adverse historical, social and economic developments, some of which are outlined earlier in this chapter. In his approach, resolute nationalist persuasion not only did not conflict with pronounced internationalism, but even required it:

> It is coming to be clearly understood also that it is on the basis of defining rather than submerging national identities that international understanding is built. The spurious opposition of national and international is therefore being undermined, though there are old-fashioned politicians among us who still cling to the shibboleths of their youth and their early reading, even if that youth is only five years distant.[70]

In analogy, a confident national state is in Thomson's view built on supporting rather than submerging regional identities and indigenous languages, and his revivalist efforts are based on a conviction that development of Scotland's languages and cultures should contribute to the

---

[69] Thomson, 'Poetry in Scottish Gaelic 1945–1992', 159.
[70] Thomson, 'Reflections after Writing *An Introduction to Gaelic Poetry*', *Lines Review* 49 (June 1974), 15.

self-confidence of the national state. This twofold and entwined commitment to regional cultural nationalism on the level of Gaelic Scotland and civic nationalism on the level of Scotland as a whole was complemented by openness towards Europe and the world, as Chapter 3 and Chapter 4 discuss in more detail in relation to international content in *Gairm* and to Thomson's work as a translator.

Essays and pamphlets on Gaelic

The following section examines in more detail several publications in which Thomson expressed his opinions on various issues related to the revitalisation of Gaelic. They are analysed chronologically, to illustrate the progression of Thomson's thought in response to historical and political developments.

'The Role of the Writer in a Minority Culture' (1966)

McLeod notes that in contrast to Ireland and Wales, there are no obvious examples of canonical texts in the Scottish Gaelic context that inspired activists involved in the language revitalisation movement, mentioning Douglas Hyde's 1892 lecture 'The Necessity for De-Anglicising Ireland' and Saunders Lewis' 1962 radio address 'Tynged yr Iaith' (The Fate of the Language) that energised the revivalist efforts on behalf of Irish and Welsh respectively and gave inspiration to action.[71] One such text in the Gaelic context that could have provided such an impetus, but its circulation and impact remained limited, was Thomson's essay 'The Role of the Writer in a Minority Culture' (1966).

It is the closest Thomson produced to a manifesto of his approach to the Gaelic revival. The paper was presented during a meeting of the Gaelic Society of Inverness on his behalf, due to forced absence, on 3 March 1966, and appeared in *The Transactions of the Gaelic Society of Inverness* in the same year. Given his inability to attend the meeting in person, Thomson included some opening explanations in the essay, foreseeing possible offences that could be taken:

> if anyone connected with the Highlands and Islands Development Board is present, I should like to say, not in a truculent but in a conciliatory spirit, that the work of rehabilitation on the Highlands should be conducted not only in the economic and social spheres, but also in the spheres of language and literature of culture generally. We want to see the *whole* of Highland society regenerated. We want to see this area regaining population, prosperity, purpose, but we also want to see it regaining a sense of its own particular identity.[72]

---

[71] McLeod, *Gaelic in Scotland*, 54–5.
[72] Thomson, 'The Role of the Writer', 256. Further references to this essay in this section are included in brackets.

Focusing on the manners in which literature and culture could contribute to this overall regeneration, Thomson sets off to examine 'certain ways in which membership of a minority culture affects the role of the writer' (257). He starts with a general classification of writers and their role in culture, pointing out that while there are undoubtedly writers 'whose work is largely independent of the size or status of the cultural community in which they work, who break into and out of a particular culture, seeming to belong to a cosmopolitan order', most writers are arguably part of a 'particular cultural environment, and to have their work defined, or restricted, or enriched, or influenced in some way, by that environment' (256).

In a culture which is not hindered or threatened, the writer's role includes communication, disseminating information and instruction, stimulating thought and provoking debate, providing entertainment, 'defining, consciously or subconsciously, the ethos of his community, or protesting against it, or satirising aspects of it', and is undertaken 'as a normal professional activity, for which they are adequately paid, and by which they can earn a livelihood' (259). The economic aspects of revivalist enterprises were never far from Thomson's mind, as attested in *Gairm* editorials and in the two publications discussed later in this section.

After sketching out this normal scenario, Thomson proceeds to consider different kinds of minorities, showing his awareness of developments in other regions and countries and his ability to draw productive parallels between them and Scotland. He differentiates between 'local-only minorities', including Italians in the USA or Pakistanis in Glasgow, i.e. those that can look to an independent country where the language is by no means neglected or suppressed, and 'specialised minorities', such as users of Nynorsk in Norway, before turning his attention to 'more absolute minorities', such as Bretons in France, Raetoromans in Switzerland and Gaelic speakers in Scotland. In contrast to local-only minorities, the absolute minorities have no metropolitan centre to refer to (257).

The role of the writer, as Thomson argues, varies according to the status of the minority culture and the attitude of the majority towards it. He mentions that for 'most of us', referring to those involved in Gaelic studies and revitalisation activities, the term 'minority culture' is loaded, as it implies 'lack of opportunity and recognition', and stresses the importance of outside forces and influences, observing that a minority culture can be 'fostered, recognised, tolerated, ignored, or persecuted' (258). Thus, he already hints at the future development of terminology and the adoption of the term 'minoritised', which suggest that the position of the culture/language is the result of a process, not a preordained state of affairs.

Even in the relatively fortunate case of Welsh-medium writers working in Wales, Thomson recognises some restrictions, such as the small maximum public, the limited offer of employment outside education and entertainment, and specific examples of the inability to make a living by writing novels or plays in Welsh. For these limitations, he proposes two solutions.

The state can provide adequate subsidies where the public market is too small; however, this step requires a much larger extent of economic and political autonomy and 'a degree of cultural interest and goodwill on the part of the government which is not apparent even in the case of Ireland' (259). Alternatively, the writer needs to combine creative work in the minority language pragmatically with another source of income. Thomson thus maintains that the ability of the minority culture to flourish, or otherwise, is not strictly dependent on the absolute number of language users but also on the overall climate in society and the political situation.

Thomson then turns his attention to less fortunate minority cultures. The limited resources of these cultures often give rise to the tendency among users of the language to seek entertainment in the majority culture, a trend which reduces and confines the role of the writer. In relation to entertainment, Thomson maintains there is a general tendency for the minority culture to 'retreat into pawkiness and cosiness, to hang on to a traditional formula long after it has lost its relevance or appeal, and so to brand itself as old-fashioned, stuffy or dull', and the writers do not have the opportunity to employ their talents and are excluded, for the minority culture 'refuses to be competitive' (261). He also points out that at the time when he is working on the essay, writers in all Celtic countries have been so far absent from the realm of the cinema, even in Ireland with all its policies and provisions for Irish, and he expresses uncertainty as to whether the cause resides in 'the lack of realism or goodwill in Irish language policy' (260).

Thomson then moves on to outline the degree and mode of contact of the minority culture with the majority one. A 'conservative and isolated minority culture' – the Aran Islands in the west of Ireland and parts of the Scottish Highlands up to the Second World War are listed as examples, may be able to preserve its ethos for a time and is likely to concentrate on conserving one or just a few selected aspects, such as 'dances, or pipe-music, or costume, or religious outlooks and mannerisms' (261). A distinct form of the language can also be retained, for example the biblical register of Gaelic and theological vocabulary in the Scottish Highlands, and in association with it a specialised form of literacy.[73] These trends, in particular the specialised literacy, naturally affect the role of the writer – positively in the sphere of theological literature, negatively in other realms. In Wales, where secular and religious activities are seen as complementary in relation to Welsh, rather than being in active opposition, the conditions for the writer are again different.

---

[73] In relation to religion, Thomson later notes that 'one section of the religious community adopted a code which was foreign to the Gaelic society', and which in turn 'eroded other aspects of that society, as for example the interest in secular literature and entertainment which was characteristic of Gaelic society' ('The Role of the Writer', 264). This ties in with Thomson's opinions on religion in relation to Gaelic and disrupts one of the stereotypical images of Gaelic culture as austere, serious and closely associated with radical Evangelical Christianity.

The rest of the essay is devoted to Scottish Gaelic, which is taken as a case history of a minority culture, and Thomson examines the role of the writer in this particular context. Writing in 1966, he classifies Scottish Gaelic culture as 'unsubsidised by the state, but still showing at least some signs of energy and enterprise' (262). He notes that although Gaelic users are more literate than in the previous century, from the point of view of the writer the situation remains unsatisfactory, for the population, educated through the medium of English, 'has come to believe that their native culture is depressed and second-rate' (264), cannot read Gaelic easily and seemingly has no need to do so. The use of Gaelic for any other purpose than for daily conversation or in a religious context is perceived as 'affected or eccentric, or pertaining to a new and odd class, that of the language revivers' (264). This observation has lasting resonance and hints at the different expectations and preferences of specific groups of Gaelic users and the possible tensions arising out of them. In relation to this state of affairs, Thomson claims that 'a process of denationalisation has been carried out with considerable success' and that 'the natural relationship between the spoken language and the written language' has been upset (264).

When commenting on the erosive influence of English education on Gaelic vocabulary and idiom, Thomson asserts that 'hand in hand with the decay of the language goes a decline in native taste, and a decline in racial loyalty' (264). The fact that Thomson's ideas as to what a 'native taste' means might be very different from more traditionally oriented revivalists is clear from his comment that secular literature and entertainment was always typical of Gaelic culture. The mention of 'racial loyalty', which brings to mind uneasy connections between language and blood, is not developed any further. Such associations of Gaelic with ethnicity are absent from Thomson's work, and, given his open and welcoming attitude that value a commitment to Gaelic and readiness to learn the language above place of origin and familial links, should most likely be read as a reproach towards people with ancestral ties to Gaelic for abandoning their language and culture, not as an attempt to limit access to it by the criteria of genetic make-up.

Thomson proceeds to comment on how the writer's own aims and attitudes to the language and culture determine their role. If one is convinced that Gaelic society should strive to regain some of its independence and wholeness, then a number of tasks and challenges arises: to strengthen the language by using it in as wide a gamut of situations and contexts as possible, thus expanding its range and flexibility, and, among other steps, to improve the provision for Gaelic in the realm of education, strengthen 'the sense of local responsibility and initiative', and bolster the musical tradition (265).

He then sketches different ways of revitalising the language, and in doing so outlines his own career, both retrospectively and prospectively.

Not surprisingly, he mentions the role of the scholar, with tasks such as 'investigating the resources of the language' and making them available to the public (265). This investigation includes editing texts, preparing dictionaries, collecting vocabulary from both oral and written sources, exploring ways of coining new words and examining language registers, thus establishing which areas of the language are 'in good health' and which are not, considering the 'psychological factors which affect the spoken and written use of the language', and contemplating the need for spelling and grammar reforms (265). Thomson himself participated in many of these activities, with varying degrees of success, as Chapter 4 examines in more detail.

The scholar's work can also help the task of the writer, and Thomson points out that 'in a situation such as the Scottish Gaelic one, it would be most useful to have a reasonably close liaison between the scholar and the writer, if the work of rehabilitation is to go ahead smoothly and quickly'; in his own case, this useful liaison was close indeed, as both conveniently met in one body. However, for the practical purposes of language revitalisation, the role of the writer is deemed more important, as the scholar might be too distant from practical considerations and 'chary of turning his energies to propaganda', while the writer is free of these inhibitions, and they should be able to use all materials and resources, and move the language to new areas of 'thought or experience', and by wrestling it into theses fresh contexts expand its 'depth, flexibility, and precision' (264–6).

Thomson also mentions the challenge of extending the range of subject matter, as 'a language which has been developed for purposes of homiletic or theological discussion does not easily adapt to the discussion of foreign policy or pop art' (266). He notes that Scottish Gaelic is currently used in 'daily news bulletins, and in descriptions of foreign travel, discussions on such topics as land improvement, drama, literary criticism, women's fashions, Japanese painting, and a host of subjects which a few years ago would have been considered unlikely, and by many impossible' (266), and a reader acquainted with the contents of *Gairm* in the first decades and Thomson's own contributions will recognise many of these examples as exact references (some of them are also referred to in Chapter 3). He points out that this has become possible in Gaelic thanks to the emergence of media open to these topics, and lists the BBC Gaelic programmes and *Gairm* as the prime representatives.

The journalistic role is proposed by Thomson as one of the most important in a minority culture, as it can boost not only the scope and flexibility of the language but also its prestige, and that of the society as a whole. The greater the range of media available, the more likely is the success of the policy, and while independent countries like Ireland have the advantage of official backing, even Gaelic Scotland 'can do much by self-help', and it could accomplish more still if even 'an additional handful of people turned their minds seriously to the task' (267), again highlighting the importance of individual commitment and effort.[74]

Thomson then turns his attention to Gaelic literature and mentions that in spite of the notable growth in the areas of modern poetry and short story over the last thirty years, there is still ample room for extension and experiment even in these two realms and much more so when it comes to the underdeveloped genres of the 'novel, biography, history, and expository writings' (267). These attempts, according to Thomson, require 'a greater than ordinary degree of effort, of dedication, of fervour' than would be necessary in a majority culture, and notes that in that context, the writer would also be enjoying more material benefits and a broader readership, returning to some of the initial observations of the essay.

The completion of new work, contributing to the strength of the minority culture and its sense of value and prestige, stems from the 'feeling of communal responsibility and pride' among the writers, and their work thus 'acquires some extra-literary characteristics', as they feel that they are helping to rebuild the language and knowing that their work 'will not be ultimately judged in isolation but as part of a communal effort' (268). Quite strikingly, Thomson likens this joint enterprise to the work of the 'masons and joiners who took part in the rebuilding of the Abbey at Iona, who, while taking pride in their individual tasks, also shared the vision of a completed building, and the satisfaction of taking part in a kind of crusade', bringing together the images of craft, devotion and holy war (268). He notes that in his view it is not 'over-fanciful to see the work of writers in a minority culture as a kind of crusade', but admits that one should be conscious of the dangers of such an attitude (268). Further military images, including those of partisanship, appear later in the article. The frequent use of concepts from biology and medicine in relation to minority languages is discussed below.

In relation to literature and the media, Thomson stresses the importance of achieving a certain bulk of work in the minority language: while absolute competition with the majority culture is impossible, it is necessary that the public 'should enjoy the luxury of choice' (268), a question that was also addressed in *Gairm* editorials and which remains relevant even today when it comes to Gaelic prose, especially to genre fiction. Thomson notes that in his view, Wales follows a commendable policy in this respect, producing publications for children and adolescents, TV parlour games and other popular formats, and recommends other Celtic countries study Welsh practice and learn from it.

---

[74] McLeod mentions the campaigns for greater provision for Gaelic on the radio and TV, and points out that Gaelic activists involved in them recognised the potentially negative impact of TV on Gaelic communities, quoting Thomson's comments on the subject, and also refers to Thomson's proposition from 1957 to establish a Gaelic television channel run by Gaelic organisations and universities. McLeod, *Gaelic in Scotland*, 170–2.

In this section of the essay, Thomson comes up with the striking image of a revivalist power plant, acknowledging that in the first half of the essay he considered the writer as part of 'an established machine, the machine that supplies power to a minority culture', and saw them as ministering to that culture, often with 'some dedication and enthusiasm' (268). At this moment, just when one might start to suspect Thomson of being too immersed in the pragmatic and practical aspects of economics and propaganda, he turns his attention to writers in a different position: to those who are 'not committed in this way, who cannot and who should not be committed', so his demands on writers in relation to minority languages are by no means absolute. The conflict between the minority and majority culture for writers who use English is acknowledged, as is the strong pull of the capital, and the danger of the writer who remains at home, if they are not from London, being labelled as regional or provincial. The market is recognised as being of no less importance for literature than for commercial affairs, and Thomson states that writers will naturally be attracted to places with facilities and business opportunities.

He comments on the 'tug-of-war', this time using a sporting image, in writers whose work is related to or influenced by two cultures, noting examples where this struggle has enriched Anglophone literature in the British Isles, including W. B. Yeats, Dylan Thomas, Neil Gunn, Hugh MacDiarmid and Gerard Manley Hopkins (the choice of authors is noteworthy in itself). He notes that similar enrichments can be seen in Welsh, Irish and Scottish Gaelic, and that some writers reflect the bilingualism of their lives and communities in using two languages in their work, such as his Bayble compatriot Iain Crichton Smith, observing that the position of the writer on a borderland between two cultures produces benefits that are sometimes claimed by the majority culture and sometimes reaped by the minority one. In this sense, he also reflects on the fact that 'fiercest partisanship occurs in the border area', which begets both the harshest attacks on the minority culture and the most extravagant defences of it (269).

Moving to another group of writers, Thomson acknowledges the contribution of second-language users of minority languages, of those who decide to learn them and use them as their creative medium, highlighting the lasting value of work done by some authors who got attracted to a different culture and approached it from an outsider's perspective. In this case, he uses the English poet, scholar and translator from Irish Robin Flower (1881–1946) as an example, and there would be more to prove him right in the following decades in the Scottish Gaelic context, including a number of *Gairm* contributors.

He notices that attitudes to minority cultures and languages often tend towards extremes, from adoration on the one hand and rejection on the other, and points out the importance of criticism, which may also come from inside and be expressed 'in satire, or irony, or some other form of protest, and a minority culture, with its tendency to ingrowing, and its incipient persecution complex, should be subjected to satire periodically', for 'a society that can learn to laugh at itself becomes more resilient, and the minority cultures need all the resilience they can muster' (270). This focus on satire, irony and humour is evident in Thomson's own writing, although it may not be the feature which is most frequently associated with it, and it is especially prominent in his contributions to *Gairm*, as discussed in Chapter 3.

In relation to criticism and satire, he picks up on another aspect of the writer's work in a minority culture, and notes that 'the very smallness of the society in a minority culture may be inhibitory', as the writer is too readily personally identified, a phenomenon which continues to influence especially the realm of literary criticism in Gaelic to the present. Taking off from the idiom 'B' aithne dhomh a sheanair' [I knew his grandfather], Thomson makes a bold statement, given the traditional ideas of Gaelic virtues of respectfulness and obedience towards one's ancestors, and compares a writer who worries too much about the reactions of their forebears to the 'good little boy who is seen but not heard', having nothing of their own to say (270).

In Thomson's view, one of the best methods of criticism and satire of society is through the medium of drama. This brings him to recall the 'abysmal history of drama' in Gaelic Scotland, and he stresses the need to devise more adequate means of putting more drama of all kinds to the public, as it could play 'the most vital role of all for the writers in a minority culture' (270). The question of Gaelic drama and its unfulfilled potential for the revitalisation of the language also received substantial coverage in *Gairm* editorials and is examined in Chapter 3. Given the variety of Thomson's activities and his usual readiness to step in and lead by example, it is intriguing to think about the reasons why he did not attempt to write any Gaelic plays himself – and if he did, why they did not appear in print or on the stage.

The essay, which summarises many of Thomson's convictions and preferences in relation to the revitalisation of Gaelic, is relevant not only for a Scottish Gaelic context, but to minoritised languages and literatures in general, as it touches on issues of continuing relevance, including cultural competitiveness, the importance of diverse reading material and reading for pleasure, and the potential of second-language users, which are now recognised as essential concerns in the development of Gaelic literature.

Gàidhlig ann an Albainn/Gaelic in Scotland *(1976)*

In 1976, Gairm Publications brought out a booklet entitled *Gàidhlig ann an Albainn/Gaelic in Scotland: A Blueprint for Official and Private Initiatives*.[75] The whole publication is bilingual, a gesture which proves that Gaelic can discuss all the progressive plans but also makes the suggestions accessible

---

[75] All page references to the booklet in this passage are included in brackets.

to those who do not have a command of the language, thus preventing excuses that politicians and civil servants cannot read it. The volume, edited by Thomson, featured the following contributions: 'Gaelic in Public Life/A' Ghàidhlig am Beatha fhollaiseach an t-Sluaigh' by Donald John MacLeod, 'The Primary School/Na Bun-sgoiltean' by Finlay MacLeod (Fionnlagh MacLeòid), 'Gaelic in Secondary Schools/A' Ghàidhlig anns na h-Àrd-sgoiltean' by Murdo MacLeod (Murchadh MacLeòid), 'Universities and Colleges/Na h-Oilthighean is na Colaisdean' by Donald MacAulay (Dòmhnall MacAmhlaigh), 'The Media (Broadcasting and Press)/Craobh-sgaoileadh is Pàipearan' by Martin MacDonald (Màrtainn Dòmhnallach) and 'Drama/Dràma' by Donnie MacLean (Donnchadh MacGillEathain). Thomson contributed the first and last chapters, on 'Gaelic in Scotland: The Background/Gàidhlig ann an Albainn: Beagan Eachdraidh' and 'Books, Literature, Publishing/Leabhraichean, Litreachas, Foillseachadh', and also the 'Salient Conclusions' (no Gaelic version given). The qualifications and experience of the individual contributors are outlined at the end, to give weight to their observations and to the proposed policies. Many of the points were later adopted in the SNP Gaelic Policy.

The booklet was produced bilingually; however, in Thomson's case, the Gaelic and English versions of his two chapters are by no means faithful translations, but rather two takes on the same subject, aimed at different audiences. The volume is preceded by a short introduction by Thomson in Gaelic and English, and these are not at all identical either. In Gaelic, Thomson notes that

> Tha creideas nan Gàidheal annta fhèin air neartachadh chun na h-ìre a leigeas leinn sealltainn pìos math romhainn. Nuair a tha sinn a' feitheamh an latha anns am bi barrachd smachd againn air ar dòigh-beatha fhèin ann an Albainn, 's e deagh àm a th' ann beachdachadh air an inbhe 's air an obair tha gu bhith aig a' Ghàidhlig 's na tha fuaighte rithe ann am beatha ar dùthcha. Chan eil seo ach toiseach tòiseachaidh. Tha sinn an dòchas gun toir e smuain air na leughas e, agus gur cuir e gu gnìomh iad ann an iomadh seagh. (iii)

> *The belief of the Gaels in themselves has strengthened to such a degree which allows us to look a fair way before us. While we wait for the day when we will have more power over our own way of life in Scotland, it is a good time to be thinking about the status of Gaelic and the work to be done on it and on related issues in the life of the country. This is but the first of many steps. We hope that it will provide food for thought for those who read it, and that they will turn that thought into action in a number of manners.*

The English introduction states:

> This is a good time for fresh analysis of Gaelic's role in the life of Scotland, and for fresh planning. [...] I have set out a series of salient

conclusions at the end, shaping these into a rough strategy which has its tactical elements. All the writers hope that these suggestions will be debated and adapted, and put into effect, some by individuals, some by groups and agencies, some by Government.

In a gesture typical of Thomson, the introductions are followed not by a motto from, say, a nineteenth-century Gaelic song but by a quote from Thomas Mann's *Doctor Faustus*, which stresses the necessity to accept new developments, and also the inevitable link between the old and the new: 'For just as little as one understands the new and the young, without being at home in the traditional, just so must love for the old remain ungenuine and sterile if one shut oneself away from the new, which with historical inevitability grows out of it.' This epigraph may be seen as a defiant pre-empting of possible criticism of the suggestions in the book as being too progressive and not mindful enough of Gaelic traditions, although it is unlikely that a quote from a German-language novel would have appeased those minded to raise such concerns in the first place.

In the opening chapter, Thomson provides a brief accessible overview of the history of Gaelic in Scotland, draws attention to the 'strong and still growing revival' (5) of the language in the last two decades, i.e. in the 1950s and 1960s, and concludes that its effect is already noticeable in the 1971 census figures. He also comments on the development of Gaelic revitalisation efforts and acknowledges the importance and varied range of activities of ACG in the early phase, noting that sometimes its desire to embrace all fields of activity was carried to extremes, and praises the later division of labour and differentiation of the field as a healthy trend which allows for the involvement of different kinds of talent and avoids 'dangers of centralisation' and the application of a 'clique vision'(7). He then moves on to structural changes and to the rethinking of Gaelic's role in the national life, and recommends that when a Scottish parliament or assembly is established, it should promptly set up a Commission on Gaelic, to conduct research into the position of the language, and also a Gaelic Secretariat to handle more practical matters and ongoing policy development (10).

In the chapter on 'Books, Literature, Publishing', Thomson provides a detailed overview of the field, including exact numbers of books published in the period 1930–74 according to genre. On the basis of these figures, he comments on the continuing scarcity of Gaelic books and their importance for education, entertainment and the competitiveness of the language, and also for the development of vocabulary for modern subjects, from astronomy and oil processing to international trade and agriculture, returning to the points he raised in 'The Role of the Writer' ten years earlier.

The 'Salient Conclusions' consist of numbered practical recommendations for specific steps and policies to be introduced in 'Education', 'Gaelic in the Life of the Nation', 'The Media and the Arts' and 'Strategic Planning', some of which have been put into practice in the following forty-five years, while others could be still picked up. The volume ends with a Gaelic-only note that expresses the hope that the opinions formulated in the chapters will not only serve as impulses for Scottish governing bodies, but also become a source of encouragement to users of Gaelic themselves, and that they will take the opportunity to carry out and implement what the nation lacks.

There is a hopeful and energetic air about the publication, inspired by the intensified discussions about a referendum at the time and by the encouraging figures from the 1971 census. Thomson notes that 'it is possible now to predict that the revival is only in its early stages, and will continue strongly for the remaining quarter of the century', stating that there can be 'little doubt now that the figures of Gaelic speakers will by then have surged well over the 100,000 mark' (5). Perhaps they would have, if the 1979 referendum had yielded a different result. Nonetheless, the authors of the booklet did their best to bring about these successes, and McLeod acknowledged its importance in 2020, noting that the HIDB Gaelic Report Group in 1981 was building on older policy proposals, especially on those formulated in *Gàidhlig ann an Albainn*.[76]

Why Gaelic Matters *(1984)*

Thomson's pamphlet *Why Gaelic Matters*,[77] subtitled 'A short discussion of the history and significance of Gaelic and its related arts in Scottish life', was published as part of the Saltire pamphlets series in 1984, in cooperation with the Saltire Society and ACG, not by Gairm Publications, and this is one of the indications of the broader outlook of the volume. Four years later, in 1988, a sister volume was brought out: *Why Scots Matters* by scholar and translator J. Derrick McClure, with whom Thomson cooperated on a number of occasions.

Why Gaelic Matters is written in a popularising tone, clearly aimed at the general public, and in English only. It can be seen as part of Thomson's efforts to promote the conception of Gaelic as part of Scottish culture and heritage in general, a component which is not only precious for historical and sentimental reasons but also viable and productive, and which could be, with regard to prospects of independence, also an important economic asset. He notes that 'the resurgence of interest in Gaelic has close links with various political aspirations for Scotland, though it would be inaccurate to suggest that there is a strict correlation between the two movements', and describes Gaelic as 'one of the touchstones of Scottish cultural and political pride' (23). He asserts that 'a gradual withering away of a vital part of Scottish history and culture is not to be regarded with equanimity by anyone who has the full interests of Scotland at heart' (33).

---

[76] McLeod, *Gaelic in Scotland*, 192–3.
[77] All page references to the pamphlet in this passage are included in brackets.

In spite of the overt propagandist focus of the pamphlet, it starts in a measured tone and acknowledges the difficulties of the situation of Gaelic:

> Gaelic has an indisputable claim to be the oldest surviving language in Scotland, the language that has been spoken longest in our country, in the course of its recorded history, and it is because of this that it is sometimes referred to as our national language. But language history is seldom clear-cut and uncomplicated, and the language history of Scotland is no exception to the rule. (5)

The booklet provides a detailed history of Gaelic in Scotland, summarising its development and the challenges it has faced, and introducing the basic points about its culture, literature and society, up to its present position and the 1981 census, including a detailed breakdown of the census figures. It stresses the general relevance of Gaelic in Scotland by listing well-known historical events that have a Gaelic connection and by explaining that many people in Scotland have Highland family links without realising them, with Gaelic only a couple of generations away. Thomson also highlights the ubiquity of Gaelic in place names and the commonly used words of Gaelic origin, especially vocabulary for the natural world of Scotland, dress, food and drink, and the general appeal of Gaelic music, poetry and dance.

Why Gaelic Matters also discusses policy directions, but while *Gàidhlig ann an Albainn* was clearly aimed at two readerships, decision makers and Gaelic users, this pamphlet is directed at the general public, rebutting widespread misconceptions and kindling positive attitudes, and thus preparing the ground for the future of the language in an independent Scotland.

Images of the language

Apart from his observations and policy proposals, the way in which Thomson writes about Gaelic in the three publications examined above and the imagery he uses is worth noticing in its own right. The language is often presented as a living organism, a bird, an animal or a human being, in which case it is exclusively personified as a woman. These images may help to induce readers to feel more affection and compassion for the language and attraction towards it, and also encourage them to action on its behalf. These rhetorical strategies are not new and Thomson's writing echoes older discourses and imagery.

In Gaelic, the grammatical gender of all languages is feminine, a fact that did not escape Alexander MacDonald in his eulogy 'Moladh an Ùghdair don t-Seann Chànain Ghàidhlig' (The Author's Praise of the Ancient Gaelic Tongue), in which he craftily plays with the personification of individual languages as female figures. Languages tend to be female in other gendered languages too, including Slavic ones, and this is reflected in discourses of national and linguistic revival in a number of countries. The homeland in revivalist discourse is frequently styled as a woman, examples of which can be found in the arts of most nations that went through a period of revival in the nineteenth century, and the personified motherland in female form can easily merge with the image of the national language envisaged as a woman, distressed and in need of support and rescue when the revival is still ongoing, or triumphant and regal once it has been accomplished.

A certain degree of personification and metaphors of life and death are common in contemporary discourse about minoritised and lesser-used languages too, including academic publications. For instance, McLeod observes that

> the decline of Gaelic became a self-fuelling argument: action to promote the language was deemed a waste of money either because it was destined to **die out** anyway or illegitimate because with so few speakers the costs of provision would outweigh any benefits (MacKinnon 2012). In a common metaphor, governmental support for Gaelic constitutes a '**life-support system**', and some commentators contend that it is time '**to pull the plug**'. (Linklater 2002; Fry 2007)[78] [emphasis mine]

Images of Gaelic as a living organism recur in Thomson's academic work, pamphlets and *Gairm* editorials, and also in his poetry, with the associated imagery of life, sickness and death, flourishing and rooting out. In 'The Role of the Writer', he states that 'the social organism which exists in the area of this minority culture, in the Scottish Gaelic area, is diseased, or that parts of it are living and parts dead' (264). Later in the same essay, he argues that Celtic communities are 'still living, developing organisms – developing in a modern, competitive world – not fossils or other exhibits to be placed in a museum', arguing against the conviction that the only interest of Celtic societies is that they are 'fossils in exposed strata of a modern landscape' (257).

He acknowledges that there may indeed come a time when 'a Celtic community ceases to develop as a living Celtic organism' and when 'the particular Celtic language goes out of currency', comparing it to a part of an organism or a human brain which is dying, and he also considers 'stunted Celtic organisms' and the writer's role in them, if there even is one in such a case. The issues surrounding language death and survival here assume a curious physical materiality, and the use of the discourse of physiology and medicine is remarkable. The imagery of fossils, excavations and museum exhibits in relation to Gaelic recurs several times in the poetry, especially in the collections *Smeur an Dòchais* and *Sùil air Fàire*, as discussed in Chapter 5.

---

[78] McLeod, *Gaelic in Scotland*, 46.

In two poems, Thomson presents the language as an animal in order to make a point about its situation. In the poem 'Dùn nan Gall' (Donegal), Irish is ironically compared to a goat which can survive on meagre pasture on hills and cliffs, referring to the prejudiced tendency to connect it exclusively with rural environment, and then it becomes a woman, and the poem imagines it dying in the arms of its sister, Gaelic. The poem 'Uiseag' (Lark) envisages Gaelic as a dying lark, a fragile creature which affects the observer by the hint of its former beauty and its near-death state. Both poems are examined in detail in Chapter 5.

Gaelic is also personified as a woman in some *Gairm* editorials. In the editorial to *Gairm* 7 (1954), Thomson and MacDonald defend themselves against criticism of the quarterly's language standards by explaining that their aim is to use contemporary Gaelic, not the Gaelic of two hundred years ago, and complain that too many people try to make the language 'seann chailleach bhochd 'ga riasladh anns an corsaidean a bh' aice an uair a bha i am blàth na h-òige' [a poor old woman trapped in the corsets which she wore in the flower of her youth]. In *Gairm* 8 (1954), they comment on the lack of respect for the language among Gaelic users themselves, noting that 'taobh a-muigh na h-eaglaise, tha a' Bheurla fhathast na banamhaighstir a tha ag iarraidh air a' Ghàidhlig bhochd neo-ionnsaichte a bhith umhail dhi' [outside the church, English is still the mistress which demands the poor unlearned Gaelic to be obedient to her]. The work of women contributors to *Gairm* and the attitude of the two editors towards them is discussed in Chapter 3.

Thomson and other figures

Several individuals who were active in Scottish culture and letters at the fin-de-siècle and in the early decades of the twentieth century are interesting to consider as Thomson's precursors in various ways. Patrick Geddes, a staggeringly prolific and interdisciplinary figure involved in the national revival and publishing activities and known for high standards and international inspirations, offers an interesting parallel, but there seems to be no proof of influence in Thomson's published output. He chose to write the entry on Geddes for *The Companion to Gaelic Scotland*, and the inclusion itself is remarkable, but he introduces him as a sociologist and town planner and mentions neither his journals, such as *The Evergreen*, which had Gaelic contributors, including the prominent folklore collector Alexander Carmichael (Alasdair MacGilleMhìcheil),[79] nor the shared interest in Ossian.[80] However, there are other cases where the

---

[79] Shaw, *The Fin-de-Siècle Scottish Revival*, 21.
[80] For a recent monograph that engages with Geddes's thought, see Murdo MacDonald, *Patrick Geddes's Intellectual Origins* (Edinburgh: Edinburgh University Press, 2020). He comments on Geddes, Thomson and Ossian on p. 77.

influence is well attested, including Ruaraidh Erskine of Mar and Hugh MacDiarmid, and these are examined in more detail in the following sections.

Ruaraidh Erskine of Mar

Stuart Richard Erskine (1869–1960), known by his own choice as Ruaraidh Erskine of Mar (Ruaraidh Arascain is Mhàirr), was a prominent nationalist, activist, editor and author.[81] As McLeod notes, 'In the early decades of the twentieth century, the most militant writers pressed for the full re-Gaelicisation of Scotland as the logical extension of this nationalist view. The central figure here was Ruaraidh Erskine of Marr [sic], a perfervid nationalist activist and founder of and prolific contributor to a number of important periodicals in Gaelic and English.'[82]

Erskine first got interested in the nationalist activities in Ireland and maintained correspondence with Patrick Pearse, whom he most likely met at the pan-Celtic Congress in Cardiff in 1899 which they both attended.[83] As Patrick Witt puts it, 'Erskine represents a nexus between Irish separatists and Scottish politicians, labour leaders, and intellectuals', and is an example of the 'underappreciated connection between Irish separatist thinking and Scottish political thought in the early twentieth century'.[84] The long-term, informed and discerning interest in developments in Ireland is one of many connections between Erskine and Thomson.

Erskine was, together with Fionn MacColla and Compton Mackenzie, one of the intellectuals who, as McLeod notes, 'tended to identify the Reformation as the great wrong turn in Scotland's history, a disastrous move away from Scotland's Catholic, Gaelic past that cut Scotland off from the mainstream of European culture' and stressed the strong link between Gaelic and Catholicism.[85] While Thomson's own background was in the

---

[81] Erskine was born into the family of William Macnaghten Erskine, the fifth Baron Erskine, descended from the Erskine Earls of Buchan. Derick Thomson, 'Erskine, Stuart Richard [known as Ruaraidh Erskine of Mar] (1869–1960)', *Oxford Dictionary of National Biography* (2004) <https://ezproxy-prd.bodleian.ox.ac.uk:4563/10.1093/ref:odnb/40311> Accessed 15 April 2023.

[82] McLeod, *Gaelic in Scotland*, 37–8, 70.

[83] Patrick Witt, 'Connections across the North Channel: Ruaraidh Erskine and Irish Influence in Scottish Discontent, 1906–1920', *The Irish Story*, 17 April 2013 <http://www.theirishstory.com/2013/04/17/connections-across-the-north-channel-ruaraidh-erskine-and-irish-influence-in-scottish-discontent-1906-1920> Accessed 15 April 2023. Pearse and Erskine shared an interest in Gaelic-medium education and the literary revival of their respective Celtic languages, and the radical Irish magazine *An Claidheamh Soluis* (The Sword of Light) that first appeared in 1899 and of which Pearse became editor in 1903, likely served as inspiration for Erskine's own journalistic ventures.

[84] Witt, 'Connections across the North Channel: Ruaraidh Erskine and Irish Influence in Scottish Discontent, 1906–1920', no page number.

[85] McLeod, *Gaelic in Scotland*, 39, 71.

Church of Scotland and his attitude to religion in general, especially to the radical Evangelical churches in the Western Isles, was critical, he and Erskine agree that the spread of Protestantism helped to sever the strong ties with Ireland, which in their view had a negative impact on the situation of Gaelic in Scotland.

In comparison with many of his contemporaries who did not connect the efforts to obtain devolution or full independence for Scotland with a specific linguistic and cultural agenda, Erskine considered the revival of Gaelic an essential component of a successful political emancipation. He himself is a remarkable representative of second-language users of Gaelic involved in the movement before the Second World War.[86] Erskine criticised his contemporaries for their indolence and unwillingness to learn Gaelic, proving by his own example that it was a manageable task. The frequent argument that the language was dying anyway and too obsolete to sustain a modern culture was in his view a mere cover-up for intellectual laziness:

> [. . .] so the Anglo-Celts being mentally lazy, and the Gaelic language hard to gain, they came to speak ascendancy about it, vowing that it must soon perish, and that though it might have some good literature in the past of long ago, yet now it was become archaic most evidently. Once the dog has been cursed to perdition any stick or stone should serve his better beating; and once sloth has overcome us, no matter what and how sorry the excuse, it will serve fine to cloak our mental inactivity.[87]

This biting comment would not be amiss in the *Gairm* editorials. It is also interesting to note Erskine's employment of the term 'Anglo-Celt', while Thomson in 'The Role of a Writer' advocates for the use of the term 'Anglo-Scottish', as a parallel to Anglo-Irish.[88]

Erskine's activities were part of the flux of political groups and small magazines in the early decades of the twentieth century. In 1920, he was involved in the foundation of the Scots National League (SNL), one of the movements which in 1928 merged into the National Party of Scotland, which is a direct predecessor of the current SNP. During the time of Erskine's involvement, the SNL, as Peter Lynch points out, focused on the status of Gaelic in Scotland and the teaching of Scottish history, and proposed the formation of a Celtic, Gaelic-speaking state in Scotland, but Erskine and like-minded members were overpowered by another faction that was concerned less with cultural nationalism and more with what they

---

[86] For a discussion of the involvement of first-language and second-language users involved in Gaelic initiatives, see McLeod, *Gaelic in Scotland*, 52.

[87] Quoted in Margery McCulloch (ed.), *Modernism and Nationalism: Literature and Society in Scotland 1918–1939* (Glasgow: Association for Scottish Literary Studies, 2004), 294–6.

[88] Thomson, 'The Role of the Writer', 269.

perceived as practical political business.[89] For some time, as McLeod notes, Erskine also considered the foundation of a political party whose aim would be to give Gaelic priority, make the teaching of Gaelic mandatory in all schools in the Highlands, and require all holders of public office in Scotland to obtain a command of the language.[90]

The most important contribution of Erskine's to Gaelic revitalisation efforts were his magazines, which are discussed in more detail in Chapter 3. In terms of literary revival, Erskine was convinced that Gaelic writers should be drawing inspiration from international practice, but without mindlessly imitating them, combining the best European trends with elements from the Gaelic tradition. Similarly to Thomson, he was both a theoretician of his revival and its practitioner, leading by example and proving that what he called for in his essays on Gaelic literature was actually feasible. One of Erskine's main concerns was the development of Gaelic drama, with a focus on non-realist modes of theatrical expression, and the complaint about the inability of ACG to use it efficiently in the revitalisation efforts runs from Erskine to Thomson, as examined in Chapter 3. Erskine himself wrote essays in Gaelic, plays and short stories,[91] combining, like Thomson did later, the role of an editor and critic with that of a practising author. Both were also interested in the international literary scene: Erskine was closely following developments especially in Ireland, Russia, France and England.

The revival stimulated by Erskine's efforts faded out in the mid-1920s, and he spent a long time in France and only returned to the United Kingdom shortly before his death. He has fallen into relative obscurity, his writing remains untranslated and up to recently, little research was devoted to his activities,[92] but Thomson knew his work and held him in high regard. He singles out Erskine in *Why Gaelic Matters*, referring to the growth of Gaelic fiction in the first quarter of the twentieth century, noting that it was encouraged by Erskine, 'energetic editor of periodicals', and that his 'long-lived periodical *Guth na Bliadhna* also encouraged radical in-depth journalism'.[93] He also contributed the entry on Erskine for the

---

[89] Peter Lynch, *SNP: The History of the Scottish National Party* (Cardiff: Welsh Academic Press, 2002), 33–4.
[90] McLeod, *Gaelic in Scotland*, 69.
[91] I discuss his Gaelic detective stories in the essay 'Snake Women and Hideous Sensations: The Strange Case of Gaelic Detective Short Stories by Ruaraidh Erskine of Mar', *Scottish Literary Review* 12:1 (2020), and his essays on Gaelic drama in 'A Fitting Offering to the Gaelic Thalia or Melpomene: Ruaraidh Erskine of Mar and Drama in Scottish Gaelic', *Litteraria Pragensia* 30:59 (2020).
[92] Donald John MacLeod comments on Erskine and his activities in his unpublished doctoral dissertation *Twentieth-Century Gaelic Literature: A Description, Comprising Critical Study and a Comprehensive Bibliography* (University of Glasgow, 1969). Recent publications on Erskine include the essay by Witt, Cairns's biography and Alex Murray's essay 'Unionism, Nationalism, Cosmopolitanism: Ruaraidh Erskine of Marr at the Fin de Siècle', *Studies in Scottish Literature* 48:1 (2022).
[93] Thomson, *Why Gaelic Matters*, 19.

Oxford Dictionary of National Bibliography and likely wrote a short piece about him for *Gairm* 16 (1956). The unsigned one-page article, accompanied by a photograph of Erskine, who was eighty-seven at the time, describes him as one of the old heroes who did much for Gaelic, but is unknown to younger generations, and acknowledges that his magazines were important predecessors for *Gairm*. It mentions the fact that Erskine is considering a return to Scotland and that he remains convinced there will be no success or improvement in the country before it separates itself from England.[94] Erskine in the end did not manage to return, but he lived long enough to see the continuation of his earlier revivalist efforts in *Gairm*.

Hugh MacDiarmid

Hugh MacDiarmid (born Christopher Murray Grieve, 1892–1978), a modernist poet of European stature and one of the leading spirits of the Scottish Renaissance in the 1920s, combined an interest in cultural and linguistic revival in Scotland and in different strands of radical politics. He was a member of the Independent Labour Party and wrote for a socialist newspaper,[95] was keenly following developments in Ireland and the 1916 Rising, observing another Celtic nation trying to assert its independence from the British Empire, and was also interested in the 1917 Russian revolution. In the 1920s, MacDiarmid flirted with fascism,[96] and throughout the 1930s, his major political concern was communism, but while being a member of the Communist Party of Great Britain, he was also one of the founding members of the NPS in 1928.

In the 1920s, MacDiarmid was experimenting with a synthetic form of Scots, which he gathered from local dialects and written documents across centuries, and he encouraged others to follow his example and revive Scots as a literary medium. MacDiarmid's cultural nationalism was remarkable in its inclusivity and willingness to incorporate many diverse aspects of Scotland into the national whole without striving to dissolve them. As McLeod notes, most authors associated with the Scottish Renaissance movement in the interwar period were strongly supportive of Gaelic, although the majority of them never achieved an active command of the language of any kind: MacDiarmid was no exception in this respect, as he was less interested in learning actual Gaelic than he was in pondering the 'Gaelic Idea', an abstract intellectual notion of national self-assertion.[97]

In 1940, he published the groundbreaking anthology *The Golden Treasury of Scottish Poetry*, bringing together poetry in Latin, Scots, English and

[94] 'Ruaraidh Arascain agus Mhàirr', *Gairm* 16 (1956), 367.
[95] 'Hugh MacDiarmid, 1892–1978', *The Poetry Foundation* <https://www.poetryfoundation.org/poems-and-poets/poets/detail/hugh-macdiarmid> Accessed 15 April 2023.
[96] Scott Lyall, 'Hugh MacDiarmid and the British State', *The Bottle Imp* 18 (June 2015), 1.
[97] McLeod, *Gaelic in Scotland*, 37–8, 118. McLeod also references McCulloch (ed.), *Modernism and Nationalism*, 270–316.

Gaelic. His readiness to include Gaelic and the choice of Gaelic material, especially of Alexander MacDonald, was influenced by his then close association with Sorley MacLean.[98] MacDiarmid also knew Erskine, who contributed Gaelic writing to his *Scottish Chapbook*, and MacDiarmid praised Erskine's efforts to modernise Gaelic letters in his 1926 collection *Contemporary Scottish Studies*.[99]

While Thomson, with a preference for practical and peaceful politics, would have little in common with MacDiarmid's far-left and far-right leanings, his interest in his works and activities concerning the revival of Scots and the national revival of Scotland in general is well attested. Over the years, he published five reviews of works on or by MacDiarmid, which is the most extensive coverage for any individual writer in Thomson's reviews, followed by Sorley MacLean and Edwin Muir.[100] The poem 'Adhlacadh Ùisdein MhicDhiarmaid, 13. 9. 78' (Hugh MacDiarmid's Burial, 13. 9. 78), which appeared in the section 'Dàin às Ùr' in the collection *Creachadh na Clàrsaich* (1982), captures Thomson's memories of MacDiarmid's funeral and stresses the resounding long-term impact of his work. MacDiarmid is also celebrated as one of the company of heroes that brings together figures associated with Scots and Gaelic in *Sùil air Fàire*. Thomson translated two of MacDiarmid's poems into Gaelic, 'Empty Vessel' as 'Soitheach Falamh' and 'Lourd on my Hert' as 'Truimead Geamhraidh air Mo Chridhe'. Both appeared in *Bàrdachd na Roinn-Eòrpa an Gàidhlig* (1990).

In *Why Gaelic Matters*, Thomson highlights the extensive exchange in the field of Highland and Lowland fiddle music and notes that 'similar borrowing across linguistic borders is common in song-melodies also – Burns took over Gaelic airs and Alasdair Mac Mhaighstir Alasdair Scots ones'.[101] The fact that Thomson was keeping an eye on developments in Scots and Scots literature is also evident from his *Gairm* reviews, and from the conference entitled *Gaelic and Scots in Harmony*, which was held at the University of Glasgow under his auspices in 1990 and after which he edited the resulting publication.[102]

---

[98] For a detailed discussion of their acquaintance and intellectual influences, see Peter Mackay, *Sorley MacLean* (Aberdeen: AHRC Centre for Irish and Scottish Studies, 2010).
[99] McLeod, *Gaelic in Scotland*, 119.
[100] Duncan Glen, *MacDiarmid and the Scottish Renaissance* (*Gairm* 52: 1965); Duncan Glen, *Forward from Hugh MacDiarmid* (*Gairm* 100: 1977); *Hugh MacDiarmid: Complete Poems* (Carcanet) (*Gairm* 162: 1993); Alan Riach (ed.), *Hugh MacDiarmid: Contemporary Scottish Studies* (*Gairm* 173: 1995); Angus Calder, Glen Murray and Alan Riach (eds), *The Raucle Tongue* (*Gairm* 182: 1998).
[101] Thomson, *Why Gaelic Matters*, 22.
[102] *Gaelic and Scots in Harmony: Proceedings of the Second International Conference on the Languages of Scotland* (Department of Celtic, University of Glasgow, 1990). Some of the papers are freely available from the website <https://www.arts.gla.ac.uk/STELLA/STARN/lang/GAELIC/gaelic.htm>. The conference was held at the University of Glasgow on 30 June–2 July 1988 and brought together a number of scholars, including Christopher Whyte, J. Derrick McClure and Kenneth MacKinnon, who discussed various linguistic and literary intersections of Gaelic and Scots.

While in a number of *Gairm* editorials and in some poems, Thomson mentions hostile attitudes and policies towards Gaelic originating from the Lowlands, he did not see the Scots language as a competitor for Gaelic, but rather as another part of Scotland's diversity and distinctiveness, which is manifested in the equal treatment of Gaelic and Scots in the SNP Gaelic Policy. In the editorial to *Gairm* 189 (1999), he suggests that the new parliament should focus on Scots, together with raising the prestige of Scottish literature in general in schools and colleges, and *Gairm* 182 (1998) featured an advert for *Lallans*, a magazine published by the Scots Language Society, to mention just some examples. This vision of an independent Scotland as a framework for future developments of not only Gaelic, but also Scots and other languages and cultures, which support the claim for independence and contribute to Scotland's cultural richness and economic strength, is one of the most salient aspects of Thomson's legacy.

International inspirations

As McLeod points out,

> Over time, Gaelic movements have been only moderately interested in and connected to efforts on behalf of other minority languages and 'small nations'. Throughout the twentieth century, for example, Gaelic periodicals published many reports on developments concerning minority communities elsewhere in Europe, but this coverage was rarely sustained and detailed. Without doubt, the main foci of interest and linkage have been the fellow 'Celtic' countries of Ireland and Wales. In relation to Ireland, these connections have mostly been cultural in nature, while Wales has been looked at enviously as the main source of policy innovation and energy. The emulation of Wales has been particularly strong since the 1960s, and most of the policies and initiatives that have been put in place for Gaelic, most notably the Gaelic Language Act of 2005, can be understood as smaller or weaker versions of existing provision for Welsh.[103]

Thomson can be considered an exception to this general trend described above, for throughout his life he retained a keen and discerning interest in developments in other Celtic countries, especially in terms of policies and activities aimed at revitalising their languages. This concern is evident in his scholarly work, organisational efforts and translations, as discussed in Chapter 4. This section considers Wales and Ireland as particular sources of inspiration for Thomson's thought, although awareness of the situation in Brittany, Cornwall and the Isle of Man is also reflected in the publications he chose to review for *Gairm*.

---

[103] McLeod, *Gaelic in Scotland*, 55.

Wales

In 1950, Thomson spent half a year at the University College of North Wales, Bangor, in order to improve his command of the language before taking on the newly established lectureship in Welsh at the University of Glasgow.[104] As Peredur Lynch of Bangor University noted, 'Thomson would have been struck by the strength and vibrant nature of the Welsh at a community level in north-west Wales, especially in the large quarrying villages of Caernarvonshire ... He would have encountered a strong cohort of native-speaking students in the Welsh Department, whose tuition would have been through the medium of Welsh.'[105] As Thomson himself noted, the foundation of The Gaelic Book Council in 1968, in which he was crucially involved, was inspired by a similar organisation in Wales.[106] Given the fact that he was acquainted with the works of the prominent author and nationalist Kate Roberts (see Chapter 4), it is also not unlikely that he knew about her involvement in the publishing house Gwasg Gee and the Welsh-language weekly *Y Faner*, which could have provided inspiration for *Gairm* and Gairm Publications.

In 'The Role of the Writer', Thomson uses Wales as one of the main cases for comparison and contrast with the Gaelic situation, and lists it as an example of a flourishing and viable minority culture. The reasons he gives for the relative viability of Welsh include the still substantial, albeit declining, number of speakers of about 650,000, widespread literacy with a long tradition, and the embeddedness of Welsh in 'many aspects of the national life of Wales', namely education, religion, literature and music, and to a lesser degree in communication and entertainment. He lists some outward signs of this strength, such as the autonomy of Welsh in education and publishing, teaching through the medium of Welsh, and the widespread use of Welsh in scholarship.[107] However, he also stresses that even Welsh has its problems, most importantly the continuing decline in the number of speakers and the constant pressure of the 'English and/or Anglo-American' majority culture.

In *Gàidhlig ann an Albainn/Gaelic in Scotland*, Thomson touches upon the question of minority language activism. He comments on the recent increase in the creation of Gaelic pressure groups in Scotland, and while noting that some suffer from insufficient command of the language and

---

[104] Thomson, 'Some Recollections', 60.

[105] Quoted in Marcus Williamson, 'Derick Thomson: Poet and Champion of the Gaelic Language', *The Independent*, 9 April 2012 <http://www.independent.co.uk/news/obituaries/derick-thomson-poet-and-champion-of-the-gaelic-language-7627275.html> Accessed 15 April 2023.

[106] Thomson, 'Some Recollections', 62.

[107] 'The Role of the Writer', 258–9. It may seem curious that Thomson singled out this particular aspect as especially important, since he did not use Gaelic for his own scholarly work to any large extent, as discussed in Chapter 4.

have been more strident than convincing in their enterprises, he expresses hope that effectiveness will arrive with time, and recommends learning from Welsh models, in terms of organising petitions and other kinds of practical activism.[108]

Wales is referred to in several *Gairm* editorials. In the editorial to *Gairm* 62 (1968), Thomson praises the refreshing effect of international travel and singles out Wales as a country from which Gaelic revitalisation efforts could take a lesson. He lists some important similarities between the two environments, such as the rising support for nationalist parties, social discontent and the growing revival of language and lifestyle. In contrast, he mentions the far greater visibility of Welsh in the public space and much more active everyday use, observing that the language is heard in the streets, in shops, and at high tables at universities, and also the more advanced provisions, including Welsh-language schools, the possibility to use the language in court, and the amount of Welsh on TV, the number of books published, catering for a substantial market of buyers which supports production, and the confidence of Welsh users. The combined focus on policies and institutional improvement and individual action and commitment is again evident here.

Publications about Wales and Welsh were also substantially represented in *Gairm* reviews: *Gairm* 5 (1953) featured a review of *Y Geiriadur Newydd* and Gwyn Williams' *Introduction to Welsh Poetry*, which likely served as one of the sources of inspiration for Thomson's own *An Introduction to Gaelic Poetry*, and he also reviewed the collection of proverbs *Diarhebion Cymru* (*Gairm* 16: 1956), *Gwerin, Journal of Folk Life* (*Gairm* 17: 1956) and *The Welsh Extremist* (*Gairm* 84: 1973), a collection of essays by intellectual and academic Ned Thomas, which examines Welsh literature and culture and describes the pressures on Welsh society. Thomson could have seen Thomas as a relatable fellow figure with preoccupations similar to those of his own.

Ireland

Although the strong connection between Gaelic Scotland and Ireland may be seen as a matter of course, due to geographical closeness and the shared literary culture which flourished until the seventeenth century, it cannot be taken for granted in the nineteenth and twentieth centuries, for, as McLeod notes, 'among Scottish Gaels more generally, attitudes to Ireland and the Irish were coloured by anti-Catholic prejudice and distaste for Irish nationalism. Scotland experienced heavy immigration from Ireland during the nineteenth century, principally in the industrial areas, and Irish immigrants and their descendants suffered significant hostility and discrimination.'[109] For Thomson, Ireland was an important source of inspiration throughout

---

[108] Thomson, 'Gaelic in Scotland: The Background', 9.
[109] McLeod, *Gaelic in Scotland*, 72. Anti-Irish prejudice, including the association with diseases, is also discussed by Ascherson, *Stone Voices*, 69.

his career, but he was also aware of the differences between the two countries and keen to stress both the links and the divergences.[110]

It is possible that Irish initiatives, like the small independent publishing house Sáirséal agus Dill (founded in 1947), which contributed to the beginning of modern Irish-language literature, and the magazine *Comhar* (established in 1942), which published new writing, cultural and social commentary, and also produced several books each year, could have inspired *Gairm*.[111] The quarterly featured a great deal of Irish-related content over the years, plus frequent commentary on Irish affairs, and also published a number of translations from Irish, including the works of Brian Merriman (*Gairm* 130–1: 1985), Flann O'Brien (*Gairm* 113: Winter 1980) and Máirtín Ó Direáin (*Gairm* 171: 1995), to list just a few out of many examples.

In the article 'Blàth Ùr air an t-Seann Stoc (A' Ghàidhlig an Eirinn)' [New Blossom on the Old Stump (Gaelic in Ireland)], which appeared in *Gairm* 29 (1959), Thomson comments on language revitalisation efforts in Ireland in more detail. He explains how difficult it is to assess the success of these initiatives, as some will say that there are but 35,000 people in Ireland who use Gaelic naturally, and were that true, then Irish as the language of family communication would be in danger, and in much worse a state than Gaelic in Scotland, where there are almost 90,000 users. However, Thomson notes that there are hundreds of thousands of people in Ireland who have some command of Irish, be it basic or advanced, which they acquired in schools, in evening classes or on trips in the Gaeltacht, with many of them equally fluent in both languages. He also mentions the importance of the recent English–Irish dictionary, edited by Tomás de Bhaldraithe and published by the Irish Stationery Office, and singles it out as one of the most important books to emerge for a long time. It is not a book of recent Irish poetry or a play that gets the praise, but this unassuming practical volume.

He also uses Ireland as a point of contrast in 'Tìr na Gàidhlig ann a Linn na h-Ola':

> Tha sinn ann a suidheachadh annasach an-dràsta a thaobh staid na Gàidhlig ann an Albainn. Tha a' Ghàidhlig, mar gum b' eadh, a' fàs 's a' crìonadh aig an aon àm, agus a rèir 's dè an t-sùil a bheir sinn oirre gheibh sinn dà shealladh dhi a tha glè aocoltach ri chèile. Gheibh duine an dà shealladh sin ann an Èirinn cuideachd, far a bheil Gaeilge

---

[110] I attempt to provide a comprehensive discussion of Thomson's involvement with Ireland and of Irish-related content in *Gairm* in the essay 'Derick Thomson and Ireland', *Litteraria Pragensia* 33:65 (July 2023), and some of the main points have been included in this section.

[111] Another possible inspiration, in terms of overall outlook and combination of literary concerns and social commentary, could have been the English-language monthly *The Bell* (1940–54), as Thomson was aware of the activities of its co-founder Seán Ó Faoláin ('The Role of the Writer', 269).

a' crìonadh air taobh an iar na dùthcha agus nas trice air beul an t-sluaigh na shaoileadh tu an iomadh àite, oir thug na h-Èireannaich rud math de dh'urram dhi 'nan obair riaghlaidh, anns na pàipearan 's mar sin. Cha robh iad ga cumail a dh 'aon ghnothaich airson Là an Naoimh Pàdraig, ach ga cur ri d' aghaidh gach uair a thadhladh tu Oifis Puist no bus-àros.[112]

> *We are in a strange situation regarding the state of Gaelic in Scotland at the moment. It is as if Gaelic was growing and withering at the same time, and depending on our perspective, we will get two very dissimilar views. The same two views can be observed in Ireland too, where Irish is withering in the west part of the country, but more than one would expect, it is spoken by people in a number of other places, for the Irish have given the language a good deal of recognition in legislation, in the papers, and in other fields. They were not keeping the language for St Patrick's Day, but rather put it in people's face every time they visit the post office or the bus station.*

The reviews in *Gairm* also testify to Thomson's awareness of the developments in Ireland. Over the years, he wrote about a number of Irish books, both poetry and prose, and discussed publications dealing with various aspects of Irish language, literature and culture, including the philosophical dictionary *Foclóir Fealsaimh* by Colmán Ó Huallacháin (*Gairm* 30: 1959) and Thomas Kinsella's *The Dual Tradition* (*Gairm* 172: 1995). One of the reviews in particular reveals an unexpected connection: for *Gairm* 13 (1955), Thomson decided to include *Drámaíocht in Éirinn* [Drama in Ireland] by Micheál Mac Liammóir (1899–1978) in an overview of recent Irish publications.

Tha Micheál MacLiammóir iomraiteach mar actar ann an iomadh dùthaich, agus tha e fhèin air dealbh-chluichean a sgrìobhadh am Beurla is an Gàidhlig. Tha esan a' toirt seachad geàrr-eachdraidh na dràma an Èirinn – araon am Beurla is an Gàidhlig – le cunntas air na prìomh thaighean cluiche, na h-actaran is na dràmairean. Tha e den bheachd gu feum dràma na h-Èireann leudachadh cuspair is spioraid, a bheir nas dlùithe don traidisean Eòrpach i, gun a gnè dùthchail a chur air chùl. Nach mairg sinne ann an Albainn nach eil dràma Ghàidhlig idir againn fhathast, is nach motha tha iarrtas aig a' mhòr-chuid againn oirre.[113]

> *Micheál Mac Liammóir is famous as an actor in many countries, and he himself writes plays in English and in Gaelic. He presents a short history of drama in Ireland – English and Gaelic together – and gives an account of the main theatres, actors and playwrights. He thinks that Irish drama should broaden in terms of subject matter and outlook, that would bring it closer to the*

---

[112] Thomson, 'Tìr na Gàidhlig ann a Linn na h-Ola', 209.
[113] Ruaraidh MacThòmais, 'An Sgeilp Leabhraichean', *Gairm* 13 (1955), 87.

European tradition, without leaving its native disposition behind. What a pity we do not have Gaelic drama in Scotland yet at all, and that the majority of us do not feel the need for it.

Gairm 38 (1961) published a substantial review of Mac Liammóir's memoir *Each Actor on His Ass* by Finlay J. MacDonald. In it, MacDonald shows detailed awareness of Mac Liammóir's multifaceted and dynamic career, and applauds his voluntary choice of Irish identity by claiming that although he was born in London and the name is a translation of Michael Willmore, 'chan eil mòran Èireannach a tha cho Èireannach ri Micheal Mac Limmaóir' [there are not many Irish who would be as Irish as Micheál Mac Liammóir].[114] MacDonald highlights the breadth of Mac Liammóir's activities and the depth of his commitment, and points out that the present volume, which describes his tours in Germany and Egypt, is actually a compilation based on two books originally published in Irish by Sáirséal agus Dill, suggesting the editors of *Gairm* were indeed closely following developments in Irish-language publishing.

The flamboyant and openly gay co-founder of the Gate Theatre, who was born in London as Alfred Willmore, learnt Irish in adulthood, and decided to become part of Irish culture and to produce creative writing in the language, might seem very far away from the serious academic who grew up in a Gaelic-speaking family in the Outer Hebrides, but there are a number of shared preferences and preoccupations. Both Thomson and Mac Liammóir focused on intellectual and creative courage and ambition to transcend national boundaries and sought to provide their cultures with fresh impulses from Europe. This cosmopolitan orientation was in both cases accompanied by a certain degree of elitism. Mac Liammóir became a proficient and eloquent writer in Irish and exhibited the degree of commitment and high standards Thomson appreciated in second-language contributors to *Gairm*. However, it is fair to keep in mind that Mac Liammóir published his most important plays in English rather than Irish, and that his involvement with Irish-language theatre was a relatively minor part of his overall work.

In his recent study of Mac Liammóir's Irish essays, Radvan Markus notes that the above-mentioned effort to open Irish-language culture as much as possible to international influences included, for instance, the publication of his travel writing, which brought new experiences into Irish-language literature, depicting his experiences from Spain, the USA and France.[115] These have an interesting parallel in Thomson's own short travelogues published in *Gairm*, which are examined in Chapter 3. Markus also highlights Mac Liammóir's focus on translation as a vital means of developing and expanding Irish-language literature, especially translations of great works

---

[114] Fionnladh J. MacDhòmhnaill, 'An Sgeilp Leabhraichean', *Gairm* 38 (1961), 183.
[115] Radvan Markus, 'Micheál mac Liammóir, the Irish Language, and the Idea of Freedom', *A Stage of Emancipation: Change and Progress at the Dublin Gate Theatre*, ed. Marguérite Corporaal and Ruud van den Beuken (Liverpool: Liverpool University Press, 2021), 123.

of literature from English and other European languages, and he himself contributed to this aim by producing a number of plays by European authors in Irish, including dramatic works by Housman, Chekhov, Molière and Lady Gregory.[116] Thomson paid substantial attention to translation into Gaelic as an active practitioner and supported it as an organiser, as discussed in Chapter 4.

Mac Liammóir lacked Thomson's nationalist motivation, and Thomson would probably disapprove of Mac Liammóir's assertion that nationality is a 'miserable thing', but they seem to meet nonetheless when arguing for the value of linguistic and cultural diversity and distinctiveness, with no religious agenda: Mac Liammóir suggests that 'the best way to create harmony in this world [...] is not to encourage the big things to destroy the weak, but to persuade them that all exist, there is difference among them, but that none of them needs to think that it is better than any other'.[117] As Markus notes, Mac Liammóir held the opinion that 'if the Irish language were to be truly revived, Irish theatre and Irish life in general should become more confident and open to foreign influences'.[118] In that case, writers would be free to engage with any topic of their choice, which comes close to Thomson's points from 'The Role of the Writer'. Neither hesitated to cause controversy and both were aware of the transgressive and provocative function of authors in minority cultures, as outlined by Thomson in 'The Role of the Writer', and the caustic tone and mischief of Mac Liammóir's essays and the readiness to voice controversial opinions are also reminiscent of some of Thomson's editorials. As much research remains to be conducted on both figures, perhaps yet more connections will come to light.

It is not known whether Thomson ever met Mac Liammóir, but he did maintain personal contacts with Irish authors and intellectuals. In the editorial to *Gairm* 76 (1971), Thomson commented on the continuation of bardic circuits in Scotland and Ireland, and mentions the upcoming visit of Irish poets, including Máirtín Ó Direáin, Caitlín Maude and Seán Ó Tuama, who were coming to Scotland for a series of readings, following on from a preceding Irish tour of Scottish poets. Thomson was involved in these literary exchanges and also reflected on his personal relationship to some Irish colleagues in his poetry. The section 'Dàin às Ùr' [Latest Poems] in Thomson's *Creachadh na Clàrsaich* (1982) includes the poem 'Do Mháirtín Ó Direáin' [To Máirtín Ó Direáin], written, according to a footnote, on 4 October 1977 in a café on Grafton Street in Dublin, on the day when Ó Direáin received the Ossian Prize for the promotion of minority languages.[119] Born and raised in an Irish-speaking family in the Aran Islands, about ten years older than Thomson himself, Ó Direáin also

---

[116] Markus, 'Micheál mac Liammóir', 125.
[117] Translated by and quoted in Markus, 'Micheál mac Liammóir', 122.
[118] Markus, 'Micheál mac Liammóir', 123.
[119] *Creachadh na Clàrsaich*, 262.

had an interest in European literatures and is recognised as one of the authors who revitalised Irish-language poetry in the middle of the twentieth century, so it is not surprising that Thomson felt a personal connection to him and held his work in high regard.

In the 1991 collection *Smeur an Dòchais/Bramble of Hope*, Thomson included the poem 'An Cuimhne Dháithi Ó hUaithne' (In Memory of David Greene). A footnote explains a dedication to David Greene (1915–81), 'Irish scholar, patriot and unforgettable character', who 'died shortly after touching down at Dublin Airport, on returning from a visit to the Faeroes'.[120] Greene was a Celtic scholar and Professor of Irish at Trinity College Dublin and at the Dublin Institute for Advanced Studies.[121] His first academic appointment was as lecturer in Celtic studies at Glasgow University, so it is possible Thomson would have met him in Scotland. They had a number of shared interests, including Wales and Scandinavia, both were active in politics and journalism, as Greene contributed regularly to the magazine *Comhar*, and Thomson's poem also reveals a deep personal affection and friendship.

In terms of comparable figures in the Irish context, the lack of references in Thomson's works to Máirtín Ó Cadhain (1906–70) is curious, as his wide-ranging activities, political engagement, commitment to literary experiment, and resolution to bring new impulses to Irish-language culture come close to Thomson's own preoccupations, and whose lecture 'Páipéir Bhána agus Páipéir Bhreaca' (White and Speckled Papers, 1969) presents an interesting parallel to 'The Role of the Writer'. As Radvan Markus has recently explored,[122] Ó Cadhain was closely acquainted with developments in Scotland and with Gaelic poetry, and wrote several articles on the subject based on his visits, and, as Markus notes, there is a specific and complimentary mention of Thomson, so the omission seems to be one-sided, but perhaps more proofs of interaction will yet be revealed, given the recent growth of scholarship on both authors.

---

[120] *Smeur an Dòchais*, 76–7.
[121] Diarmaid Ferriter, 'Greene, David William', *Dictionary of Irish Biography*, October 2009 <https://doi.org/10.3318/dib.003606.v1> Accessed 15 April 2023.
[122] Radvan Markus, 'Máirtín Ó Cadhain and Scotland', *Litteraria Pragensia* 33:65 (July 2023).

CHAPTER THREE

Gairm

This chapter examines the quarterly *Gairm* which Thomson co-founded and (co-)edited for fifty years, as one of his most influential contributions to the revitalisation of Gaelic in the second half of the twentieth century. It comments on the role of periodicals in the Gaelic revival before the magazine, with special focus on those with a similar outlook. Most of the chapter is devoted to a detailed account of *Gairm* itself: its foundation and funding arrangements; the gradual transformation of its aims and focus; topics related to Gaelic revitalisation addressed in the editorials; and contributors who provided content for the magazine. It concludes with an overview of Thomson's own writing which appeared in the quarterly and the way these pieces reflect his revivalist preoccupations.

Periodicals in the Gaelic revival

Due to the relative cheapness of production, regularity, collective nature, capacity to promote new writing and ability to quickly respond to contemporary issues, the magazine has been an important tool in the revitalisation of minoritised languages in the nineteenth and especially in the twentieth centuries. Similar examples of revivalist media ventures can be found in Celtic countries other than Scotland. In Wales, Kate Roberts (1891–1985) published the weekly *Y Faner* as part of the Welsh-language press Gwasg Gee. In the Isle of Man, activist, folklorist and poet Mona Douglas (1898–1987) founded the periodicals *Manninagh* and *The Manxman* with similar aims in mind.[1] In Brittany, author and scholar Roparz Hemon (1900–78) ran the periodicals *Gwalarn*, *Sterenn* and *Arvor*, with the aim to prove that high culture could emerge in Breton and which stimulated the production of new literature in the language, representing an interesting parallel, but their appreciation has been overshadowed by the founder's wartime involvement with Nazi Germany.[2]

---

[1] Fenella Bazin, 'Douglas, (Constance) Mona (1898–1987), folklorist', *Oxford Dictionary of National Biography*.

[2] Hemon went into exile in Ireland where he was employed at the Institute for Advanced Studies in Dublin and continued to work for the Breton language, producing teaching materials, academic studies and creative works. Gwenno Piette, 'Breton Literature During the German Occupation (1940–1944): Reflections of Collaboration?', conference paper, University of Ulster, 'Celtic Literature in the 20th Century' (2000) <https://www.aber.

As McLeod notes, in comparison to other European minority languages, 'the Gaelic periodical press has been distinctly underdeveloped', which 'has had significant consequences for Gaelic language movements in terms of limiting the opportunities for ideological, policy and cultural debates'.[3] In this realm of distinct underdevelopment, several magazines stand out. Donald John MacLeod observes that 'at the centre of each was one man or a very small nucleus of enthusiasts, usually motivated by nationalistic fervour' who 'ran periodicals in which Gaelic was used for discussing the latest intellectual problems and in which the work of experimental writers of fiction was welcomed'.[4] In these ventures, the founder often served as the editor and strove to procure money for the publication, either by means of subscriptions or donations or from their own resources, and contributed a significant part of the content.

The first of these personalities was Reverend Norman MacLeod (Tormod MacLeòid, 1783–1862)[5] and his magazines *An Teachdaire Gaelach* (The Highland Messenger) and *Cuairtear nan Gleann* (The Traveller of the Glens),[6] which attempted to provide their readers with information and instruction that had so far only been available in English and contained articles on various subjects, from history and religion to agriculture and current affairs, poetry, fiction and book reviews. As MacInnes observes, MacLeod intended to 'develop from the pre-existing traditions, written and oral, a formal standard Gaelic prose which could handle a wide range of subject matter', and succeeded in creating a 'genuinely popular readership' and standards that influenced Gaelic writers for more than a century.[7] Thomson singles out MacLeod in his brief overview of Gaelic literature in *Why Gaelic Matters* as an editor of periodicals and a prolific essayist, and notes the strong radicalism that informs much of his writing.[8]

Other nineteenth-century Gaelic periodicals were inspired by MacLeod's efforts, although they exhibited less religious leaning, including *An Gàidheal* (The Gael), a bilingual monthly edited by Angus Nicolson (Aonghas MacNeacail), and *Mac-Talla* (Echo), the very first Gaelic newspaper in Nova Scotia, which was published by Jonathan G. MacKinnon.[9] Both these periodicals published not only new Gaelic literature, but also translations from other languages, especially from English, into Gaelic – for instance,

---

ac.uk/mercator/images/breton_literature_during_German_Occupation.pdf> Accessed 15 April 2023.
[3] McLeod, *Gaelic in Scotland*, 54.
[4] Donald John MacLeod, *Twentieth-Century Gaelic Literature*, 53.
[5] MacLeod was a minister of the Church of Scotland, nicknamed 'Caraid nan Gàidheal' (friend of the Gaels). He organised material relief in the Highlands in the difficult decades of the 1830s and 1840s, and also promoted Gaelic in education.
[6] Donald John MacLeod, 'Gaelic Prose', *Transactions of the Gaelic Society of Inverness* XLIX (1976), 203–4.
[7] John MacInnes, 'Caraid nan Gàidheal', *The Companion to Gaelic Scotland* (1983), 35.
[8] Thomson, *Why Gaelic Matters*, 19.
[9] MacLeod, 'Gaelic Prose', 204–5.

Stevenson's *Treasure Island* and short stories by James Hogg.[10] ACG started to issue the magazine *An Deò-Ghrèine* (The Sunbeam) in 1905, and it appeared under the title *An Gàidheal* (The Gael) from 1923 until 1967.[11] The magazine was designed as a bilingual publication but English content prevailed.[12] From 1958 to 1962, James Thomson, Derick Thomson's father, served as editor.[13]

The magazines founded and edited by Ruaraidh Erskine of Mar, which combined a broad cosmopolitan outlook, political radicalism and popular appeal, set an especially important precedent for Thomson's own efforts. In Donald John MacLeod's words, Erskine 'deployed his own capital and his remarkable resources of ideas and of energy to rid Gaelic literature of the influence both of its "peasant origins" and its new "enthusiasm for the music hall"' and to raise it to the best European standards of the time.[14] To this end, he founded several magazines that he edited, contributed to and sponsored: the bilingual monthly *Am Bàrd* (The Poet, 1901–2), the quarterly *Guth na Bliadhna* (The Year's Voice, 1904–25, bilingual until 1919, all-Gaelic afterwards), the weekly *Alba* (Scotland, 1908–9), a magazine devoted to fiction, *An Sgeulaiche* (The Storyteller, 1909–10 monthly, 1911 quarterly), and a book-length annual, *An Ròsarnach* (The Rose Garden, 1917, 1918, 1921, 1930).[15]

The most influential of Erskine's publications was *Guth na Bliadhna*, which lasted for an impressive twenty-one years. Erskine also sought to make information of all sorts available to Gaelic readers, but his focus was on much more intellectual and elite audiences, and the choice of subjects to an extent was governed by his own interests. In response to a complaint that *Guth na Bliadhna* was too highbrow for the majority of Gaelic readers, he pointed out that the aim of the magazine was to

> [. . .] deagh litreachas anns a' chànain Ghàidhlig a chur a-mach, agus mar an ceudna spiorad fìor thuigseach lèirsinneach a thaobh nithean àrda an t-saoghail seo a dhùsgadh anns na Gàidheil air fad. Ma ghabhas seo dèanamh ann an dòigh a bheir tlachd agus toileachadh don mhòr-chuid de na Gàidheil, tha sinn toilichte; ach mur toir, tha sinn coma, is gur iad is motha leinn daonnan prionnsabalan seach daoine.[16]

---

[10] Donald John MacLeod, *Twentieth-Century Gaelic Literature*, 38.
[11] Donald John MacLeod, *Dualchas an Aghaidh nan Creag: The Gaelic Revival 1890–2020* (Inverness: Clò Bheag, 2011), 11. McLeod, *Gaelic in Scotland*, 64–5.
[12] McLeod, *Gaelic in Scotland*, 64–5.
[13] Derick Thomson, 'An Gaidheal', *The Companion to Gaelic Scotland*.
[14] MacLeod, 'Gaelic Prose', 210.
[15] Derick Thomson, 'Erskine, Stuart Richard [known as Ruaraidh Erskine of Mar] (1869–1960)', *Oxford Dictionary of National Biography* (2004) <https://ezproxy-prd.bodle ian.ox.ac.uk:4563/10.1093/ref:odnb/40311> Accessed 15 April 2023.
[16] Quoted in MacLeod, 'Gaelic Prose', 211–12 (my translation).

[. . .] *publish good literature in the Gaelic language, and also to awake the spirit of true understanding and intelligence towards the elevated things of this world in all the Gaels. If it can be done in a way that brings pleasure and happiness to most of the Gaels, we are glad; if not, we do not care, for principles are more important to us than people.*

Guth na Bliadhna published treatises on a wide range of topics, including Scottish and European politics, philosophy, folklore and ethnology, literature, and also book reviews and criticism. In tune with Erskine's own religious persuasion, it strove to promote Roman Catholicism by featuring prayers and biographies of saints. Erskine wrote a good deal of the content himself, but he managed to assemble a small team of regular contributors, including the professional journalist Angus Henderson (Aonghas Mac Eanruig), who often addressed topics related to land use and education, and Donald Sinclair (Dòmhnall Mac na Ceàrdaich) contributed poetry and drama. John MacCormick (Iain MacCormaig) and Angus Robertson (Aonghas MacDhonnchaidh), authors of the first two Gaelic novels, *Dùn-àluinn* (Dunalin, 1912) and *An t-Ogha Mòr* (The Great Grandson, 1913) respectively, regularly wrote for *Guth na Bliadhna* and enjoyed Erskine's support and encouragement. In accordance with his pan-Celtic interests, Erskine had a number of Irish contributors, including Pearse and the famous lexicographer and leader of the Gaelic revival Padraig Ua Duinnín, and in later years he published texts by Breton revivalists Pierre Mocaër and Paul Diverrès.

In 1948, a bilingual English–Gaelic periodical, *Alba*, was launched by Malcolm MacLean (Calum MacGill-Eain) and T. M. Murchison (Tòmas MacCalmain) but appeared only once due to a lack of funding.[17] Thomson contributed the poem 'An Loch a Tuath' (The North Loch) and the short story 'Ri Taobh an Teine' [By the Fireside] to the first issue of the magazine, and he likely appreciated some of the radical opinions expressed in it, such as the caustic essay 'Uisge-beatha agus Uisge-bàis: Reflections on Gaelic Drama' on the insufficient employment of theatre in the revitalisation efforts, by Hector MacIver (Eachann MacÌomhair), a close acquaintance of Thomson's from 1948 onwards, as discussed later in this chapter. The realisation of *Alba*'s demise and its implications for the future of Gaelic writing might have been one of the immediate impulses for the foundation of *Gairm*.

Thomson had a lifelong interest in journalism. His magazine debut, entitled the *Bayble Herald*, was founded by the ten-year-old editor and issued in the Bayble schoolhouse, 'admittedly for very local circulation' (i.e. his parents, brother and aunt). When 'copy was short and inspiration failed', large sketches of Cotrìona, a local woman who came to help with the cleaning filled the space.[18] His second venture into journalism was a

---

[17] Thomson, 'Some Recollections', 60.
[18] Thomson, 'A Man Reared in Lewis', 135; Thomson, 'Some Recollections', 57. Thomson talks about his childhood journalistic projects in the documentary film *Creachadh na*

student nationalist periodical entitled *Alba Mater*, which he co-founded at the University of Aberdeen in 1945: it was short-lived but enjoyed initial commercial success, as a number of buyers mistook it for the regular literary magazine *Alma Mater*.[19] Six years later, he embarked on a journalistic project which proved to be one of the major achievements of his career, a venture with profound influence on some parts of the Gaelic world in the second half of the twentieth century, and also a venue where his political opinions and his vision of the Gaelic revival could be both formulated and carried out in poetry, essays and other forms.[20]

Founding and funding *Gairm*

The project started in 1951[21] when Thomson, who was at the time often involved in broadcasting, approached Finlay J. MacDonald,[22] since 1945 of the Gaelic department of the BBC, with the idea of establishing a Gaelic quarterly magazine, seeing the gap and the need for such a publication. They spent the first year gathering funds from various supporters: in the first editorial (*Gairm* 1: 1952), they mention that they were certain of the need to procure all the means related to the effort themselves, by asking people and organisations for donations. At the end of the first issue, a list of supporters, both individuals and groups, was published, including the folklorist John Lorne Campbell of Canna (Iain Latharna Caimbeul, 'Fear Chanaidh'); the novelist Compton Mackenzie; Sam MacLean (i.e. Sorley); his brother, the classicist and translator John MacLean (Iain MacGill-Eain); and, not surprisingly, Ruaraidh Erskine of Mar. They managed to collect £1,000, and since the first issue cost only £300, the magazine had a solid start in terms of financial management and could produce two more issues relying only on the initial contributions.[23]

 Clàrsaich (BBC Alba, 2000, prod. A. Mhoireasdan), which also shows some pages from his handwritten and hand-drawn periodical.
[19] Thomson, 'A Man Reared in Lewis', 134.
[20] Among the longest-running and most influential periodicals, McLeod lists ACG's monthly *An Deò-Ghrèine/An Gaidheal* (1905–67), Erskine's quarterly *Guth na Bliadhna* (1904–25) and *Gairm* (1952–2002). *Gaelic in Scotland*, 54.
[21] In some sources, the date is given as 1952: the confusion springs from the fact that while the magazine was established in 1951, the first issue appeared in 1952. Since *Gairm* 65 (1968), the first page of the magazine included 'stèidhichte 1951' [founded 1951] under the title *Gairm*.
[22] MacDonald was a native Gaelic speaker born and raised in Harris. A radio and television producer by profession, he worked on films such as *A Boy in Harris* (1966) and *The Highlander* (1959). He published three volumes of memoirs in English dealing with his childhood in Harris between the two world wars: *Crowdie and Cream* (1982), *Crotal and White* (1983) and *The Corncrake and the Lysander* (1985). For *Gairm*, he wrote reviews; articles on music; an extensive series 'As Aithne Dhuibh ... ?' [Do You Know ... ?], introducing interesting people; translations (poetry by Boris Pasternak); travelogues; and humorous pieces, including advice on how to knit stockings.
[23] Thomson, 'Some Recollections', 60.

The issue of funding and the importance of support from readers recurred in the editorials. In *Gairm* 17 (1956) and *Gairm* 29 (1959), the editors stress that two things keep *Gairm* 'on the perch': loyal readers who buy it and companies that advertise in it and see the benefit of being visible in the journal, although they may have no interest in Gaelic. Like Erskine's journals before it – *An Sgeulaiche*, for instance, promoted Vauxhall's Stout and the celebrated 'Mandarin' razors on the title page – *Gairm* featured all-Gaelic advertisements for goods ranging from whisky to electric cookers, jewels and cutlery, and services of various establishments. These represent an insight into the fashion and trends of the period, but also make a statement regarding the commercial potential of Gaelic, presenting it as a language that can help to boost trade, not only as one that needs subsidising.

In terms of funding, as MacAulay points out, *Gairm* was initially 'independent of all the elements of the Gaelic establishment – church, state and Comunn Gàidhealach'.[24] This allowed the editors to express critical views on many issues, including the work of possible sponsors such as ACG, the Western Isles Council (Comhairle nan Eilean) and the Highlands and Islands Development Board (HIDB). In *Gairm* 56 (1966) the editorial recognises a contribution from the Scottish Arts Council and also mentions the promise of state financial support for Gaelic publishing. In *Gairm* 90 (1975), the Scottish Arts Council is acknowledged again, noting that the support enables editors to pay a modest fee to contributors, not only meet the costs. The growing support of *Gairm* from official Scottish bodies corresponds with the gradual increase of institutional provisions for Gaelic in Scotland.

Until *Gairm* 47 (1964), Thomson and MacDonald steered the magazine as co-editors, and up to *Gairm* 56 (1966), MacDonald remained involved as a member of the trust. From the next issue (1966), Donald John MacLeod (Dòmhnall Iain MacLeòid)[25] is listed as Thomson's co-editor, and the editorial to *Gairm* 56 announces that a new voice will be heard in the editorials – perhaps sweeter, perhaps more bitter to some ears, and MacLeod indeed brought with him pronounced political focus.[26] He stayed as co-

---

[24] MacAulay, 'Introduction', *An Rathad Cian*, 4.
[25] Donald John MacLeod (1943), a native Gaelic speaker from Ardhasaig, Harris, completed a doctorate under Thomson's supervision at the University of Glasgow and wrote an extensive thesis on twentieth-century Gaelic literature, which still remains one of the most comprehensive sources of information on Gaelic writing between 1900 and 1960. He was a lecturer in Celtic at Glasgow when Thomson served as Head of Department, published a number of articles on Gaelic fiction, and edited the collection of short stories *Dorcha tro Ghlainne* (Through a Glass Darkly, 1970). Several of his academic publications are quoted throughout this study.
[26] A prolific and versatile author, MacLeod wrote essays and opinion pieces on a number of topics, ranging from the Vietnam War, Christianity and politics, John Knox, the thought of Mao Tse-Tung; to education, drugs and cinema, and also contributed short stories, poems, travelogues from the USA and Nova Scotia, reviews and several editorials.

editor until *Gairm* 97 (1976). Although both MacDonald and MacLeod shaped the magazine by their own viewpoints, talents and personal interests, Thomson was clearly the major force behind the whole venture, and even more as sole editor from 1977.

Intended readership and thematic focus

As Edna Longley notes, 'Irish and Scottish circumstances ensure that, more than elsewhere, periodical and magazine overlap', and she mentions *Gairm* specifically as an example of this overlap, caused by the 'need to maximise resources (financial and human) in a small country':

> Derick Thomson's Scottish Gaelic magazine *Gairm* (1952–2002) also catered for the extra-literary concerns of a linguistic community. An ideological cause – which generates conceptual tension as well as holistic possibility – is the founding role of literary nationalism, and poetry's founding role in that. Poetry magazines belong to a history of speaking for Ireland or Scotland.[27]

The magazine's title, *Gairm* [Cry, Call, Cock-crow], was meant as a wake-up call to users of Gaelic to take more interest in their own language and culture and also in contemporary Scottish and international affairs, and as a summons that attracts people from abroad to the Gaelic world. From the first issue, the cover featured the drawing of a cockerel, a symbol which went through different artistic renditions but remained associated with the magazine until the last issue, and the editorials often played with galline imagery.[28]

One of the radical aspects of *Gairm* was to make this 'call' in Gaelic only from the very beginning, a decision which was kept throughout the fifty years of the quarterly's existence. As McLeod notes, 'for much of the twentieth century, Gaelic organisations, especially An Comunn [Gaidhealach], tended to conduct their affairs in English, and most Gaelic periodicals were actually bilingual rather than all-Gaelic'.[29] One of the aims of the magazine was clearly to prove that Gaelic is flexible enough to sustain diverse content that reflects the varied interests and concerns of its users, in Scotland and increasingly also abroad.

The thematic focus of *Gairm* transformed throughout the years, with a changing ratio of the literary and extra-literary. Thomson and MacDonald were clearly aiming to attract a substantial and broad readership, and

---

[27] Edna Longley, 'Phoenix or dead crow? Irish and Scottish Poetry Magazines, 1945–2000', *Modern Irish and Scottish Poetry*, ed. Peter Mackay, Edna Longley and Fran Brearton (Cambridge: Cambridge University Press, 2011), 295.

[28] In her essay, Longley presents an overview of periodical naming tendencies, listing *Gairm*, together with *The Dark Horse, Mongrel Fox, Blind Serpent* and others, as part of the Irish/Scottish magazine menagerie (309).

[29] McLeod, *Gaelic in Scotland*, 54.

combined radical new literature and comments on contemporary affairs with more light-hearted content and traditional writing. In the first editorial, they claim: 'gun leugh daoine leabhraichean ma lorgas iad rudeigin inntinneach annta, agus cuideachd, mura leugh daoine leabhraichean 'nan cànan fhèin, gun tèid a' chànain leis an t-sruth ann an ùine nach bi fada' [that people will read books when they find something interesting in them, and that unless people read books in their own language, the language will be gone in a short time].[30] They state that Gaelic survives on the lips of ordinary people in the Gàidhealtachd – crofters, fishermen, housewives – and when they stop using the language, scholars will be unable to save it, and therefore they dedicate *Gairm* especially to these readers.[31]

In the early issues, the commitment to this promise was evident enough. *Gairm* 1 (1952) included, among other content, a description of St Kilda, a history of fishing in Lewis, poems, cartoons, a song with a complete score and lyrics, a 'women's page' discussing fashion and household management, a dedicated section for learners of Gaelic, book reviews and a crossword puzzle. During the years, the magazine also featured travelogues, advertisements, portrayals of interesting people with photographs, humorous stories and traditional community poetry: Ronald Black fittingly compared *Gairm* in this period to the Gaelic *Picture Post*.[32] In this respect, some roots of *Gairm* can be traced to the Portree high school magazine *An Cabairneach* (The Tattler), where Gaelic prose, as MacLeod points out, at last broke free of Norman MacLeod's 'sombre formality' and the 'earnest idealism' of Erskine and his circle.[33] It is no accident that young Finlay J. MacDonald, while studying in Portree, served as the first editor of *An Cabairneach*.[34] In the later decades, *Gairm* gradually transmuted into a more exclusive literary magazine, publishing mostly poetry, short stories and reviews, but still retaining some of its initial variety.

The editorial to *Gairm* 98 (1977) stresses the inclusivity of *Gairm* and states that it is designed for everyone, black and white, Protestant and Catholic, islanders and mainlanders, educated or not, and that it is able to welcome in the same issue Jorge Luis Borges, funny local news and many kinds of poetry, so that all readers would find something interesting in it. In the editorial to one of the last issues, *Gairm* 198 (2002), Thomson again draws attention to the diversity of *Gairm* contributors that mirrors the variety of its readers. He notes with gratification that new poets are being

---

[30] 'As a' Chathair', *Gairm* 1 (1952), 13.
[31] 'As a' Chathair', *Gairm* 1 (1952), 13.
[32] Ronald Black, '*Gairm*: An Aois Òir', *Aiste* 2 (2008), 95.
[33] MacLeod, 'Gaelic Prose', 213, 215.
[34] Anne Loughran, 'Bibliography of the Non-Traditional Creative Gaelic Skye Prose: *An Cabairneach*', *Gaelic Literature of the Isle of Skye: an Annotated Bibliography*, 2018 [website based on the author's MA dissertation, University of Aberdeen, 1986], available at <http://www.skyelit.co.uk/prose/creat2.html> Accessed 15 April 2023.

drawn to Gaelic from all over the world and expresses the hope that this new poetry will be read in Gaelic schools (and ever the shrewd businessman, he offers that *Gairm* will send to them a packet of issues at a reasonable price).

In the first years, *Gairm* organised Gaelic classes and encouraged readers to use the magazine as a study resource in order to spread the command of the language. In *Gairm* 3 (1953), the editors announce that Gaelic lessons for children, based on the quarterly, are held in Glasgow every Saturday, and suggest to readers they could and should conduct their own classes with the help of the material published in the magazine – giving the example of Manchester, where thirty readers meet every week to learn Gaelic with the help of *Gairm*. In *Gairm* 42 (1963), a new specialised section aimed at young people was announced, led by Chrissy Dick (Criosaidh Dick), with the hope that young contributors would in time provide some of the content themselves. In the 1990s, Thomson was running a specialised section for learners entitled 'Theab Mi a Leughadh (Earrann do Luchd-ionnsachaidh)' [I Almost Read (A Piece for Learners)], the first one appearing in *Gairm* 160 (1992) and the twentieth in *Gairm* 179 (1997), proving that even in the last decades of the quarterly's existence, when it transformed into a mostly literary magazine, the educational and revivalist agenda was never far from Thomson's mind. Gairm Publications also brought out Thomson's *Gaelic Learners Handbook* (1973).

Engaging readers

In the editorials, readers were repeatedly encouraged to share their opinions, submit their own contributions, and invest their energy and resources not only in *Gairm*, but also in the revitalisation of Gaelic in general. In *Gairm* 164 (1993), the editorial asks people to sell some copies of the quarterly in their community – not to make the venture more financially profitable, but to broaden the reach of the journal, especially in places where the language is still strong, so that people would read more Gaelic and thus empower it further.

Often, the editorials reproached readers, in both humorous and serious manner, addressing regional rivalries in the Gaelic world, the lack of commitment, and the inability of Gaelic users to stand up for their rights and articulate their demands. At the same time, these critical points were articulated in the first person plural and highlighted a sense of community and shared effort and responsibility. The editorials also featured various practical and feasible tips for grassroots initiatives and private action on behalf of Gaelic.

In *Gairm* 7 (1954), Thomson and MacDonald remark bitingly that plenty of those who tend to be most vocal about Gaelic and even give *Gairm* unwanted advice have not lifted a finger to help the magazine. In their words,

Faodaidh *Gairm* a bhith cho beairteach ri Carnegie agus cho glic ris an Fhàidh Isàiah, ach fhad 's a thatar a reic barrachd dheth an am Manchester's a thatar a reic anns na Hearadh tha rudeigin ceàrr. Chan eil ach dà leabhrachan Gàidhlig a' tighinn am follais gu h-aimsireil an Albainn – *Gairm* agus *An Gàidheal.* Le chèile cha chosgadh iad do neach sam bith 'sa bhliadhna ach prìs cairteal tombaca. An fhiach iad an uiread sin? Sin a' chiad cheist a bu chòir do dhuine sam bith a chur ris fhèin mus fhosgail e a bheul mu 'Ghàidheil ri guaillibh a chèile' no mu 'chor na Gàidhlige'.

Gairm *could be as rich as Carnegie and as wise as the prophet Isaiah, but as long as there are more copies sold in Manchester than in Harris, there is something wrong. There are just two Gaelic magazines being issued in Scotland at present,* Gairm *and* An Gàidheal. *Together, they would not cost one per year more than a quarter of tobacco. Are they worth that? This is the first question people should ask themselves before they open their mouth and say anything about 'the Gaels standing shoulder to shoulder' or about 'the state of Gaelic'.*

In *Gairm* 8 (1954), they return to this lack of commitment, pointing out that while children are no longer beaten for speaking Gaelic in schools, Gaelic users still hesitate to give their language the respect it deserves and are reluctant to employ it in other than family contexts, and propose that it is time to speak it all the time and everywhere. In the following issue, *Gairm* 9 (1954), they also add a reproach about the laxity in relation to politics, maintaining that the lack of engagement with local government leads to misrepresentation of the Gaelic-speaking areas and results in inadequate policies.

In *Gairm* 36 (1961), the editors express their gratefulness to all contributors, readers and sellers of the quarterly in the nine years of its existence and acknowledge the enjoyable challenge of keeping the venture going. They explicitly ask readers for their help in attracting new writers to keep *Gairm* fresh, and acknowledge that while they are able to engage people from their circles, they might be missing contact with the younger generations, revealing a healthy awareness of the risk of creating a clique, and a desire to avoid it. The editorial to the next issue, *Gairm* 37 (1961), formulates some of the quarterly's principles, including its effort to remain neutral in terms of class and religious differences. Its main aim is proclaimed as drawing attention to the situation of Gaelic and of the Highlands and Islands, and to present possibilities for how even small individual decisions followed on a daily basis can contribute to the revivalist effort. It mentions that the editors are receiving letters from people of all ages and from different parts of the world, including Africa, Hong Kong and London, and mischievously expresses the hope that one day they might even receive a letter from the big offices of state in Edinburgh, which would be the ultimate confirmation of *Gairm*'s success.

The editorial to *Gairm* 44 (1963) is one of several that respond to conflicting complaints about the quarterly – its alleged excessive lightness or seriousness or perceived bias towards some part of Gaelic-speaking Scotland. The editors note that while voicing complaints is useful, it is much better to be proactive, and ask their readers to submit a hymn or a philosophical essay to the magazine if they find the content too light, and a humorous piece if they consider *Gairm* too serious. They encourage people from different parts of the Gàidhealtachd to contribute and lend their own accent, 'blas', to *Gairm*. Regional rivalries between individual islands and parts of the Highlands are a recurring topic in the editorials, including *Gairm* 88 (1974) and *Gairm* 164 (1993).

Spring 1965 saw the publication of the anniversary issue: *Gairm* 50. The editorial acknowledges that the quarterly indeed feels a bit old, noting that some might consider it too old and advise it to take a nap near the fireside, which cannot happen unless someone starts another magazine and raises another call, a better one or a more suitable one for the present age. They assure the public that they would take no offence at such an initiative, on the contrary, and while waiting for competition, they confirm their dedication to continue with *Gairm*, 'an fheusag againn a' dol am bogadh anns an inc, agus chan eil teagamh nach bi sinn a' dèanamh mabladh eagalach air a' Ghàidhlig' [dipping our beard in the ink and undoubtedly making a terrible mess of the Gaelic]. They also envisage that the Gaelic Development Board will take ten pages for advertising in each issue, trying to attract the attention of the knights and landlords who have lost English, and of the old Liberals, and follow this jibe on the lack of official backing with an expression of sincere gratitude to those who do support *Gairm*.

The editorial to *Gairm* 85 (1973) again responds to readers' feedback, noting that some write to the editors to tell them how much they appreciate *Gairm* and others to communicate how little they enjoy it, and observes that it is from the first group that the quarterly gets most contributions, while the latter provides only little in the way of actual submissions. The editorial cheekily suggests that perhaps they are saving their writings until they establish a new magazine of their own, and while it expresses the support of such a venture, the implication clearly is that the written complaint is going to be the only outlet of these energies. It concludes that *Gairm* is open to all people who have anything to say and the knack to say it.

Editorials

The editors themselves certainly had the knack, and a great deal to say. Every issue of *Gairm*, with very few exceptions,[35] included an editorial. In the first few issues, they were entitled 'As a' Chathair' [From the Chair] and signed both by Thomson and MacDonald, though in a number of issues no signature was included. *Gairm Air-loidhne* now provides a comprehensive

---

[35] There is no editorial in *Gairm* 75 (1971), *Gairm* 77 (1971) and *Gairm* 78 (1972).

overview of the editorials, listing Thomson as the author of most of them.[36] From spring 1956, the editorials bore the heading 'Air an Spiris' [On the Perch] and have been affectionately referred to as 'na Spirisean' [the perches]. The editorial to *Gairm* 28 (1959) points out that the quarterly gives freedom to contributors, and if someone is looking for the opinions of the editors, they will find them expressed in 'Air an Spiris'. In terms of style, they are characterised by fluent colloquial tone sprinkled with sarcasm and tongue-in-cheek humour directed at various phenomena of the Gaelic world, including the journal itself and its editors. After MacDonald's departure, the editorial basically served as Thomson's opinion column, providing a space to discuss what preoccupied him most at the moment, be it political events, social ills, developments in Gaelic publishing or football.[37]

In the editorial to *Gairm* 200, the very last issue, Thomson notes the thousands of pages in the individual issues and in the books published by Gairm Publications that bear witness to the many changes in the Gaelic world, in Scotland, the UK and the world between 1952 and 2002. As Black observed, Thomson's life and career was affected by 'the Cold War, the decline of Gaelic in its heartland, the flawed ideology of the Highlands and Islands Development Board, the rise of pop culture, the iron grip of religious extremism on Thomson's native island of Lewis, far-off foreign wars or famines, and the slow, agonising steps towards Scottish home rule and independence',[38] and many of these phenomena were reflected in the 'Spirisean'. The following section attempts to sketch some aspects of that history on the basis of *Gairm* editorials and examines a selection of major recurrent topics related to Gaelic revitalisation.

Policies, resources and language planning

A number of the editorials commented on the development of Gaelic and the position of the quarterly in relation to these trends. The editorial to *Gairm* 7 (1954), appearing slightly more than two years after the venture had been established, responds to complaints that the Gaelic employed in the quarterly is not sufficiently pure. Thomson and MacDonald retort that their aim is to use contemporary Gaelic, not the idiom of the eighteenth century, and profess that Gaelic has to be as free as any other language, allowed to make loans if necessary, and that what it needs is more recognition in the public space, rather than puristic interventions. The editorial

---

[36] When Alexander John MacAskill (Alasdair Iain MacAsgaill) guest-edited the whole issue, *Gairm* 31 (1960), he also supplied the editorial. Donald John MacLeod co-wrote the editorials for *Gairm* 70, 71, 72 and 73 (1970).

[37] *Gairm* 177 (1996), *Gairm* 183 (1998), *Gairm* 199 (2002). The game surfaces in Thomson's poetry several times, including 'A' Cluich air Football le Fàidh' (Playing Football with a Prophet) from *An Rathad Cian* and 'Alba v. Argentina 2/6/79' from *Creachadh na Clàrsaich*.

[38] Ronald Black, 'Sorley MacLean, Derick Thomson, and the Women Most Dangerous to Men', *The Bottle Imp* 21 (July 2017), 1.

to *Gairm* 35 (1961) picks up the topic of the public visibility of Gaelic and suggests it could be employed more efficiently in outdoor advertising in the Highlands and Islands, which would have the double benefit of drawing people's attention to their own language and of attracting visitors. It notes that ACG could do more in this respect – and that *Gairm* could contribute more substantially too.

The editorial to *Gairm* 87 (1974) responds to the newly published results of the 1971 census, observing with joy that for the first time since the census started to count Gaelic speakers, the number has increased, and it also commends the growth of Gaelic in the Lowlands. Four years later, in *Gairm* 102 (1978), the editorial criticises the general registry, suggesting that when it became clear the numbers of Gaelic speakers were finally growing, suspicions were raised about people merely pretending to have competence in the language, but when the numbers went down in previous years, no one seemed to think people might be just too shy to say they were fluent. It protests strongly against removing questions related to Gaelic from the census and invites readers to complain both to the registry and to their MPs on the subject, once more promoting individual commitment and grassroots activism.

In the late 1970s and early 1980s, several editorials (*Gairm* 105 and 116) commented on the newly introduced changes in Gaelic spelling, which were hailed as an improvement and adopted, and Thomson tried to explain the rationale behind the reform and its benefits, expecting resistance to these developments. In *Gairm* 128 (1984), he returned to the topic and argued that standardised Gaelic spelling is essential for the future of the language and its use in official contexts, following up on the recommendations included in the 1978 SNP Gaelic Policy. However, he makes it clear there is no need to introduce a standardised pronunciation, to appease the fears of those who imagined that an official committee would try to deprive them of their accent.

When read chronologically, the editorials capture the gradual diversification and professionalisation of Gaelic initiatives in the second half of the twentieth century. Several editorials from the late 1960s discuss the work and outlook of the HIDB and its activities in relation to Gaelic. In the 1980s, they reflect on the emergence of several new bodies, including the establishment of Comunn na Gàidhlig (CNAG), Comann an Luchd-ionnsachaidh (CLÌ), a dedicated organisation for Gaelic learners, and the publication of a Gaelic National Policy. The editorials have a common theme of criticising what Thomson perceived as a lack of rigour and engagement with existing resources, including the 1978 SNP Gaelic Policy and *Gàidhlig ann an Albainn*, when it came to planning language policies, and the preference for founding new structures and commissioning further reports, rather than carrying out actual efficient work on behalf of the language in those realms where it was most urgently needed.

Over the years, Thomson reflected on the trends in terms of places where Gaelic was used, the background of the speakers and the changing attitudes to the language. The editorial to *Gairm* 99 (1977) turns its attention to the substantial growth of Gaelic in the Lowlands and the demands for classes and books, noting that many contributors to *Gairm* are second-language users of Gaelic, which should be a source of encouragement for everyone, including hereditary speakers: 'gu bheil a' chlach a dhiùlt na clachairean a-nis ann am prìs, agus daoine a' dèanamh cuimse air a bòidhchead 's air a h-ealantachd' [that the stone which was refused by builders is now appraised and that people admire it for its beauty].

In *Gairm* 130 (1985), he examined the paradoxical simultaneous developments in the situation of the language that had occurred during the quarterly's existence: after the Second World War, when it was founded, the language was still relatively strong in the traditional areas but there was little provision for it in terms of publishing and official support. In the following thirty years, much had been achieved for Gaelic in terms of national recognition, international reputation and publishing, and Gaelic had started to be used in geographical areas where it had never been strong before, but the foil of this progress had been its withering in the former strongholds in the Highlands and Islands. Thomson also observed that when people were discouraged from communicating in the language, they tended to adhere to Gaelic, whereas with the official incitements to use it, many of them seemed to prefer English.

In the editorial to *Gairm* 147 (1989), Thomson comments on the precarious position of Gaelic in relation to language standards and the related threat of English. He notes that in other countries where local languages are strong, such as Italy and Germany, the English influence is not as dangerous, suggesting it should not be universally demonised, but stresses the special care needed regarding the spread of English literature in Gaelic-speaking areas, and also the perils of dubious standards in Gaelic education in terms of grammar and spelling. In relation to that, he criticises the low standards of Gaelic materials published in *The Scotsman*, stressing the need to balance revivalist efforts with quality.

The editorial in *Gairm* 161 (1992) commented on the 1991 census, which showed a fall of 17 per cent in the numbers of Gaelic speakers since 1981, and a worrying drop in the numbers of Gaelic-speaking children in the Western Isles. Thomson states that Comhairle nan Eilean made a mistake in introducing a bilingual policy in the Western Isles, which not all schools and teachers were even committed to, and that only the adoption of a 'Gaelic first' approach can save the language. He balances these negative observations by mentioning the positive developments in the realm of broadcasting and publishing, and the growing interest in Gaelic outside Scotland, but stresses the danger of Gaelic disappearing as the main spoken language in the traditional communities.[39]

---

[39] The same contrary trends are described in greater detail by McLeod in *Gaelic in Scotland* in the chapter 'Institutionalisation, 2006–20'.

The return of the Scottish parliament made Thomson consider the impact of this momentous political change on Gaelic revitalisation activities. In the editorial to *Gairm* 189 (1999), he refers to the opinion that the Gaelic bodies and initiatives should be brought together into one organisation, so that funds could be distributed and used more efficiently, but asks cautiously how this overall organisation would be directed, and whether it would have politically appointed management. He argues for a diversity of Gaelic initiatives, and states how encouraging it is to witness new bodies active in new areas, clearly not wishing to retain a monopoly on Gaelic journalism and publishing.[40] He also suggests that the parliament should focus not only on Gaelic, but also on Scots, and on raising the prestige of Scottish literature in all languages in schools and colleges, another indication of his growing engagement with Scots in the 1990s, as discussed in Chapter 2.

Education

Provision for Gaelic in education has long been recognised as an essential aspect of the survival of the language, and as Ian Grimble points out, Thomson 'used his editorials from the outset to pioneer improvements in the educational system of the Highlands and Islands, and particularly the establishment of proper Gaelic streams in the schools'.[41] The editorials consistently advocated Gaelic-medium education over bilingual arrangements, and stressed the importance of schools and job opportunities for the viability of communities in the Highlands and Islands in preventing further depopulation.

The editorial to *Gairm* 19 (1957) turns its attention to Gaelic in universities in response to the appointment of the first professor to the Chair of Celtic at the University of Glasgow, Angus Matheson (1912–62). McLeod mentions the symbolic value of Gaelic in universities and the foundation of dedicated chairs in relation to the prestige of the language.[42] *Gairm* 152 (1990) comments on changes in universities in relation to Celtic and Gaelic. Thomson notes that in the past, the curriculum tended to concentrate rather on classical Gaelic of the seventeenth century, and that there would be little focus on the later major figures of Scottish Gaelic poetry, including the great figures of the eighteenth century, and that students usually studied some Gaelic, especially in Glasgow, but did not follow the interest further. He observes, drawing on his own experience, that in recent years, more students have been opting for Gaelic or Celtic Honours, combining it with other Celtic languages and other subjects, and hails

[40] Appreciative comments about the growing diversity of the Gaelic movement are also included in *Gàidhlig ann an Albainn/Gaelic in Scotland* (see Chapter 2).
[41] Ian Grimble, 'Poet and Scholar as Journalist', *Scottish Gaelic Studies* XVII (1996), 160.
[42] McLeod, *Gaelic in Scotland*, 96.

this trend as a healthy development which shows that the Gaelic world is opening up more to Europe and to the whole world.

Publishing

A number of *Gairm* editorials commented on the topic of Gaelic books, their contents, the market for them, and available support both from the reading public and from various institutions. Expanding the thematic range, quality and also the sheer bulk of Gaelic literature was also presented as vital in order to prevent users of Gaelic from turning to the huge and easily accessible English-language market for both information and entertainment. One of the proclaimed aims of associated Gairm Publications was to fight against the perceived dichotomy of tedious, outdated, instructive Gaelic books and attractive, modern, entertaining English productions, and the related association of Gaelic with duty, obsolete topics and the past, and of English with fun, contemporary concerns and the future.

The editorial to *Gairm* 6 (1953) responded to a letter addressed to the quarterly from a pupil from Inverness who complained about the scarcity of Gaelic reading for schoolchildren. Thomson and MacDonald stressed the crucial importance of systematically building a bigger corpus of enjoyable reading suitable for children and called for the foundation of specialised Gaelic magazines. In *Gairm* 16 (1956), they returned to the problem:

> Is fhada bho bha aithnichte do dhuine smaoineachail sam bith gum b' ann fìor dheireil a bha teagasg na Gàidhlig anns an sgoil-bhig, an uair nach leughadh ach corra dhuine a' Ghàidhlig le tlachd, aig aois ceithir-bliadhna-deug. Aig an aon àm, feumar aideachadh nach eil ach criomag de leabhar an siud 's an seo, ann an Gàidhlig, a tha freagarrach do chloinn na h-aoise seo.
>
> *For a long time, it has been manifest to every thinking person that teaching of Gaelic in primary schools is truly wretched, when only a few people at the age of fourteen read Gaelic with pleasure. At the same time, one has to admit that there is a mere handful of Gaelic books here and there that are suitable for children of this age.*

Only recently has the importance of producing a broad enough corpus of books for young readers that would encourage reading Gaelic for pleasure been addressed by publishing houses and parents' groups, due to the boom in Gaelic-medium education. As early as 1956, Thomson and MacDonald realised that reading habits are formed in childhood and that attracting young readers to Gaelic meant there would later be a larger market for Gaelic poetry, short stories, novels and non-fiction.

The editorial to *Gairm* 10 (1954) lists several reasons for the scarcity of Gaelic books at that time, the first being that users of Gaelic are 'ro leisg, no ro spìocach, gus ceannach an fheadhainn a thig am follais' [too lazy or too miserly to buy the few that have been published]. After this biting reproach, the editors add that many people have not received enough Gaelic education to read in the language with ease, and that the choice of attractive books is too small to cater for the tastes of all readers. The editorial states that although the obvious suggestion for improvement would be to obtain funds from the government and raise Gaelic teaching standards in schools, both these options entail difficulties, and maintains users of Gaelic need to utilise all means already at their disposal and create others, such as book clubs based on Irish and Welsh models, estimating that if there were two thousand members of these clubs, four new books could be published every year. The editorial also includes a barb directed at ACG, expressing the hope it will realise that investments in books are more important to people and to the language than a preoccupation with meetings.

In *Gairm* 64 (1968), the editorial announces the sum of £5,000 in support of Gaelic books from the government has been allocated, and will be received by the University of Glasgow, leading to the establishment of a dedicated Gaelic Books Council (Comhairle nan Leabhraichean). The editorial acknowledges the amount of struggle this achievement took, and this is likely a personal note from Thomson, as he was involved in the process, as discussed in Chapter 5. Again, the editorial urges *Gairm* readers to write, so that there would be new Gaelic literature for the Council to publish and to promote. The editorial for *Gairm* 66 (1969) returns to the topic of the Council in more detail (the issue also featured its first advertisement) and expresses the hope that at least three new Gaelic publishers will emerge, in order to foster healthy competition, and announces that *Gairm* intends to be more active in this respect too, noting that if the quarterly has proved anything during its existence so far, it is that Gaelic writers are able to address almost any topic in existence, and that there are readers and buyers for Gaelic material of all kinds.

In *Gairm* 70 (1970), the editorial focuses on the topic of libraries, proposing that a survey should be conducted on the topic, and argues that libraries in the Highlands and Islands should by default purchase every new Gaelic book, and so should libraries in cities where the language is taught, thus ensuring basic sales for the publications that emerge thanks to the new support mechanisms, and encourages readers to petition their local libraries to this effect. In *Gairm* 110 (1980), Thomson reflects with gratification on the increasing number of Gaelic books, noting that Gairm Publications are no longer the only player in the field, and mentions that the Gaelic Book Council organises a competition for the best books in terms of design, marking a move from the bare requirement to have books to a sustained effort to raise production standards. He maintains that while a substantial corpus of textbooks and learning resources for children and young people has been created, there are still major deficiencies in the area of reading for pleasure that would strengthen their relationship with the language and encourage them to associate it with enjoyment, and not only with education and a sense of duty.

The media

A number of the editorials discussed the situation of Gaelic in the media, proposed new policies, criticised certain developments and commanded others. In *Gairm* 8 (1954), the editorial notes that both Welsh and Irish are being used in film and suggests that research should be conducted into the possible costs of Gaelic films, in order to prevent the prevalence of English on TV. The editorial to *Gairm* 21 (1957) returns to the issue of TV, with reference to the establishment of a new station in Scotland, STV, and points out that it is difficult to get any TV signal in the north-west of the Highlands and Islands. It acknowledges that people who live in remote places naturally seek every interesting pastime available, but notes that when TV reaches the Gaelic-speaking areas, it will pose a danger to the language in terms of influence on the young generation, for they will be encountering the amusing and pleasant new phenomena through the medium of English. It outlines several preventative steps, such as the creation of appealing Gaelic books and magazines and investment in Gaelic drama, recommends that a broadcasting survey should be conducted, and proposes the idea of obtaining permission for various bodies, such as universities and regional organisations, to put on all-Gaelic broadcasting in the evenings.

The editorial to *Gairm* 26 (1958) comments on the Gaelic news broadcast by the BBC for an hour per week, and notes sarcastically that since the Gaels have had no news since the Battle of Culloden in 1746, it is gratifying to get reporting on current affairs. It recalls the promise made by the BBC governor at the Royal Mòd in Glasgow that the corporation will do justice to Gaelic, and considers the meaning of the concept in this respect, in comparison to the availability of services such as the post and telephone. Six years later, the editorial to *Gairm* 48 (1964) was able to reflect on a changed situation. It gives an account of developments in the BBC Gaelic department and notes that its work in the Highlands is growing, with new stations being built and new programmes recorded, including some aimed at schoolchildren. It asserts that these new initiatives do not imply neglect of traditional culture, but that it is necessary to keep up with modern developments and make provisions for young people. It asks viewers of Gaelic BBC to write to it with both praise and criticism, and to petition state authorities for the creation of more Gaelic content.

The editorial to *Gairm* 84 (1973) follows up the topic and notes that it would be beneficial to decentralise the Gaelic BBC by setting up an additional office in the Western Isles, to avoid concentrating the activities and related opportunities in Glasgow only, and proposes a great variety of content, including stories, discussions of current issues, recordings of literary works, and traditional and new Gaelic music (even a bit of pop!).

A similar issue is raised in *Gairm* 123 (1983), where Thomson reflects on the new management of the Gaelic BBC and claims that it should be directed by people who ensure that Gaelic broadcasting is inclusive and belongs to all listeners, irrespective of age and place of origin, with both traditional and modern preferences and of various intellectual demands, including dedicated programmes for learners.

In *Gairm* 143 (1988), Thomson comments on the STV Gaelic programmes, which are kept for the early morning hours, but he still praises the content, which includes recordings of poetry, and compares it favourably with the BBC, which has not broadcast a Gaelic play for a long time and does not even feature proper reporting about the Mòd. He concludes by asking whether there should be an independent Gaelic TV channel.

Many of these demands and ideas were brought into practice with the establishment of BBC Alba in 2008, which was however the work of a later generation of Gaelic activists and Thomson was not personally involved. This step meant, as McLeod notes, that Scotland finally had 'a universally available dedicated Gaelic television service, the long-sought objective of Gaelic language planners and campaigners', and points out that 'this milestone was reached almost thirty years later than in Wales, where the Welsh channel S4C was launched in 1982, and fifteen years later than in Ireland, where Teilifís na Gaeilge (renamed TG4 in 1999) was launched in 1996'.[43]

Drama

Several editorials deal specifically with the problem of the scarcity of Gaelic drama. This is a call that goes back to Erskine of Mar and his series of essays on Gaelic drama in *Guth na Bliadhna* in the 1910s, and to the biting article 'Uisge-beatha agus Uisge-bàis: Reflections on Gaelic Drama' written by Hector MacIver and published in the magazine *Alba* in 1948. In it, MacIver notes that 'it would be good to think that Gaelic drama would at last drive the bogus orators and maudlin songsters from the stage. We would then have, in the Gaelic movement, some of the strong water of life instead of the present tasteless water of death.'[44] The criticism is directed, similarly to that of *Guth na Bliadhna*, at ACG and its perceived inordinate focus on the Mòd, while the vast potential of Gaelic drama for revitalisation of the language remains unexploited.

The editorial to *Gairm* 15 (1956) refers to MacIver's article eight years later[45] and makes it clear that the unsatisfactory situation continues, with the Mòd focusing on ceilidhs and singing competitions. While some claim that there is no such thing as Gaelic drama, the editorial refutes

---

[43] McLeod, *Gaelic in Scotland*, 315–16.
[44] Hector MacIver, 'Uisge-beatha agus Uisge-bàis: Reflections on Gaelic Drama', *Alba: A Scottish Miscellany in English and Gaelic*, ed. M. MacLean and T. M. Murchison (Glasgow: An Comunn Gàidhealach, 1948), 43.
[45] Mistakenly, it gives the publication year of *Alba* as 1946.

these notions, and states that drama is 'cho dual don Ghàidheal agus a tha na gugachan do na Nisich, ach is e mullach na truaighe nach do dh'èirich drama, mar bu chòir dhi a bhith air èirigh, à làraichean nan seann tighean cèilidh' [as natural to the Gaels as the gugas are to the people of Ness, but regrettably drama did not arise, as it should have, from the ruins of the old ceilidh houses], due to various historical and social factors. It suggests that to remedy this situation, Gaelic drama groups and a number of dedicated local festivals should be established, going beyond Glasgow and reaching townships in the Highlands and Islands. In *Gairm* 52 (1965), the editorial reflects on some new developments in the field, mentioning that drama groups will be starting again soon and putting on new plays, and notes that these will only be accessible for audiences in Glasgow, Aberdeen and Portree. It acknowledges that the Fèis Dràma Ghlaschu [Glasgow Drama Festival] is a commendable enterprise but claims that it could and should be made more accessible to audiences through television, even if only two or three times a year, and that this demand should be presented to the Secretary of State for Scotland (the Scottish Secretary).

Two more editorials reflect on news in the realm of Gaelic drama (*Gairm* 67 and *Gairm* 103), including the foundation of the new drama group, Fir Chlis [Northern Lights], with support from the Scottish Arts Council in the late 1970s, and the topic crops up several times in relation to ACG, but during the existence of *Gairm*, the wished-for breakthrough that would make drama a major force in the revitalisation efforts was not achieved, although a substantial amount of diverse new plays emerged in the 1960s and 1970s.[46] Even in *Why Gaelic Matters*, published in 1981, Thomson maintains that 'professionalism is almost entirely lacking in the sphere of Gaelic drama', pointing out that the most vital contribution was made in the late 1950s and 1960s by the Glasgow Gaelic Drama Association, whose technical support for amateur producers and actors led to the production of a number of new plays. He observes that 'a fairly elaborate scheme to set up a professional Gaelic repertory company, Fir Chlis, generously funded by the Scottish Arts Council, was badly mismanaged, and came to an early end'.[47]

Apart from discussing the topics in the editorials, Gairm also advertised a competition for new Gaelic drama (*Gairm* 20: 1957) and published a short play in verse by Allan MacDonald (Maighstir Ailean, 1859–1905) edited by John Lorne Campbell (*Gairm* 26: 1958), an extract from Aeschylus' *Agamemnon* translated by John MacLean (*Gairm* 62: 1968), 'Dealbh-chluich as a' Ghàidhlig' [A Play in Gaelic] (*Gairm* 71: 1970) by John Murray (Iain Moireach), and essays devoted to the subject by Murray and Cailean Spencer (*Gairm* 87: 1974).

---

[46] For a summary, see Ian Brown, *Scottish Theatre: Diversity, Language, Continuity* (Amsterdam: Rodopi, 2013), 186–7.

[47] Thomson, *Why Gaelic Matters*, 31.

While, even nowadays, drama is still not a central force in Gaelic revitalisation efforts, some of the demands presented in *Gairm* editorials have been fulfilled in the form of the company Theatre Gu Leòr [Galore], which focuses on contemporary innovative drama in Gaelic, employs multimedia and digital technologies, and encourages the creation of new repertoire, both original plays and stage adaptations.

Economics

For all the interest in literature and education, *Gairm* editor(s) were aware of the importance of the economic wellbeing of the Highlands and Islands for the survival of the language and called for new local industries and infrastructure which would prevent people from leaving the region in search of better opportunities, but at the same time stressed the need to introduce these innovations carefully with regard to the threatened status of the language. Recommendations to bodies such as the Crofters' Commission, HIDB and CnE were thus formulated on the basis of this conviction. As McLeod notes, starting in the late nineteenth century, 'the distinct social and economic needs of the Highlands and Islands were recognised by the government and the economic development of the region became a defined official priority' but 'language issues tended to have little explicit role in these policy processes and the debates that accompanied them', and 'Gaelic was implicitly understood as the cultural reflex of the outdated economic structure that needed to be replaced'.[48]

Gairm editorials were trying to negotiate these two concerns and suggest ways in which they could complement each other. Several of them discussed the problem that new industries and projects bring in people from outside the region, which is not a negative phenomenon in itself, but their presence dilutes the Gaelic-speaking communities further and encourages users of Gaelic and whole communities to favour English. A similar point is raised by Thomson in *Why Gaelic Matters*, where he argues that 'economic pressures still continue to take their toll, in the forms of both emigration and immigration. As the Gaels move out of the Gaelic area in search of work their lands and houses are bought by English-speaking immigrants retiring on pensions or attracted by HIDB largesse or opting out of congested environments elsewhere.'[49]

The editorial to *Gairm* 47 (1964) suggests Gaelic could play a vital role in stressing the distinctiveness of the region and in boosting cultural tourism. In *Gairm* 57 (1966), the editors commented on the internalised perception of the language as a career hindrance on the part of some Gaelic users, urging readers to leave these nineteenth-century prejudices behind and capitalise on their command of the language, noting the lack

---

[48] McLeod, *Gaelic in Scotland*, 34.
[49] Thomson, *Why Gaelic Matters*, 26.

of people with degrees in Gaelic who could apply for the emerging jobs in a number of realms, from education to the media. The progressive idea of treating Gaelic as an economic asset and supporting it not only on the grounds of cultural nationalism but also for financial reasons is only gradually being embraced both by language planners and by users of the language.

An Comumm Gàidhealach and other bodies

Over the years, many editorials in *Gairm* discussed the work of other bodies involved in Gaelic revitalisation efforts, and these comments reveal Thomson's position on a number of issues and chronicle the development of the Gaelic movement. The organisation whose work was addressed most frequently, and often critically, was An Comunn Gàidhealach (ACG). As McLeod notes, 'from its establishment in 1891, An Comunn stated that its work would be non-political', and it came 'under attack almost from its inception from critics who challenged its non-political stance and general lack of vehemence'.[50] The perception of ACG as a ponderous, conservative body which cares mostly about formal meetings conducted in English and organising concerts, rather than coming up with radical ideas and progressive policies that would keep Gaelic alive and bring it into the modern world, is a complaint that echoes back to Erskine of Mar, and it resounds many times in *Gairm* editorials.

A recurring claim in these critical comments is that the organisation of the Mòd, the annual Gaelic festival and competition which focuses primarily on music, became ACG's chief preoccupation, and many felt that it was not doing enough to promote the actual use of the language.[51] *Gairm* kept challenging ACG to introduce a more modern programme to its competitions, to engage in Gaelic publishing and to lead by example in terms of using Gaelic in its own activities, from internal meetings to public events and print materials. In *Gairm* 22 (1957), the editors suggest that Gaelic will not be saved by being talked about in English, and recall the promise of ACG to produce books for children, but observe that not much has happened in that respect so far and conclude that 'chan fhuirich am bàs idir ri là math' [death does not wait for a good day].

The editorial to *Gairm* 28 (1959) responds to criticism of the quarterly published in the *Stornoway Gazette*, provoked by a caricature of ACG by Calum Ferguson (Calum MacFhearghuis) featured in the previous issue. The editorial acknowledges that the caricature did not comment on some positive developments but maintains that it also captured part of the truth, and that ACG will not get attention and respect by making proclamations

---

[50] McLeod, *Gaelic in Scotland*, 49–50.
[51] For an overview of the criticism of ACG in relation to using too much English and the cultural orientation of the Mòd, see McLeod, *Gaelic in Scotland*, 61.

but by being active in the Highlands and Islands. In *Gairm* 38 (1961), the editorial comes up with further suggestions as to what ACG should be doing and where – to focus not only on those areas where Gaelic is already threatened, but also on those where it still thrives, to ensure this situation does not change, for instance by providing local people with modern facilities in Gaelic, including radio and TV programmes. The editorial to *Gairm* 46 (1964) maintains that ACG will face substantial challenges in terms of changing the design of the organisation, if the Mòd is to survive in the age of television. It recommends that writers and composers could be encouraged to produce new music and that the festival could incorporate competitions in literature, drama and art.

In *Gairm* 104 (1978), the SNP Gaelic Policy was published,[52] and two years later, in *Gairm* 113 (1980), it resurfaced in connection with ACG. The issue featured a reprint of a leaflet distributed by ACG at the National Mòd in Perth, together with Thomson's commentary. The document, entitled 'Your MP and Gaelic' (apparently produced in English only), sums up the main promises made by the Conservative, Labour and Liberal parties and the SNP prior to the 1979 General Election in relation to Gaelic, noting that ACG 'maintains impartial contact with all parties in Parliament', and, apart from 'urging the Government of the day to meet its commitments', endeavours to 'keep Members briefed on Gaelic affairs and to claim their support'.[53] In the leaflet, it lists 'members of both Houses with an interest in Gaelic', encouraging people to contact their MP and demand more engagement from them, join party discussions about their Gaelic policies, and try to influence candidates and parties by means of individual lobbying.

Although the leaflet may at first look productive enough and in line with *Gairm*'s calls for individual political engagement and grassroots activism, the commentary on it, 'Propaganda a' Chomuinn Ghàidhealach' [Propaganda of the Gaelic Association], is scathing. It points out that upon reading the leaflet, nobody would have known that long before ACG started to lobby the parties, the SNP had established a committee to put together a Gaelic Policy, that the policy was adopted publicly at the 1978 party congress, that it was published in *Gairm* 104, and that it has much more substance than the empty promises of the other parties, without actually putting them to their congresses. It asks, why is ACG afraid to communicate this to people, who prepared the leaflet for ACG and who sanctioned its production? No answers are provided for these questions, and the article closes with a simple statement that there are still copies available of *Gairm* 104, where the SNP policy can be read, and that they can be purchased at the affordable price of fifty shillings.

For all this acidic commentary, it is important to note that there were

---

[52] A summary of the policy is included in Chapter 2.
[53] 'Your MP and Gaelic', *Gairm* 113 (1980), 60.

personal connections between the management of *Gairm* and ACG – Thomson's father James was involved in the association and served as editor of its magazine, *An Gàidheal*, and Thomson contributed to it frequently, so it would be misleading to imagine that the relationship of the quarterly and its editors to ACG and its activities was inherently hostile. In *Gairm* 7 (1954), the editorial responds to accusations that the quarterly was seeking to replace *An Gàidheal*. It argues that most people who come up with these insinuations likely never saw either of the periodicals in question before and asserts that *An Gàidheal* has not lost a single reader because of *Gairm*; moreover, that the magazines have been even sharing content. The same editorial stresses that these are at the moment the only two Gaelic periodicals issued in Scotland and reminds readers that the yearly price of both of them is negligible in comparison with their other expenses, implying there is no excuse for not buying and supporting both. In *Gairm* 111/112 (1980), Thomson published an article entitled 'Ave Atque Vale', quoting a phrase associated with paying tributes to heroes, which praises the departing president of ACG, Calum MacLeod (Calum MacLeòid), and also his successor in the post, Dolina MacLennan (Dolina NicIllFhinnein). The editorial to *Gairm* 140 (1987) shows solidarity with ACG on its upcoming hundredth anniversary, with Thomson explaining that it struggles with financial problems and urging readers who are members of the association to pay their membership fee to help to stabilise the situation.

Even when it comes to the Mòd, the position of *Gairm* and of Thomson was not unremittingly critical, and already *Gairm* 97 (1976) presents a surprisingly different take on the topic. It summarises the grounds on which some people criticise the event but points out that those who speak against it might be more profitably employed if they actually did something for the language themselves. According to this logic, *Gairm* has a strong mandate to criticise, as its efforts on behalf of Gaelic are evident, and Thomson makes it clear that the quarterly was in many ways supplying what ACG failed to do. Several editorials from the 1990s (*Gairm* 153, 157, 169, 173) discuss issues related to the Mòd, commenting on the latest instalments of the festival and their positives and shortcomings. In general, they acknowledge it as a precious part of Gaelic culture and thank ACG for organising it, which may sound incongruous with the earlier jibes, but it proves that those were not directed primarily at the event itself, but mostly at the other activities ACG did not pursue, due to its preoccupation with the Mòd. By this time, Gaelic revitalisation efforts were much more diversified, and many of the gaps had been filled in. In the editorial, Thomson also mentions that the choice of the location of the Mòd is important, as it continues to move around Scotland, with regard to how much Gaelic is going to survive in the area afterwards. The last editorial on the topic (*Gairm* 173: 1995) suggests that the Mòd should receive more coverage in the major Scottish media, as its main aim is to promote Gaelic heritage as part of Scotland's heritage, in line with the broadening of perspective of Scotland as a whole, which is evident in the editorials from the 1980s and 1990s.

While some of the comments directed at ACG, HIDB and other organisations were quite critical, *Gairm* was also quick to acknowledge positive developments and changes of policies on the part of bodies and initiatives the editors had previously found fault with, and joined forces with them. The quarterly kept urging readers to take direct action and offered feasible specific suggestions as to what users of Gaelic could demand of their elected representatives, such as dedicated employees who would focus on Gaelic at the National Library of Scotland and Ordnance Survey, higher numbers of Gaelic teachers and examiners, increased funding for Gaelic publishing, and more Gaelic coverage on TV and radio.

Some of the Gaelic policies proposed in *Gairm* were quite ahead of their time in Scotland, and they often drew on successful Irish and Welsh models, be they making short Gaelic films, founding a Gaelic book club, so that more new books could be published using private funding, or establishing Gaelic drama groups and theatre companies. The *Gairm* editorials were the space where Thomson continued to comment on developments related to Gaelic even during the decades when he was no longer personally involved in them, including the major improvements that occurred in the period from 1985 onwards, when he was already in his mid-sixties, a paradoxical consequence of the fact that many of the propositions were so progressive. Most of them have been carried out in some form, some quickly, some only decades after Thomson called for them, and some still await realisation.

Literature in *Gairm*

When recalling the beginnings of the quarterly, Thomson mentioned the aim was to

> iomadach seòrsa nòs sgrìobhaidh a chleachdadh ann an *Gairm*, rudan meadhanach seann-fhasanta agus rudan cho ùr 's a ghabhadh agus thog sin rud math de dheasbad anns na bliadhnaichean tràth co-dhiù. Bha daoine a' sgrìobhadh thugainn agus ag ràdh, chan eil sinn ag iarraidh an còrr dhen rubbish a tha sin fhaicinn, gu h-àraidh ann am bàrdachd. Cha robh e a' còrdadh riutha idir gu robh dòighean ùra a' nochdadh ann am bàrdachd agus tha mi a' creidsinn gu bheil na beachdan sin beò fhathast ann an iomadach àite.[54]

> *employ various styles of writing in* Gairm, *fairly old-fashioned things and things that were as modern as possible, and this raised quite some debate, at*

---

[54] Ruaraidh MacThòmais, 'Mar a chaidh an ràitheachan *Gairm* a chur air chois', BBC Alba *Làrach nam Bàrd*, available at <http://www.bbc.co.uk/alba/foghlam/larachnambard/poets/ruaraidh_macthomais/am_bard> Accessed 15 April 2023.

least in the early years. People were writing to us, protesting they did not want to read that sort of rubbish, especially in poetry. They did not like at all that new styles were appearing in poetry, and I believe that these views are still common in a number of places.

In *The Future of the Highlands*, he made a similar point, asserting that the foundation of *Gairm* was sympathetic to new literature, and that it was indeed established chiefly to make the publication of such writing possible.[55] Promoting contemporary writing was part of the magazine's effort to contribute to the revitalisation of the language, some of the principal works of modern Gaelic literature appeared in *Gairm* for the first time, and a number of emerging authors who had the chance to publish in the magazine also had their debut collections or novels produced by Gairm Publications.

However, the focus on modern experimental writing was not exclusive, and several *Gairm* editorials commented on this mixture of the old and the new, the traditional and the innovative, in the pages of the magazine. The editorial to *Gairm* 34 (1960) mentions that the issue features two stories in a modern fashion, one of them influenced by George Orwell, the other by Jules Verne, and both are hailed as important pointers for new directions in Gaelic literature. It maintains that since more than thirty years have elapsed since the renaissance of Scottish writing in English, it is high time to instigate a similar revival in Gaelic and move it away from 'thigh mo sheanair' [my grandfather's house] and 'shitig mo sheanmhair' [my grandmother's dung heap], driving at what seemed to the editors as an excessive preoccupation with local and domestic topics. At the same time, the editorial acknowledges the validity of more traditional ways of writing, and asserts that there is a need for both, including suitable literature for children, and that *Gairm* tries to produce a mixture which would please most people. The following sections trace the editorial decisions of *Gairm* in relation to poetry, fiction, reviews, and the way it navigated between tradition and experiment.

Modern poetry and short story

As Longley observed, 'poets need magazines more than do other writers',[56] and *Gairm*, co-founded and steered for fifty years by a poet, proved instrumental in supporting the flourishing of modern Gaelic poetry, including Thomson's own work. The editorial to *Gairm* 34 (1960) notes that Gaelic poets have become bolder when it comes to engaging with new forms and subjects, and that modern poetry is now well established in Gaelic, in spite of those who mocked Sorley MacLean when he published *Dàin do Eimhir*

---

[55] Derick Thomson, 'Literature and the Arts', *The Future of the Highlands*, ed. Derick Thomson and Ian Grimble (London: Routledge & Kegan Paul, 1968), 215.
[56] Longley, 294.

(Poems to Eimhir) in 1943, and it acknowledges with gratification that the quarterly has not been suffering from a shortage of contributions. Apart from Thomson's own writing, it also featured the work of the four other poets who made up the 'Famous Five', the collective term for the major voices of modern Gaelic poetry, including MacLean, whose iconic poem 'Hallaig' first appeared in *Gairm* (*Gairm* 8: 1954), Donald MacAulay, George Campbell Hay (Deòrsa Mac Iain Dheòrsa) and Iain Crichton Smith – all regular contributors, in poetry and in other genres. Over the years, the quarterly provided space for the upcoming generations of Gaelic poets, some of whom brought radical new agendas with them. In the 1980s, *Gairm* featured poetry by Christopher Whyte, the author of some of the earliest published Gaelic poems dealing openly with being gay. Gairm Publications often produced the debut collections of poets whose works previously appeared in the magazine, which is the case of Crichton Smith's *Bìobuill is Sanasan-Reice* (Bibles and Adverts) (1965), MacAulay's *Seòbhrach as a' Chlaich* (Primrose from a Stone) (1967), Christopher Whyte's *Uirsgeul* (Myth) (1991), Anne Frater's *Fon t-Slige* (Under the Shell) (1995) and others.

Although short stories were already appearing in the journals edited by Erskine in the 1910s and 1920s, Gaelic short story in the modern sense, i.e. as a self-contained, compact form focused on mood and character psychology, truly emerged only in the 1950s and 1960s.[57] In Donald John MacLeod's view, this period was 'characterised by the activity of a small group of enthusiasts and by the emergence of important periodical media', chiefly thanks to the BBC Gaelic Department and *Gairm*.[58] Both provided venues not only for the stories themselves but also for literary criticism, encouraging 'a greater consciousness of literary techniques, more awareness of standards other than the traditional Gaelic ones, and a consequently more professional attitude on the part of Gaelic writers'.[59]

As MacLeod, notes, from around 1953, the modern type of short story, in which 'psychological insight is more important than plot development', started to appear in *Gairm*.[60] Early proponents include Hector MacIver and Paul MacInnes (Pòl MacAonghais). One incentive Thomson and MacDonald used to attract more contributions were the short story competitions: in 1956 (*Gairm* 18), the editors offered a prize of ten guineas for the best short story 'anns an nòs ùr' [in the new vein], and another competition was advertised in 1961 with a prize of £20. Colin MacKenzie (Cailean T. MacCoinnich) won the first round with his mystery story, 'An Sgàthan' [The Mirror], and the winner of the second one was Crichton

---

[57] This general introduction on the Gaelic short story and the role *Gairm* played in its birth is partly based on the opening part of my essay 'Old Women, Dreams, and Reversed Revivals: Derick Thomson's Gaelic Short Stories'.
[58] MacLeod, *Twentieth-Century Gaelic Literature*, 93.
[59] MacLeod, *Twentieth-Century Gaelic Literature*, 94.
[60] MacLeod, *Twentieth-Century Gaelic Literature*, 100–1.

Smith with his futuristic story 'An Solus Ùr' [The New Light].[61] Almost all authors of Gaelic short fiction active in the second half of the twentieth century published something in the magazine, including some of the most acclaimed writers such as John Murray and Eilidh Watt. Both editors wrote short fiction themselves – Thomson's short stories are discussed in more detail below, and MacDonald contributed three stories of his own: 'An Càr' [The Car] (*Gairm* 17: 1956), 'Air Beulaibh an t-Sluaigh' [In Front of the People] (*Gairm* 23: 1958) and 'Am Putan Dearg' [The Red Button] (*Gairm* 34: 1960).

Similarly to poetry, the first collections of *Gairm* short story contributors were often produced by Gairm Publications, including milestones in the genre such as Crichton Smith's *Bùrn is Aran* [Water and Bread] (1960) and Murray's *An Aghaidh Choimheach* [The Mask] (1973). The publishing venture also brought out two seminal short story anthologies intended to promote the form even further – *Dorcha tro Ghlainne* [Through a Glass Darkly], edited and introduced by Donald John MacLeod (1970), and *Eadar Peann is Pàipear* [Between Pen and Paper], edited and introduced by Donald John MacIver (Dòmhnall Iain MacÌomhair), which appeared in 1984.

In the editorials, Thomson repeatedly stressed the importance of the short story in twentieth-century Gaelic literature, and in retrospect reflected on the role the quarterly played in its development. In the editorial to *Gairm* 160 (1992), he wrote:

> Tha fianais anns na duilleagan sin air iomadh car is tionndadh a thachair fad nam bliadhnachan, is fianais air eachdraidh is beul-aithris, air saoghal ùr 's air seann saoghail. Agus dhaibhsan aig a bheil ùidh ann an litreachas, tha fianais air leth prìseil annta air mar a leudaich 's a dhoimhnich sgrìobhadh na Gàidhlig, gu h-àraidh ann am bàrdachd 's ann an sgeulachdan-goirid. Tha e glè shoilleir nach robh pàirt den leudachadh seo air tachairt idir mura b' e gu robh comas air a thoirt do luchd-sgrìobhaidh na sgrìobhaidhean aca fhaicinn an clò, agus obair an co-aoisean 's an seanairean fhaicinn.[62]

These pages give evidence of the many twists and turns that occurred over the years, about history and folklore, about the new world and the old one. Those who are interested in literature will find precious evidence here as to how Gaelic literature grew in scope and depth, especially in the realm of poetry and the short story. It is very clear that some part of this growth would not have occurred, if the writers did not get the opportunity to see their work published, and to see the work of their contemporaries and predecessors.

---

[61] MacLeod, *Twentieth-Century Gaelic Literature*, 98.
[62] See also the editorial in *Gairm* 139 (1987).

In the editorial to the final, two hundredth, issue of *Gairm* (2002), he noted:

> 'S ann anns na bliadhnachan sin a thàinig an sgeulachd ghoirid gu ìre ann an Gàidhlig. Bha na h-uiread de sgeulachdan ghoirid air nochdadh anns na deicheadan roimh 1950, ach chunnaic sinn leudachadh is fosgladh mòr, le sgrìobhadairean air am misneachadh gu rudan a sgrìobhadh gach ràithe, agus corra chruinneachadh a' tighinn on chlò cuideachd.[63]
>
> *It was during those years that the short story grew up in Gaelic. A number of short stories had appeared in the decades before 1950, but we saw a great growth and opening afterwards, as writers were encouraged to produce something every season, and several collections appeared in print too.*

As Moray Watson observes, the great bulk of Gaelic short stories in the second half of the twentieth century, several hundred in all, indeed appeared in *Gairm*,[64] and the quarterly served as one of the main platforms thanks to which the short story achieved such high standards and gained a prominence in Gaelic literature which continue to this day.

Women contributors

In previous Gaelic periodicals, the overwhelming majority of the content was supplied by male authors. This is true both for the publications run by Norman MacLeod and Erskine of Mar, as is evident even from a cursory glance over the lists of contents for the individual issues. In the early years of *Gairm*, male writers prevailed to a large extent, but even the first issue featured several contributions by women: a cartoon of the two editors by Morven Cameron (Morven Chamshron), who became a regular contributor, and a section entitled 'Gnothuich Bhoirionnach' [Women's Issues] by Christine Mackay (Cairistiona NicAoidh), which gave advice on fashion, cosmetics and household management. Given the title and focus of the last-mentioned section, it seems that the quarterly was still relegating women to the realms and interests traditionally assigned to them, but it may also be seen as an attempt to cater for as broad a readership as possible, including those who would appreciate a discussion of such topics through the medium of Gaelic, not as a statement on the assumed scope of female interests and capacities. Even the earliest issues featured reviews, translations and short fiction by women writers, such as Anna Mackenzie (Anna NicCoinnich), Murdina Mackenzie (Murdag NicCoinnich) and Margaret MacCodrum (Mairead NicCodruim).

---

[63] 'Air an Spiris', *Gairm* 200 (2002), 297–8.
[64] Moray Watson, *An Introduction to Gaelic Fiction*, 61. The third chapter of Watson's monograph provides a useful overview of Gaelic periodical fiction from 1952 up to the present. *Gairm Air-loidhne* allows to browse through all the contributions made by individual writers.

In *Gairm* 14 (1955), the editorial complained about the scarcity of women contributors:

> Tha e duilich dhuinn a thuigsinn carson a tha luchd-sgrìobhaidh cho gann, air neo cho doirbh an lorg, am measg mnathan na Gàidhealtachd. Chan e idir nach eil taobh air fir-deasachaidh no dhà thuca, is coireach gun deach cho beag an clò bho am pinn anns an leabhar seo. [. . .] bha sinn a-riamh den bheachd gum b' ann mar bu mhotha a chuireadh duine (no boireannach) tàlant gu feum a thigeadh piseach air an tàlant sin. 'S fheudar a rèisd gu bheil mòran de rosg agus de bhàrdachd Ghàidhlig a' dol a dholaidh ann an cisteachan is ann an dreasairean air feadh na Gàidhealtachd, gun luaidh idir air na seòmraichean sin anns a' bhaile mhòr [. . .] Dh'fhalbh an là anns am biodh na mnathan riaraichte a bhith fon chlèibh, no a' deasachadh bidhe, no a' nighe shoithichean. Tha iad a-nis a' dleasadh an aon inbhe ris na fir, agus feumaidh mar sin pàirt den chòmhradh aca a dhol an clò. Tha airgead 'ga chur a-mach orra anns na sgoiltean is iad 'nam pàisdean, is feumaidh iad pàirt dhe sin a phàigheadh air ais anns an aon chùinneadh a ghleidheas beagan de a luach anns an là a th' ann' – 's e sin facail, agus gu h-àraid facail ann an clò.

> *It is difficult for us to understand why writers are so scarce, or so difficult to find, among women of the Gàidhealtachd. The fact that so little from their pen has been published is not at all caused by lack of favour towards them on the part of the editors. [. . .] we have always been of the opinion that the more a man (or a woman) uses a talent, the more this talent grows. It is possible that much fiction and poetry in Gaelic is rotting away in the coffers and dressers all over the Gàidhealtachd, not to mention the rooms in the big cities [. . .] The day is gone when women were content to be hauling creels, preparing food or washing the dishes. They are now claiming equality with men, and thus part of their argument has to go to print. Money is spent on them in schools from childhood, and they need to pay some of it back in the same currency which still retains a bit of value in these days – and that is in words, and especially in printed words.*

The editorial proceeds to list a miscellany of illustrious Gaelic women poets of previous centuries as an example: 'Cha robh Màiri Nighean Alasdair Ruaidh 'na tàmh anns an t-seagh so, is cha motha bha Dìorbhail Nic a' Bhruthainn, is Sìlis na Ceapaich, is Mairead Nighean Lachlainn, no Màiri Mhòr nan Òran' [Màiri Nighean Alasdair Ruaidh was not idle in this respect, and neither were Dìorbhail Nic a' Bhruthainn, Sìlis na Ceapaich, Mairead Nighean Lachlainn or Màiri Mhòr nan Òran].

The editors note that there are indeed active women poets and authors, and make it clear that their complaint is directed at those women across the country who conceal their talents. They thank Christine Mackay and Murdina Mackenzie for their contributions so far, and ask others to join them and submit stories, poetry and other kinds of writing to *Gairm*. The same editorial features some further tongue-in-cheek comment, including the observation of an unnamed friend who says some women may spend most of their words in talk and have little left to put on paper, hinting at the stereotypical image of women as garrulous and gossiping, and also notes that the other editor who is not writing the editorial (a joke referring to the editorial double-act of Thomson and MacDonald) asks prospective women contributors to attach their best photograph to the submission. The mixture of serious commitment and incisive criticism with mischief and jibes, also self-directed, is typical for the style of the 'Spirisean' in general and is not reserved to this particular discussion.

Moreover, the editors proved true to their word, and over the years featured a number of women contributors. Some of them, including Mary Jane Mackay (Màiri Sìne NicAoidh), wrote for children and young people, which is again a role traditionally expected from a woman writer, but many published their own poetry and short fiction aimed at an intellectual readership, including short stories by Eilidh Watt and Chrissy Dick, and poems by Catrìona Montgomery (Catrìona NicGumaraid), Mary Montgomery (Màiri NicGumaraid), Meg Bateman and Anne Frater. Gairm Publications brought out some of their debut collections.

Translations

Gairm also proved to be an important medium for bringing out and encouraging translations from other languages into Gaelic. Thomson formulated his conviction of the importance of translation into Gaelic for the development of the language in the editorial to *Gairm* 119 (1982):

> Anns an àireamh seo de *Ghairm*, tha dithis de ar luchd-sgrìobhaidh ag eadar-theangachadh bho chànanan eile 's bho luchd-sgrìobhaidh às an Eadailt 's às an Spàinn. Bha bàrdachd againn à Ameireaga-a-deas anns an àireamh mu dheireadh, sgeulachd ghoirid às an Fhraing agus iomradh air an Nirribhidh. [. . .] A bheil cus de thaobh thall an t-saoghail againn 's ro bheag mu ar teallaichean fhèin? [. . .]
>
> Ach leis an fhìrinn innse, chan ann ag iarraidh leisgeul a dhèanamh a tha sinn, a thaobh nam boillsgidhean mhòir ann an litreachas. 'S ann a tha e tuilleadh is furasda do na Gàidheil smaoineachadh gun dèan iad an gnothach ann an cùil leotha fhèin, agus tha sin dualtach a' chùil fhàgail cumhang, 's a' dol nas cumhainge.
>
> 'S e aon dòigh air a' chùil a leudachadh boillsgidhean a leigeil a-steach innte bhon iarmailt mhòir air an taobh a-muigh, agus 's ann tren mhac-meanmain a tha sinn, cha tèid sinn ga shireadh, saoilidh mi, air luchd-poileataigs no luchd-fòghlaim no air naidheachdairean, ach air luchd-sgrìobhaidh bàrdachd is sgeulachdan is dhealbhan-cluiche.
>
> Mar sin, is dòcha nach bu mhisde sinn, aig an àm seo, fada barrachd

fhaighinn bhon taobh a-muigh, ach e bhith air a shìoltachadh tren chànan fhìn, agus is dòcha a' sìolachadh ann cuideachd.

In this issue of Gairm, *there are two writers translating from other languages and from authors from Italy and Spain. In the last issue, we had poetry from South America, a short story from France, and a mention of Norway. [. . .] Do we have too much of the world and too little about our own hearths? [. . .]*

But to be honest, we do not want to make excuses about the big flashes in literature. It is too easy for the Gaels to think that they will make do in their own corner, and it is customary for us to make the corner narrow and let it become even narrower.

One of the ways to let in the beams from the big sky beyond is through imagination, and I think that we will not go seeking it from politicians, scholars or journalists, but from the writers of poetry, stories and plays.

Thus, perhaps we should be at this time getting much more from the outside, but filtered through our own language, and perhaps fertilising it too.

Over the years, translations from a number of European languages were featured in the quarterly, mostly poetry, ranging from the classics and Shakespeare's sonnets through Robert Burns to Constantine Cavafy, Ezra Pound, Pablo Neruda and Anna Akhmatova. Thomson also edited the anthology *Bàrdachd na Roinn-Eòrpa an Gàidhlig* (European Poetry in Gaelic, 1990), largely based on the pieces that appeared in *Gairm* throughout the years, which is discussed in more detail in Chapter 5. In terms of fiction, the readers of *Gairm* were able to read samples of the work of a wide range of authors in Gaelic, including Arthur Conan Doyle, J. R. R. Tolkien, Guy de Maupassant, Kate Roberts and Pádraig Ó Conaire.

International and second-language contributors

The interest in energising impulses from other literatures went hand in hand with an openness to people who came to the Gaelic world from the outside – be it as second-language users of Gaelic from Scotland or from other countries. In the editorial to *Gairm* 99 (1977), Thomson notes that many writers who contribute to the quarterly have learnt Gaelic, and stresses that this should be perceived as a source of encouragement, not as a threat to the purity of the language and the exclusive position of traditional speakers. One of the most prominent second-language contributors was Christopher Whyte, and other examples include Meg Bateman, Norman Burns (Tormod Burns), Dennis King, Girvan McKay (Garbhan MacAoidh), Fergus MacKinlay (Fearghas MacFhionnlaigh) and William Neill (Uilleam Nèill).[65] International champions of Gaelic, such

---

[65] Information as to the first-language/second-language status of a number of prominent writers is included in the PhD dissertation by Susan Ross, *The Standardisation of Scottish Gaelic Orthography 1750–2007: A Corpus Approach* (University of Glasgow, 2016), available from <https://theses.gla.ac.uk/7403>.

as the Norwegian linguist Magne Oftedal and the Japanese scholar Tokusaburo Nakamura, were also given space in *Gairm* and Thomson reviewed and commended their work.

Reviews

Contributions to the *Gairm* review section 'An Sgeilp Leabhraichean' [The Bookshelf] and essays on literature constitute one of the most substantial volumes of criticism on Gaelic literature in the language itself, as most new publications of note were reviewed on the pages of the magazine, which helped to promote these new works and encourage discussion about them. As many of the reviews were written by Thomson himself, they bear witness to his preferences and interests. Other prolific reviewers include Finlay J. MacDonald, Iain Crichton Smith, Donald John MacLeod and John MacInnes.

The *Gairm* reviews chronicle the progress of Gaelic literature in the second half of the twentieth century and reflect the development of critical approaches. Besides, the section was not limited to Gaelic works only and regularly featured reviews of new works concerning Scottish literature in English and Scots; Scottish history, ethnology and politics; scholarly works in Celtic studies; and new publications concerning Irish, Manx, Cornish, Welsh and Breton. Thomson and other reviewers too felt free to examine books with no Scottish or Celtic connections at all, signalling unobtrusively that the world did not end at the edge of the Celtic realm. His reviews are discussed in more detail below.

Given the numerical smallness of the world of Gaelic letters, the contributors to *Gairm* often wrote about each other's works, and these close relations and the limited number of possible critics for new writing could not but affect the tone and content of the reviews. The inevitability of being easily personally identified, one of the challenges of the writer's position in a minoritised culture as pinpointed by Thomson, is thus complemented by limited access to more impersonal critical evaluation of one's work, a pattern which continues to affect the Gaelic literary scene to this day. The reception of Thomson's own work as a poet was affected in this way, since he was in charge of the magazine which would have been one of the most natural venues for its evaluation, and his prominence and influence in the field might have discouraged more daring and open critical responses.

Thomson's own contributions to *Gairm*

Apart from editing the magazine and (co-)writing most of the editorials, shaping its policies and inviting contributors, Thomson also provided a substantial amount of content for the quarterly in a number of genres and formats, including crossword puzzles and photo reportage. His poems often appeared initially in *Gairm* and only later in the collections, and eight of his ten short stories were first published in the quarterly: 'Foghar 1976' [Autumn, 1976], *Gairm* 17 (1956); 'Bean a' Mhinisteir' (The Minister's Wife), *Gairm* 22 (1957); 'Mar Chuimhneachan' [As a Keepsake], *Gairm* 31 (1960); 'Tea Feasgair' ['Evening Tea'], *Gairm* 35 (1961); 'Mòd Thorgaboil' [The Mòd in Torgabol], published under the pseudonym 'Tormod MacNèill' in *Gairm* 36 (1961); 'An Staran' [The Stepping Stone Path], *Gairm* 38 (1961); 'Aig a' Phump' [At the Pump], *Gairm* 173 (1995); and 'Seann Iain' [Old John], *Gairm* 186 (1999).[66] The short stories and poems that comment on Gaelic and revitalisation efforts are discussed in detail in Chapter 5. The following section covers most of his contributions that are not examined in detail in other parts of this study.

Travel writing

Thomson's work often took him abroad to conferences and poetry readings, and he wrote up the impressions from three of these trips for *Gairm*. These short pieces, which were accompanied by Thomson's own photographs, often with humorous captions, are remarkable for their vivacity, sense of wonder and anecdotal dimension, such as when the famous linguist truthfully relates how he became overly confident about his command of Swedish and ended up ordering a bowl of semolina instead of a portion of porridge in Stockholm. They often speak about food and sensual impressions, give space to encounters with people, ideas and recollections, and provide a valuable and rather rare insight into Thomson's personality. They also reveal a lively and open-minded curiosity about other countries, especially as far as local languages and cultures are concerned, and a readiness to pick up on progressive ideas and approaches and to suggest them for adoption in Scotland.

The first of these, entitled 'Deich Là anns an t-Suain' [Ten Days in Sweden], appeared in *Gairm* 24 (1958). Thomson does not specify the occasion of the visit, only that he stayed with a relative from Bernera and was able to speak Gaelic, and continued to Norway afterwards. He makes fun of himself for being seasick, noting he would have made an incompetent Viking, as he was unable even to keep a camera straight, not to mention

---

[66] The very first known short story, 'Dubhsgeir', was recorded for the BBC on 9 August 1945. 'Ri Taobh an Teine' [By the Fireside], appeared in *Alba* (1948). 'Dubhsgeir' and 'Mòd Thorgaboil' were located among Thomson's papers by Ian MacDonald after this monograph was first published. 'Seann Iain', although published for the first time in 1999, was, according to Thomson's note, written some fifty years previously and he had come across it when going through old papers: this would date it to the late 1940s or 1950s, together with the rest of the corpus. The ten extant short stories have been included in the collection of Thomson's Gaelic prose *An Staran*, ed. Petra Johana Poncarová (Stornoway: Acair, 2025).

a sword, hinting at the firm association of his native Lewis with sea travel and the far-reaching Scandinavian influence. He includes various pieces of information about the history of Sweden for the benefit of readers and highlights its connections to Scotland and the Gaelic world, including the presence of Gaelic-speaking mercenaries from the Hebrides in the army of Gustavus Adolphus and references to these wars in Gaelic song. He also turns his attention to the environment and everyday life, praising the cleanliness of Swedish trains powered by electricity, the focus on physical culture and the prominence of sports, possibly as an inspiration to Scotland.

The next travelogue, 'O Canada' [From Canada], was written almost twenty years later and appeared in *Gairm* 108 (1979). It recalls a summer visit to Canada for the Meeting of the Clans and the Scottish Canadian Literary Festival, which Thomson attended with other poets, including Sorley MacLean, Iain Crichton Smith and Donald MacAulay. He acknowledges that it would be rash to try to make an opinion of the country after such a short time but presents some of his own impressions. Cape Breton, the local Gaelic heritage and the Gaelic-speaking minority, which would have been much more numerous in the 1970s, were naturally of major interest. During the trip, Thomson visited a collection of Gaelic manuscripts in Halifax, the University of St Francis Xavier in Antigonish, which also has strong Gaelic connections, and a museum of Cape Breton history. He notes how strange it was to see Scottish and Gaelic place names transported to Canada and hearing Gaelic spoken with recognisable Highland and Hebridean accents by people who have never been to Scotland. He commends the positive attitude to Gaelic and the pride of Canadian people in their Scottish heritage but notices the lack of visibility of Gaelic in Cape Breton, the weakness of the language in people under fifty, and the population draining out of towns and the countryside in favour of the cities.

Reflecting on Canadian bilingual policies, he describes the focus on English and French and the fact that French is forcing out Gaelic in towns, but also suggests that some of the policies, such as the consistency of using bilingual texts on food and drink packaging, could also be adopted for the benefit of Gaelic, if only the state were more positive towards the language in Scotland. Observations on lifestyle in parallel to Scotland include the absence of visibly drunk people in public and less explicitly sexual content in the newspapers and advertisements, and some space is again devoted to the question of food, especially fish.

In the last paragraph, Thomson turns his attention to another minority, and draws the reader's attention to the Canadian First Nations, stating openly that these are the people to whom the land belonged before the arrival of the English, Scottish and French immigrants, acknowledging the roles of Scottish settlers, including the Gaelic-speaking ones, in the dispossession of the aboriginal populations. He points out that their language is still alive and that the members of the Micmac tribe continue to live in Nova Scotia in substantial numbers. This parallel to the situation of Gaelic speakers and Gaelic, which however draws attention to their own complicity in the dispossession and suppression of other cultures and languages, is reminiscent of Thomson's poems which focus on the same paradox. The article is concluded by a poem written in Halifax, 'Aodannan' (Faces),[67] in which Thomson comments on the presence of the First Nations people in Canada and compares their situation to that of Scotland. Later, it was published as part of the section 'Dàin às Ùr' in *Creachadh na Clàrsaich* (1982).

The last travelogue, 'Sùil air Suòmi' [A Glance at Finland], appeared in *Gairm* 124 (1983). Thomson explains that he attended the second international congress on minority languages in Turku, at Åbo Academy.[68] In relation to the congress, he reminds readers that the first event of this kind was held at Glasgow University in 1980 and that the resulting publication, *Minority Languages Today*, edited by Einar Haugen, J. Derrick McClure and Thomson himself, was published a year later by Edinburgh University Press. According to the travelogue, Thomson delivered a paper, 'Foillseachadh leabhraichean Gàidhlig ann an Albainn' [Publishing Gaelic Books in Scotland], at the congress in Finland, and presented copies of several books to the delegates, most likely volumes produced by Gairm Publications.

He mentions friends in attendance, including Magne Oftedal, and the titles of some of the presentations, illustrating the diversity of the delegates and the topics, and the refreshing and inspiring effect of meeting researchers who were deeply involved in their subjects. In particular, he singles out a young woman academic in attendance who had a command of seven languages, and notes that such examples should make Scottish people reconsider their reluctance to use even two different languages, and the fear of Scottish schools to provide them such an opportunity. He also states how ashamed he felt of his limited command of Finnish, in comparison with the local people's fluency in English.

Naturally, he turns his attention to the linguistic situation in Finland and refers to the presence of Swedish as a minority language there, and the supportive policies towards it, observing that the same amount of good will is not available for the language of the Sámi minority. He also describes some

---

[67] Not to be confused with the poem of the same title which appeared in *Sùil air Fàire* (2007).
[68] The article also reveals an interesting personal link: Thomson describes coming across the bust of Otto Andersson, professor of music at the Åbo Academy, whom he met in Lewis in 1938, when Andersson was researching Scandinavian musical traditions preserved on the island, and received a copy of the volume *Eilean Fraoich* from Thomson's father James. Later, the scholar published the pamphlet *On Gaelic Folk Music from the Isle of Lewis* (Åbo, 1953). This prompts Thomson to stress the importance of cultural and historical links between countries, and of such personal connections.

details of the life of the Sámi, making comparisons between them and the life of the traditional communities in Lewis. Basic information about the history of Finland is summarised, including the former influence of Russia and Russian (comparing the custom to speak Russian when noblewomen of Turku met for tea to the use of English in Stornoway), its struggle for independence, and its current economic situation and political system. Turku is described in comparison to Aberdeen and Thomson praises the neatness of the city, the lack of Russian influence and, again, the absence of visibly drunk people in the streets.

He notes that although Finland may be bigger than the UK in terms of area, it is nonetheless very small in terms of population, and suggests that Scotland could learn from it in several areas, namely the support for minority languages, especially for Swedish and for Sámi to a lesser extent; the policies at schools and universities, which also support the minority language; the impressive number of daily newspapers (and the fact that twelve out of ninety-four are published in Swedish); and finally the healthy attitude to work which combines productivity with self-esteem. This particular travelogue also features some of his most effective descriptions of the local landscape, especially from a night train from Sweden to Norway, and these are some of the most winning examples of Thomson's command of Gaelic prose.

Apart from these three travelogues, *Gairm* also featured a number of photo reportages by Thomson, mostly from Scotland but also one from Wales, 'Rud air na Laigh Sùil' [Things That Caught the Eye] (*Gairm* 81: 1972), which documents the presence of Welsh in the public space and thus illustrates the local language policies, and another from France, with snapshots of everyday local life (*Gairm* 141: 1987). Thomson's authorship is recognisable not only thanks to the abbreviation RMT, but also through the witty, wry captions that accompany the photographs.

Tributes

Over the years, Thomson published three tributes to recently deceased people he knew and who were in different ways involved in promoting Gaelic: Hector MacIver (*Gairm* 71: 1970), Iain Fraser (*Gairm* 77: 1971) and Duncan Livingstone (*Gairm* 119: 1982). These measured, generous essays reveal a more private and sensitive side of Thomson, his keen interest in other people and his ability to appreciate them. Iain Fraser (Iain Friseal, 1882–1945) was a professor at Oxford University who focused on comparative linguistics, old Celtic languages and the study of the Picts. Thomson opens the article by mentioning the lack of recognition for his achievements in the Gaelic world and proceeds with an overview of his career and his character, including personal recollections of people who knew him, thus introducing to the reader a major scholar who was a Gaelic speaker, worked on Gaelic and related subjects, and also taught the language. Duncan Livingstone (Donnchadh MacDhunlèibhe, 1877–1964), a native of Mull who spent most of his life in South Africa, was a poet, a contributor to *Gairm* and the author of some scathing criticism of the apartheid policies in South Africa. In the essay, Thomson pays tribute to his achievements and provides a detailed examination of his poetry.

The most personal of these obituaries is that for Hector MacIver, which takes the form of a review of a festschrift published in his honour, *Memoirs of a Modern Scotland* (ed. Karl Miller). Apart from the essay, Thomson also published an elegy for MacIver in *Gairm* 56 (1966), 'Eachann MacÌomhair (Marbhrann)'. MacIver (1910–66) was a writer, reviewer and poet who grew up in Shawbost, Lewis.[69] He taught English at the Royal High School in Edinburgh and was a friend and associate of many literary figures, including Hugh MacDiarmid, Dylan Thomas, Louis MacNeice and Sydney Goodsir Smith. Thomson recalls that he first encountered MacIver twenty-five years previously at a political gathering in Stornoway, and that they started to meet more often in Edinburgh after 1948, spending many an evening together joking and discussing politics, history and especially poetry. The article is much less of a review, although Thomson gives an overview of the contributions to the festschrift, and more of a personal tribute to a friend, which, while acknowledging some of the more challenging aspects of MacIver's personality, also shows great fondness for the man and gratefulness for his acquaintance. MacIver's name appears in connection with Thomson a number of times: he receives an acknowledgement in the preface to *An Dealbh Briste*, his article on Gaelic drama is referred to in the editorial to *Gairm* 17, as discussed in the section on Gaelic drama in *Gairm* above, and he also contributed several articles and one short story to *Gairm*.

Satire, humour, entertainment

A number of Thomson's contributions to *Gairm* reveal his sense of humour, dry wit and delight in mischief, which he also employed when discussing the situation on the Gaelic world and the revitalisation initiatives. In general, *Gairm* was instrumental in developing modern humorous writing in Gaelic. In *Gairm* 49 (1963), for instance, Thomson published a satirical piece entitled 'Cagailte Còmhradh', a scathing response to an article in the *Stornoway Gazette* that criticised modern poetry and other new trends in art, under the nickname

---

[69] Iain Smith, 'A Hebridean Bohemian in Rose Street', *Scottish Review*, originally published 2014, republished online on 8 August 2018, available from <https://www.scottishreview.net//IainSmithannals441a.html> Accessed 15 April 2023.

'Donn Dòmhnall', referring to the *Gazette* series as 'Còmhradh Cagailte, le Dòmhnall Donn'.⁷⁰

Another notable example of the wry style is the deliberation about the Gaelic ombudsman in the editorial to *Gairm* 53 (1965), co-written by Thomson and MacDonald, which serves as a pretext to pillory the putative capacity of Gaelic users to complain about various things without providing an alternative:

> A bheil Ombudsman a dhìth oirnn air a' Ghàidhealtachd? Chan eil sinn idir a' ciallachadh an duine sin a tha Pàrlamaid Lunnainn an dùil a chur an sàs, ach Ombudsman dhuinn fhìn, fear a bheireadh am follais gach cànran a th' againn an aghaidh ar luchd-riaghlaidh 's ar luchd-stiùiridh air a' Ghàidhealtachd, agus ann an àite sam bith far a bheil caitheamh agus ana-caitheamh gan dèanamh air a' Ghàidhlig. Tha sinn dùil gur h-e duine feumail a bhiodh ann. Nach iomadh gearain a dh'fhaodadh e dhèanamh. [. . .] Chan eil teagamh cuideachd nach fheumadh e dèiligeadh ris an fheadhainn a bhios a' sgrìobhadh mu ghnothaichean eaglaise ann an *Gasaid Steòrnabhaigh*. Cha bhiodh leigheas orrasan ach an cur cola-deug do dh'eaglais Easbuigeach a dhustadh 's a ghlanadh nan ìomhaighean. Tha rithist ann na daoine nach cùm camara TV còmhnard air Oidhche Dhihaoine a' Mhòid. Dè ghabhas dèanamh riuthasan? Chan eil a' cheist seo duilich a fuasgladh. An cur fad mhìos do Sheòmar nan Naidheachdan anns a' BhBC, a leughadh nan naidheachdan Gàidhlig, fhad 's a bhios Cailein MacCoinnich agus Coinneach MacDhòmhnaill a' leigeil an anail ann am Majorca. Bu mhath leinn cuideachd gun togadh an duine seo gearain an aghaidh nan daoine nach bi a' leughadh *Gairm* – agus gun cuireadh e orrasan mar pheanas *Gairm* a leughadh. Ach cò thaghadh an duine seo, agus dè an t-ainm a bhiodh air? Nam b' e an Comunn Gaidhealach a thaghadh e cò dhèanadh casaid an aghaidh a' Chomuinn? A thaobh ainm, cha bhiodh sin duilich a lorg. Gheibheadh e ainmeannan gu leòr aon uair 's gu rachadh e an sàs anns an obair seo air Ghàidhealtachd.

> *Are we lacking an ombudsman in the Gàidhealtachd? We do not mean at all the person the parliament in London hopes to put in place, but our own*

---

⁷⁰ The entry on the article in *Gairm Air-loidhne* includes detailed information with reference to Ronald Black's forthcoming article 'Gairm: An Aois Òir (2)'. Another reflection of the exchange between *Gairm* and the *Stornoway Gazette* is the editorial to *Gairm* 43 (1963), which discusses the Gaelic material featured in the *Gazette* and states that a periodical issued in the centre of Lewis should naturally promote the language. It mentions that the *Gazette*, under the editorship of 'Dòmhnall Donn', is reputedly planning to publish a Gaelic translation of Stevenson's *Kidnapped* with strip-cartoon, and *Gairm* asks its readers to support the effort, write to the *Gazette*, and demand that the booklet should indeed be produced.

ombudsman, someone who would bring into the open all our complaints about the governance and administration in the Gàidhealtachd and in any place where Gaelic is wasted and misused. We think it would be a useful person. He could raise so many complaints. [. . .] Undoubtedly, he could deal with those who write about church matters to the Stornoway Gazette. *There is no remedy but to send them for a fortnight to the Episcopal Church and make them dust and clean the statues. There are also those who cannot keep a TV camera straight on Friday night at the Mòd. What should be done with them? It is not a difficult question to resolve. Put them for a month into the BBC newsroom to read the Gaelic news, while Colin Mackenzie and Kenneth MacDonald take some time off in Majorca. We would also like this person to complain about the people who do not read* Gairm *– and to make them read it as a punishment. But who would choose this person and how would he be called? Should he be chosen by An Comunn Gàidhealach, who would then complain about the association itself? As to the name, it should not be difficult to find – he will be called names enough, as soon as he becomes involved in this sort of work in the Gàidhealtachd.*

Further illustrations of this satirical tone can be found in the editorial to *Gairm* 182 (1998), where Thomson takes the then-current plans to erect a Millennium Dome in London as a pretext to critique the waste of public resources, regional rivalries in Lewis and corruption in local politics. He suggests that with every Londoner donating twelve pounds, the capital could keep the Millennium Dome, and proceeds to consider that many other places surely deserve a dome too, for example Lewis, proposing a special black house worth two million pounds, but wonders where it would be located, given the local rivalries. If in Garrabost, the people of Ness and the West Coast would not be happy about it, although they already have a Dùn in Carloway. He also observes that if a referendum should be held in Lewis, three instead of two possible answers would be needed: tha / chan eil / tha + chan eil [yes / no / yes + no]. In the end, he proposes that if half a million is sent to *Gairm*, it will erect a small cairn close to the office, or perhaps change the name of the street from Waterloo Street to Sràid Ghairm [Gairm Street], and there will be enough left for council members to go to Trinidad or another attractive place.

The already-mentioned section for learners, 'Theab Mi a Leughadh' [I Almost Read], which Thomson ran in the 1990s, also included some tongue-in-cheek content, such as his advice in *Gairm* 160 (1992) to learners of Gaelic who suffer from a scarcity of interlocutors:

Ach cuimhnich: ma tha cù no cat agad, faodaidh thu Gàidhlig a bhruidhinn ris. 'Ach,' arsa tusa, 'am bruidhinn esan Gàidhlig riumsa?' Well, bruidhnidh e a Ghàidhlig fhèin riut, agus cha bhi e fada gus an tuig e dè tha thu ag ràdh. Agus rud eile: cha bhi eagal ort gun tòisich e a' fanaid, no a' gàireachdaich. Bruidhinn thusa ris a h-uile là airson còig no deich mionaidean. Agus mur eil cù no cat agad, faigh fear, no dealbh de dh'fhear.[71]

But remember: if you have a dog or a cat, you could talk in Gaelic to them. 'But,' you say, 'will they speak Gaelic to me?' Well, they will speak their own Gaelic to you, and it will not take long for them to understand what you say. And another thing: you will not be afraid that they will start to mock you or laugh at you. Speak to them every day for five or ten minutes. And if you do not have a dog or a cat, get one, or at least a picture of one.

Thomson further suggests that while walking the dog, the learner can speak about football, whereas cats are not keen on walks, and prefer lying in the sun and eating fish.

Faighnich dha dè an seòrsa as fheàrr leis: adag no sgadan no breac no trosg no sgait. Is iongantach gun can e dad ach 'Miaow', ach tha sin a' ciallachadh 'Is caomh leam a h-uile iasg a chunnaic mi riamh. Falbh is faigh iasg a-nis agus cha bhi mise fada ga ith.' Nuair a bhios tu a' dèanamh sin, feuch gu seinn thu 'Balaich an iasgaich', no gun dèan thu dannsa bheag le na facail 'Adagan is sgadan agus breac is trosg is sgait', no 'Sgait is breac is sgadan agus adagan is trosg.'

Ask the cat what it prefers: haddock, herring, trout, cod or skate. I expect that it won't say anything but 'Miaow', but that means 'I like every sort of fish I have ever seen. Go and get me fish now and I will be quick to eat it.' And while you do that, try to sing 'Balaich an iasgaich' [The Fisher Boys], or do a wee dance with the words 'Haddock and herring and trout and cod and skate', or 'Skate and trout and herring and haddock and cod'.

These learning suggestions, which reveal Thomson's sense of humour and fondness of animals (and, again, interest in football), can be of course followed seriously too, and they also suggest that while the revitalisation efforts should be conducted with high standards and intense commitment, those involved in them should not take themselves too seriously.

According to entries in *Gairm Air-Loidhne*, Thomson was also the author of the anonymously published humorous photo captions, including 'Seann Nòs aig a' Mhòd' [Old Style at the Mòd], *Gairm* 121 (1982); 'Vote S.N.P.', *Gairm* 145 (1988); 'Òrdughan Urramach' [Honorary Orders], *Gairm* 148 (1989); and others. In the 1990s and 2000s, he wrote an extended series of short pieces of political satire and amusing prose for the quarterly, showing his sense of humour and commitment to bring a satirical edge to Gaelic revitalisation efforts and to Scottish politics did not leave him even in later life.

---

[71] MacThòmais, 'Theab Mi a Leughadh', *Gairm* 160 (1992), 312–13.

Reviews

The *Gairm* reviews provide a unique insight into Thomson's opinions on various topics and also into his reading. In some cases, the reviews may reveal less about the volumes in question and more about Thomson's own take on their subject matter, but he usually provides a fair and supportive assessment of the given book as well. According to the records in *Gairm Air-loidhne*, many of the early anonymous reviews were written by Thomson. Starting from *Gairm* 8 (1954), the reviews are signed, and thus it can be said that Thomson indeed did most of the reviewing work for the quarterly, and that he influenced readers both by the choice of books and by the opinions he expressed about them.[72] While some of the publications he reviewed for *Gairm* have a straightforward enough connection to the Gaelic revitalisation agenda, other choices reveal Thomson's own reading preferences and bring forward preoccupations and concerns which might otherwise go unnoticed, but which in connection with other pieces of evidence, for instance his translations and references in the editorials, provide a new perspective on Thomson as a reader who was especially interested in, among other authors, Edwin Muir, W. B. Yeats, R. M. Rilke and Alexander Solzhenitsyn.

Naturally, works dealing with various aspects of the Gaelic world and with Gaelic revitalisation efforts were covered extensively in the reviews. Thomson was keeping an eye on all new publications dealing with the history of Gaelic in Scotland, the Gaelic movement and also folklore and linguistics, such as Kenneth MacKinnon's *Lion's Tongue: Story of the Gaelic Language*, John Prebble's *The Highland Clearances* and Margaret Fay Shaw's *Folksongs and Folklore of South Uist*. The reviews also covered works in English but with strong connections to the Gaelic world in terms of authorship and subject matter, such as the three seminal novels dealing with the Highland Clearances (Iain Crichton Smith's *Consider the Lilies*, Neil Gunn's *The Butcher's Broom* and Fionn MacColla's *And the Cock Crew*) and MacColla's radical autobiography *Too Long in This Condition*.

In accord with the pronounced support for modern Gaelic writing in *Gairm*, Thomson paid much attention to new work by Gaelic poets, many of whom he encouraged by giving them the opportunity to publish in *Gairm* and by reviewing their books, and he also examined some of the major works of modern Gaelic fiction, including the novel *Deireadh an Fhoghair* (The End of Autumn) by Norman Campbell (Tormod Caimbeul) and supernatural short stories by Eilidh Watt. What may be more surprising, given the widespread idea of a personal animosity between the two poets, is that Thomson's reviews testify to a sustained and discerning interest in the work of Sorley MacLean, and a dedication to comment on it seriously. Thomson reviewed the translation of *Poems to Eimhir* by Iain

---

[72] A complete overview of all reviews by Thomson is now available via *Gairm Air-loidhne*.

Crichton Smith and also the collections *O Choille gu Bearradh* and *Reothairt is Contraigh*. Together with the respect for MacLean's achievements expressed in the editorial to *Gairm* 178 (1997), published upon the older poet's death, and the fact MacLean was invited to contribute to *Gairm* and indeed published in it, these suggest that when it came to opportunities connected to the quarterly, it seems MacLean was not slighted by Thomson in any way.

A substantial number of the reviews in *Gairm* by Thomson discussed Scottish writing in English and Scots, and also academic works on Scottish literature, including *Scottish Poetry: A Critical Survey* by James Kinsley and *History of Scottish Literature* edited by Cairns Craig. The reviews also attest to Thomson's long-term preoccupation with both Muir and MacDiarmid, who famously clashed over the issue of the language in which Scottish national literature should be created. His interest in Muir is indicated by the translations he included in the anthology *Bàrdachd na Roinn-Eòrpa* and by three *Gairm* reviews: Muir's *Autobiography*, his collection *One Foot in Eden* and the anthology *New Poets 1959*, featuring Iain Crichton Smith, Karen Gershon and Christopher Levenson, which Muir edited. Apart from the extensive coverage of MacDiarmid, discussed in Chapter 2, Thomson also reviewed literature dealing with the Scots language, including Billy Kay's *Scots: The Mither Tongue* and William Neill's *The Tungs o Scots*. The fact that a number of books Thomson chose to write about for *Gairm* deal with Scottish history and nationalism is not at all surprising, but the range of the reading reveals how much he was following the publications on the topic and the discussions outside the Gaelic world, and the reviewed publications, such as James G. Kellas' *Modern Scotland*, H. J. Hanham's *Scottish Nationalism*, and *The Scottish Debate*, edited by Neil MacCormick, indicate a remarkable breadth of outlook.

Thomson's engagement with Ireland and Wales and their revitalisation efforts is discussed in detail in Chapter 2 and Chapter 4, and there is plentiful evidence of his interest in other countries where minority languages are present beyond the Celtic world, in the *Gairm* travelogues and also in the anthology *Bàrdachd na Roinn-Eòrpa*. *Gairm* reviews corroborate this interest further. Over the years, Thomson commented on a number of books dealing with Celtic languages and languages of the British Isles. Naturally Meic Stephens' magnum opus *Linguistic Minorities in Western Europe* did not escape his attention. The *Gairm* 'Bookshelf' also provides evidence of his awareness of publications covering Cornwall, the Isle of Man and even the Faroe Islands.

In the editorial to *Gairm* 160 (1992), Thomson acknowledges the happiness of seeing six million words in the 160 issues that bear witness to the changes and developments in the Gaelic world, including the development of a broader and more varied literary scene, especially in the realm of poetry and short fiction, which arguably would not have happened if the writers had not had the advantage of a suitable and supportive venture for publishing their work, and Donald John MacLeod considers *Gairm* the basis of the revival which took place in Gaelic literature in the second half of the twentieth century.[73] Gairm Publications became one of the most prolific Gaelic publishers of the era, bringing out new literature, teaching materials, non-fiction and books for children, and thus preparing the ground for later and more diversified initiatives such as the publishing houses Acair, CLÀR and Stòrlann, a body that coordinates the production of teaching materials.

As Donald MacAulay noted, 'Had Thomson made no other contribution to Gaelic than the work he has put into *Gairm*, in formulating its policy and in putting that policy into effect, his contribution would have been of remarkable importance.'[74] As this chapter tried to illustrate, with its extra-literary concerns and ambitions, the quarterly contributed to the revitalisation of Gaelic by discussing issues related to the language and proposing specific steps and policies; encouraging individual action and grassroots activism; and supporting second-language users and the teaching and employment of the language beyond the traditionally Gaelic-speaking areas. The aftermath of *Gairm* and the realm of the Gaelic periodical press in its wake is examined as part of Chapter 6.

---

[73] MacLeod, *Dualchas an Aghaidh nan Creag*, 23.
[74] Donald MacAulay, 'Introduction', *Derick Thomson: The Far Road and Other Poems, Lines Review* 39 (December 1971), 4.

CHAPTER FOUR

Scholarship, Activism and Translations

Many of Thomson's activities as a scholar, editor, organiser and translator can also be conceptualised as part of the Gaelic revitalisation efforts. As this part of his work is one of the least explored, this chapter summarises Thomson's scholarly output, organisational work, activism and translations in the first comprehensive overview, and discusses their intended and possible connections to the promotion of the language. MacAulay remarked that Thomson's Gaelic activism, such as the foundation and maintenance of *Gairm* and The Gaelic Books Council, spring from the same motivation that pushed him into active participation in nationalist politics, for he saw those activities as 'offering at least a marginal possibility of the survival of Gaelic culture'.[1]

Scholarship

Thomson's main career was that of a university lecturer and academic, and throughout his life he continued to write and publish research on various aspects of Gaelic literature, from medieval poetry to developments in Gaelic verse that were occurring in his own lifetime. His scholarly oeuvre includes publications designed as reference works that are accessible both to Gaelic scholars and to an international readership, and also detailed specialised studies that resonate most within the field of Gaelic literature.

The vast majority of Thomson's purely academic work was published in English, which contrasts with the importance he accredited to conducting research on Gaelic topics through the medium of Gaelic, noting that 'a contemporary living literature needs a contemporary criticism in its own language', and the conviction that published criticism in Gaelic could provide the needed impetus for more university courses and school classes conducted through the medium of the language.[2] As McLeod notes, until the late 1990s almost no scholarly work was published in Gaelic, which was a general trend in academia, and the practice of delivering lectures and papers and publishing academic essays on Gaelic topics in Gaelic only became more common in more recent decades.[3] Thomson followed his

---

[1] MacAulay, 'Introduction', *The Far Road* 4.
[2] Thomson, 'Reflections after Writing *An Introduction to Gaelic Poetry*', 19.
[3] McLeod, *Gaelic in Scotland*, 327.

own advice mostly through the contributions to *Gairm*, where essays on Gaelic literature and an extensive corpus of reviews in Gaelic appeared across fifty years, but all these articles are relatively short, running to about five pages maximum. Thomson's Gaelic prose also remains uncollected and untranslated, and constitutes one of the least studied parts of his work.

Thomson's scholarly works can be seen as part of the revivalist effort in terms of filling in at least some of the numerous gaps in the field of Gaelic studies. In this sense, Thomson's academic output is remarkable for its rigour and the refusal to extol all works in the history of Gaelic literature for their mere existence, in order to provide arguments for its value and boost the confidence of the speakers. Rather, he seeks to offer a thorough examination of the literary merit of Gaelic writing and the context of its emergence, so that both readers and authors can get a clear understanding of the tradition. There is a marked preference for topics that have a political and nationalist dimension, that reach out to international inspirations, and aspire to a high intellectual standard.

Two reference works by Thomson, one authored and one edited, remain indispensable to most scholars working in the field: *An Introduction to Gaelic Poetry* (1974)[4] and *The Companion to Gaelic Scotland* (1983, edited). They have played a crucial part in providing the basic framework for further research and in making Gaelic literature and culture more accessible to the international public. After the former study appeared, Thomson wrote an essay for *Lines Review* entitled 'Reflections After Writing *An Introduction to Gaelic Poetry*', on the invitation of the then editor of the journal Robin Fulton, which explains the cultural and nationalist motivation behind his scholarly work, and can be used as a fruitful introduction to this whole section. In the opening part of the essay, Thomson states:

> The time seemed absolutely right to offer some exposition to the non-Gaelic world, especially in Scotland, of the Gaelic tradition, and poetry is a surprisingly important part of that tradition. Scotland is engaged in some reappraisal of itself, and quite clearly sees that the Gaelic part of its identity is valuable.[5]

He continues by pointing out the necessity of bringing together the various spheres of the reappraisal and the importance of connecting literature, culture and language policies with economics, politics and planning. In his view, this needed cross-fertilisation could be achieved through at least one 'undogmatic periodical' with at least a monthly frequency. Much more work in 'clearing a view in specific areas' needs to be

---

[4] The first edition was published in 1974. In 1989, a new one was issued, with some additions to the final chapter and an updated bibliography.
[5] Thomson, 'Reflections after Writing *An Introduction to Gaelic Poetry*', 15.

done in the background and Thomson asserts this was one of the functions of producing *An Introduction to Gaelic Poetry*. He also mentions the lingering prejudices against Gaelic in Lowland Scotland, which similar studies could help to dissipate, and maintains that the quality of Gaelic poetry speaks so strongly for itself that it was not even necessary to stress how easily it undermines the old claims about the 'barbarism' of Gaelic Scotland.

The essay also touches on the widespread misconception that Gaelic is obsolete and unable to cope in terms of vocabulary with the modern world, having no terms for 'asset stripping' and 'carbohydrate', a feeling of inadequacy common also among the users of the language themselves, and Thomson notes mischievously that 'often they have no idea how many such words can in fact be called into service in Gaelic. I may have been under some small temptation to react to such initiatives, but (not surprisingly) we have no Hugh MacDiarmid to produce from the Gaelic hat, so I have largely let it be.'[6] This comment is of substantial relevance to Thomson's major translation project, the rendition of a complete biology textbook in Gaelic, which is discussed below. He stresses that such a study of poetry is also inevitably an examination of the language, not only of the lexical meaning of the individual words but of the history of the language and the social context, thus situating it directly into the revivalist framework.

He states that he wrote *An Introduction* with the vision of Gaelic studies becoming integrated into 'a total Scottish context' and proposes a move 'towards thinking of the country as a bilingual one', not by introducing compulsory Gaelic or compulsory English, but by making more space for the language in academia and in the public space, including bilingual road signs and notices, and by allocating more support to Gaelic bodies. He concludes that it is 'against such a background, Scottish and international, and also more specifically Gaelic, that my recent book takes, or doesn't take, its place'.[7] It is profitable to locate Thomson's scholarship against this backdrop of the twin concerns of Gaelic revitalisation and Scottish independence, and it is what this chapter attempts to do.

An Introduction to Gaelic Poetry traces the history of poetry as a form which dominated Gaelic letters until the mid-twentieth century. Thomson states that he aims to 'discuss and illustrate as many traditions, styles and individual bodies of verse as possible', starting from the bardic schools and oldest, mostly anonymous songs and continuing to a more detailed account of 'the poetry of clan and politics in the seventeenth–eighteenth centuries'.[8] Generous space is devoted to the eighteenth century, traditionally seen as the golden age when much brilliant verse was produced,

---

[6] Thomson, 'Reflections after Writing *An Introduction to Gaelic Poetry*', 16.
[7] Thomson, 'Reflections after Writing *An Introduction to Gaelic Poetry*', 19.
[8] Thomson, 'Reflections after Writing *An Introduction to Gaelic Poetry*', 16–17.

and Thomson describes it as a period when Gaelic poetry 'breathes a new air' and 'shows a new vigour'.[9] The poetry of the three great poets of the eighteenth century, Alexander MacDonald, Duncan Ban Macintyre and William Ross, is given generous space, and the account leads up to the middle of the twentieth century. The study reflects Thomson's above-mentioned preferences for intellectually aspiring and politically outspoken poetry, especially for the works of Alexander MacDonald and John Smith (Iain Mac a' Ghobhainn) of Iarsiadar, Lewis.

The Companion to Gaelic Scotland, the very first volume of its kind, as no dictionary of Gaelic biography or a dictionary of Gaelic writers preceded it, was first published in 1983 by Blackwell.[10] In the introduction, Thomson explains that the idea for the companion came in late 1978 from John Davey of the Blackwell publishing house, who asked Thomson to prepare it. He recalls that he was 'immediately attracted to the idea', as he noticed 'great curiosity about Gaelic Scotland', with no 'readily available way of satisfying it, and even for professional students of Gaelic matters there has been no set of tools that will produce quick results for a variety of enquiries'.[11] Thomson acknowledges the help of a large number of people in its making and the difficulties of choosing what to include and what to omit. He concludes though that in spite of some inevitable shortcomings, the volume 'can be used with profit by scholar and layman, Gaelic writer and French tourist, in fact by anyone who is interested in any aspect, past or present, of Gaelic Scotland'.[12] The bulk of the companion is devoted to the individual entries, which are accompanied by a chronological chart covering the main events in the history of Gaelic Scotland and by an extensive bibliography.

The volume is broadly conceived and does not show preference for any particular strain of Gaelic culture, be it rural or urban, Catholic or Protestant, and covers, among other areas, agriculture, architecture, dance, geology, history, the visual arts and material culture, literature, music, religion, social developments, and the Gaelic world in Scotland and abroad. The list of contributors is diverse too, featuring representatives of Scottish universities and independent researchers, but also scholars based at universities in England, in Continental Europe and in the USA and Canada, including Thomson's long-term collaborators such as John Lorne Campbell, Ian Grimble and Magne Oftedal.

Apart from editing the volume, Thomson contributed tens of entries, from very short accounts of historical incidents, documents and various persons to more extensive discussions. Apart from general entries (an

---

[9] Thomson, *An Introduction to Gaelic Poetry* (1977), 156.
[10] In 1987, a paperback edition with small updates appeared, and in 1993 a more substantially revised edition was prepared, including recent developments and an updated bibliography, and published by Gairm Publications.
[11] Thomson, 'Preface', *The Companion to Gaelic Scotland*, vii.
[12] Thomson, 'Preface', *The Companion to Gaelic Scotland*, vii.

overall survey of Gaelic; Gaelic orthography), he naturally chose to write those on some of his major interests: Gaelic manuscripts and collections (Book of the Dean of Lismore; The Book of Deer; Carmina Gadelica), the poetry of the eighteenth century (Duncan Ban MacIntyre; Alexander MacDonald; William Ross), the Ossian controversy (James Macpherson; Rev. Donald MacNicol), the works of his contemporaries (Donald MacAulay; Sorley MacLean; George Campbell Hay); and the developments in Gaelic scholarship, publishing and media (coverage of current affairs in Gaelic; Gaelic-language organisations; the magazine *An Gàidheal*; Gaelic press, periodicals and publications; literary history and criticism).

There are also some surprising entries written by Thomson which reveal interests he is not so frequently associated with. Prosaic reasons may have been involved in the allocation, and as the editor he may have needed to write up what his contributors failed to provide, but the selection indeed seems to reflect Thomson's less-known preoccupations. He wrote on Gaelic folksong (extensive entries on 'early folksong' and 'folksongs, collections of'), on 'humour (post-1600)' and on Gaelic prose, including early non-literary prose and the Gaelic novel. In terms of biographical entries, he supplied those on the architect and designer Charles Rennie Mackintosh and the polymath Patrick Geddes. Their links to Gaelic Scotland may seem less prominent, but by their inclusion Thomson would have stressed the international dimension of Scottish culture, in terms of both receiving and providing new impulses. It is also interesting to note what Thomson did not contribute himself – he left the entry on Ruaraidh Erskine of Mar to T. M. Murchison and the one on Iain Crichton Smith to Donald MacAulay. The entry on Thomson himself was supplied by Ronald Black.

Major research topics

Thomson's scholarly output beyond the two general volumes is large and diverse.[13] In terms of twentieth-century developments, he published several studies of modern Gaelic poetry, including 'Tradition and Innovation in Gaelic Verse since 1950' (*Transactions of the Gaelic Society of Inverness LIII*: 1982–4) and 'Gaelic Renaissance *c.* 1900–1930' (*Transactions of the Gaelic Society of Inverness* 60: 1997–8). Although he reviewed works of the latest Gaelic fiction for *Gairm*, and was keen to support the development of the short story in Gaelic and wrote some himself, he published no academic studies of Gaelic prose, apart from two entries in *The Companion to Gaelic Scotland*. One summarises early Gaelic non-literary prose, while the other, quite extensive, covers the development of the Gaelic novel, revealing Thomson's acquaintance with the field and showing a preference for the

---

[13] An overview of Thomson's published academic output up to 1993 is available in 'Bibliography', *Fèill-sgrìbhinn do Ruaraidh MacThòmais*, 4–23.

prose works of Iain Crichton Smith as well as an appreciation of Tormod Caimbeul's experimental novel *Deireadh an Fhoghair.*

The core of his academic interest was, however, the eighteenth century and earlier eras. He published extensively on classical Gaelic poetry, late-medieval learned culture, manuscript collections, such as the Books of Clanranald and the Book of the Dean of Lismore, and the poets represented in these collections, including the MacMhuirich bards. He contributed entries on these topics to *The Companion to Gaelic Scotland* and wrote a number of substantial essays on them, such as 'Gaelic Learned Orders and Literati in Medieval Scotland' (*Scottish Studies* 12: 1968), 'The MacMhuirich Bardic Family' (*Transactions of the Gaelic Society of Inverness* XLIII: 1966), 'The Poetry of Niall MacMhuirich' (*TGSI* XLV: 1971) and 'Niall Mòr MacMhuirich' (*TGSI* XLIX: 1977).

Two particular concerns, both within the eighteenth century, can be traced throughout his career, and as both have a profound political dimension and are related to the position of Gaelic in Scotland and of Scotland in Europe, they are examined here in more depth: they are the Ossianic publications of James Macpherson and the works of Alexander MacDonald.

James Macpherson and the Ossian controversy

At the beginning of his career, James Macpherson (Seumas Mac a' Phearsain, 1736–96), a native of Ruthven from Badenoch, published three volumes of poetry – *Fragments of Ancient Poetry* (1760), *Fingal* (1761) and *Temora* (1763) – which proved to be a major success with the reading public, played a crucial part in the early phase of the European Romantic movement, and sparked a controversy that raged mostly in Macpherson's own time but which continues in different forms to this day.

Fiona Stafford has argued that Macpherson's activities were influenced by his experience in his native region, where he witnessed post-Culloden repression, and by a desire to achieve more prestige for Scottish Gaelic culture at a time of profound crisis by providing it with a national epic poem, a proof of long-standing history, and cultural refinement according to the standard of his time.[14] The success of the poems and the question of their 'authenticity' were from the beginning connected with the prestige of Scotland as a nation,[15] and the nationalist dimension continued to influence the controversy, together with different and changing attitudes towards authorship.[16]

---

[14] Fiona Stafford, *The Sublime Savage: A Study of James Macpherson and the Poems of Ossian* (Edinburgh: Edinburgh University Press, 1988).

[15] See, for instance, Richard B. Sher, 'Percy, Shaw and the Ferguson "Cheat": National Prejudice in the Ossian Wars', *Ossian Revisited*, ed. Howard Gaskill (Edinburgh: Edinburgh University Press, 1991), 207–45.

[16] I develop the argument in the essay '"Many More Remains of Ancient Genius": Approaches to Authorship in the Ossian Controversy', *Authors That Matter: Authorship after*

Given the political and nationalist dimension, the European impact, and the close relationship to the perception of Scottish Gaelic and its literature in Scotland and abroad, it is not surprising that the topic attracted Thomson from the very beginning of his career.[17] The thesis he submitted as the conclusion of his degree in Anglo-Saxon, Norse and Celtic at Cambridge is entitled simply *The Gaelic Sources of Macpherson's 'Ossian'* (1952). The title itself makes an important and radical statement, suggesting there were Gaelic sources Macpherson could use – and that he did use them. A similar conclusion had been proposed already by the nineteenth-century folklore collector and polymath John Francis Campbell (Iain Frangan Caimbeul, also known as Iain Òg Ìle, 1821–85) in the introduction to the fourth volume of his *Popular Tales of the West Highlands*,[18] but Thomson was the first scholar who undertook the task of identifying particular passages in specific ballads Macpherson had drawn on and devoted a monograph to the subject.

In the introduction, Thomson sums up the controversy over two hundred years and notes that the debate was 'misdirected for more than a century', as 'the point of issue was taken to be whether there existed Gaelic poems, preferably in ancient MSS, composed by a bard called Ossian in the third century A.D'.[19] These, he states, clearly did not exist but what was extant were the Ossianic ballads, common throughout the Highlands and Islands in the eighteenth century and long before. He describes the volume as an 'attempt to illustrate Macpherson's manner of working' and 'to identify particular sources which he may have used', stressing that the innovative aspect is not the evidence employed, but the approach, consisting of 'a detailed comparison of Macpherson's texts with authentic Gaelic ballads'.[20]

His verdict is that it can be proved, conclusively in most cases, that Macpherson used about fourteen or fifteen ballads and that the manner of utilising this source material varies greatly, ranging from passing references in one or two instances to very close engagement in other cases, where the exact source or sources can be identified with some confidence. Thomson concludes that Macpherson probably arranged his material in his own way, a trend he could have adopted from traditional cultural practices of his native community in Badenoch, just like the tendency to merge motifs

---

Barthes and Foucault, ed. Martin Procházka (London: University College London Press, 2024).

[17] I discuss his engagement with the topic in the essay 'Derick Thomson and the Ossian Controversy', *Anglica* 29:3 (2020), and some of the observations from the essay are incorporated here too.

[18] John Francis Campbell, *Popular Tales of the West Highlands*, Vol. 4 (Middlesex: Wildwood House Ltd, 1984), 5–23.

[19] Thomson, *The Gaelic Sources*, 3.

[20] Thomson, *The Gaelic Sources*, 9–10.

and characters from the Ulster cycle and the Fenian cycle.[21] These findings go against the widespread impression that there were no sources to be employed and that Macpherson was a shrewd trickster who worked with no existing material, and that the whole existence of old Gaelic literature was spurious.

After bringing out *The Gaelic Sources of Macpherson's 'Ossian'*, Thomson continued to publish both scholarly and popularising articles on the subject almost until the end of his life. His academic work on the topic includes, among other essays and monograph chapters, 'Bogus Gaelic Literature c. 1750–c. 1820', *Transactions of the Gaelic Society of Glasgow* 5 (1958); 'Ossian, MacPherson, and the Gaelic World of the Eighteenth Century', *Aberdeen University Review* XL (1963); 'Macpherson's Ossian: Ballad Origins and Epic Ambitions', *Religion, Myth, and Folklore in the World's Epics*, edited by Lauri Honko (De Gruyter, 1990); and 'James Macpherson: The Gaelic Dimension', *From Gaelic to Romantic: Ossianic Translations*, edited by Fiona Stafford and Howard Gaskill (Rodopi, 1998). He also contributed the entry on 'Ossian' to *Cassell's Encyclopaedia of World Literature* (1972) and *The Companion to Gaelic Scotland* (1983, 1994), and the entry 'Macpherson and Ossian' to *A Companion to Scottish Culture* (1981), edited by David Daiches.

In these academic works, Thomson discusses the details of Macpherson's work and the various aspects of the ensuing controversy, and stresses one vital aspect of the phenomenon that tended to be overlooked in many other contributions, i.e. the Gaelic dimension, and the necessity to be aware of the Gaelic context if one ventures into the subject. Especially in the earlier stages, although examples can be found even in the latter half of the twentieth century, many contributors to the Ossian controversy came to the debate with a strong pre-existing agenda. With Thomson, given his dedication to the Gaelic revival and to the Scottish national movement, one could expect a certain bias and efforts to further the cause at the expense of research integrity, but he retains his scholarly rigour and level-headedness, and the differences in his take on the controversy spring from pragmatic regard for specific audiences.

In terms of outreach, one of the most influential pieces Thomson wrote on the subject is the entry in *The Companion to Gaelic Scotland*. In the limited space, Thomson chose to say the following:

> Macpherson was neither as honest as he claimed nor as inventive as his opponents implied. In *Fingal*, his most elaborate work, we can identify at least twelve passages, some of them fairly lengthy, in which he used genuine Gaelic ballad sources, sometimes specific versions. He used, for example, ballads dealing with Garbh mac Stairn and Manus for the groundwork of his plot, and three other ballads ('Fingal's Visit to

[21] Thomson, *The Gaelic Sources*, 11.

Norway', 'Duan na h-Inghinn' and 'Ossian's Courtship') for important episodes or sub-plots; other ballads were exploited in a more restricted way. He used many names from the ballads, often distorting them violently, and he juggled historical data to suit his own ends.[22]

Thomson also discussed Macpherson in his works aimed at the general public and in pamphlets. While there are no contradictions in opinions or distortions of positions stated in his academic works, these popularising works exhibit a marked tendency to stress the European dimension of the phenomenon, its lasting cultural impact, and the positive aspects of Macpherson's influence on the Highlands and Islands and on Scotland as a whole, including the boost of interest in Gaelic manuscripts and the resurgence of national confidence.

In *Why Gaelic Matters* (1983), Macpherson is mentioned in the brief overview of the history of Gaelic and Thomson sums the whole matter up in the following manner:

> In the mid-eighteenth century, James Macpherson became aware of this strong tradition [of Gaelic ballads], added his own nationalistic interpretation to it, and published his supposed translations as *Fingal* and *Temora* (1761–3). He knew some of the Gaelic ballads and traditions, but invented some himself. His work had a wide-ranging influence on literary fashion at the time, and many European repercussions.[23]

A remarkable account in Gaelic can be found in the publication for older children *Ainmeil an Eachdraidh* (Famous in History, 1997), which Thomson edited and published at Gairm Publications. The book, according to the subtitle, presents the lives of twelve people who were famous: 'ann an caochladh sheòrsachan eachdraidh, gu h-àraid an Albainn' [in different kinds of history, especially in Scotland]. It is an intriguing list and Macpherson receives the honour of appearing alongside his famous countrymen and countrywomen, such as the inventor James Watt and the great nineteenth-century Gaelic poet Mary MacPherson (Màiri Nic a' Phearsain, known as Màiri Mhòr nan Òran), and a curious selection of non-Scottish worthies, including Michael Faraday and Julius Caesar. The short volume was aimed at older school pupils and likely intended for use in teaching history and Gaelic.

In the article, Thomson does not pass over the controversial aspects of Macpherson's career and the ongoing debate, but stresses the following points:

> Cha robh cus de Ghàidheil a rinn ainm cho mòr dhaibh fhèin 'nan latha ri Seumas Mac a' Phearsain. [...] Chaidh an obair aige

---

[22] Thomson, 'James Macpherson', *The Companion to Gaelic Scotland*, 189–90.
[23] Thomson, *Why Gaelic Matters*, 16.

eadar-theangachadh gun dàil gu Eadailtis is an ùine ghoirid gu cànanan Eòrpach eile, is bha fear dhe na leabhraichean sin aig Napoleon ri a làimh mus deidheadh e gu blàr. Tha fhios gur h-e seo a thug air Napoleon Acadamh Ceilteach a stèidheachadh ann am Paris. Cha chreid mi gun cuala mi dad mu dheidhinn Mhic a' Phearsain anns an sgoil, ach dh'innis Gearmailtich dhomh gum biodh iadsan ga leughadh anns an sgoil anns an linn seo fhèin.[24]

> *There were not many Gaels who made such a name for themselves in that period as James Macpherson. [. . .] His work got translated without delay into Italian and shortly into other European languages, and Napoleon had one of those books with him before he went into battle. It is known that this motivated Napoleon to establish the Celtic Academy in Paris. I think I did not hear anything about Macpherson when I was in school, but a German told me that they were reading him in schools in this century still.*

In the opening paragraph, Thomson thus stresses the magnitude of Macpherson's success, his Gaelic background, and also the curious lack of information about such a personality in the Scottish education system, even in schools in Gaelic-speaking areas which Thomson attended. He continues with an account of Macpherson's life and motivations which corresponds with the latest scholarly accounts of the time, including Stafford's monograph, although presented, on this particular occasion, in a language accessible to younger readers:

> Balach a chaidh a thogail faisg air gearasdan Ruadhainn ann am Bàideanach, far an deach an t-arm Seumasach ma sgaoil an dèidh Blàr Chuil-lodair, chan eil rian nach biodh e eòlach air a' chreich 's air a' bhriseadh-dùil a dh'fhuiling na Gàidheil an dèidh Bliadhna Theàrlaich. A-rèir coltais, chuir e roimhe, airson beagan bhliadhnachan co-dhiù, cliù nan Gàidheal a thogail às ùr troimh a sgrìobhadh. Tha fhios gu robh buaidh cuideachd aig teagasg Thomas Blackwell air, nuair a bha e 'na oileanach an Obar Dheathain. Bha Blackwell air leabhar a chur a-mach ann an 1735 air beatha is bàrdachd Hòmair, agus a-rèir coltais chuir Mac a' Phearsain roimhe epic a dhèanamh do na Gàidheil mar a rinn Hòmair do na Greugaich.[25]

> *As a boy who was brought up near the Ruthven barracks in Badenoch, where the Jacobite army was dispersed after the Battle of Culloden, it is impossible that he would not have been aware of the destruction and disappointment the Gaels suffered after the Year of the Prince. It seems that he decided, for a couple of years at least, to raise the prestige of the Gaels again through his writing. It is known that he was influenced by the teaching of Thomas Blackwell when he studied in Aberdeen. Blackwell published a book in 1735 on the life and poetry of Homer,*

---

[24] MacThòmais, 'Seumas Mac a' Phearsain', *Ainmeil an Eachdraidh*, 88.
[25] MacThòmais, 'Seumas Mac a' Phearsain', 88–9.

and it seems Macpherson decided to provide the Gaels with an epic, in the way Homer did for the Greeks.

He explains Macpherson's manner of working, the attractivity of the material for readers, and mentions some of the major artists whom Macpherson inspired:

Do dhuine aig a bheil eòlas air litreachas na Gàidhlig tha e soilleir gu robh eòlas aig Mac a' Phearsain air grunn math de na laoidhean Oiseanach. [. . .] Uaireannan tha a' Bheurla meadhanach faisg air a' Ghàidhlig, ach gu tric chan eil iad ach a' suathadh ri chèile. Agus chuir Mac a' Phearsain mòran de rudan eadar-dhealaichte an taice ri na bloighean eadar-theangachaidh: nìghneagan ainglidh, ceò is stoirm, glinn is beanntan, tursachan is uamhan. Chòrd am measgachadh seo gu mòr ri luchd-litreachais a bha air an tarraing gu cuspairean romansach, agus bha gu leòr dhiubh coma co às a thàinig na duain seo: b' e an rud bu mhotha prìs gu robh iad ann, 's gun dùisgeadh iad sgrìobhaidhean ùra. Bha bàird Ghearmailteach mar Ghoethe is Herder den fheadhainn sin, Byron is Gray gu ìre, is ri tìde W. B. Yeats. Agus ghluais obair Mhic a' Phearsain mac-meanmain luchd-ciùil mar a bha Brahms agus Mendelssohn, is dealbhadairean leithid Alexander Runciman. Chan eil teagamh ann gun tug an obair 's an leudachadh farsaing seo inbhe às ùr do dh'Albainn, 's gu h-àraidh don Ghàidhealtachd, ann am beachd an t-saoghail. Chan eil an ùidh sin air sìoladh air falbh eadhon anns an là a th' againn. Chan eil cho fada bho chaidh eadar-theangachadh Seapanais a dhèanamh (1971), agus eadar-theangachadh Ruiseanais (1983), agus reiceadh mìltean mòra dhe na dhà sin.[26]

To people who are acquainted with Gaelic literature it is clear that Macpherson knew a fair deal of Ossianic ballads. Sometimes the English is moderately close to the Gaelic, but often they merely rub against each other. And Macpherson added many different things to those bits of translation: angelic maidens, mist and storm, glens and bens, standing stones and caves. This mixture was very pleasing to literary people who were drawn to romantic subjects, and many of them did not care much whence it came: the important thing was that it existed, and that it was inspiring new writing. The German poets such as Goethe and Herder belonged to this group, Byron and Gray to an extent, and in time W. B. Yeats. And Macpherson's work stirred the imagination of composers such as Brahms and Mendelssohn, and of painters like Alexander Runciman. There is no doubt that his work and its broad reach gave a new prestige to Scotland, and especially to the Gàidhealtachd, all over the world. And this interest has not subsided even to our times. It is not so long ago that a Japanese translation

---

[26] Thomson, 'Seumas Mac a' Phearsain', 91.

was made (1971),[27] and Russian translation (1983), and many thousands of them were sold.

Thomson concludes by touching on various activities Macpherson's work provoked in Scotland, including the boom of Gaelic poetry collecting and the number of literary monuments saved in this process that would otherwise likely have disappeared. He also notes that the controversy did not end Macpherson's career, and that he moved to other areas, became a member of the parliament, and enjoyed prosperity, and that his legacy in general merits more research and recognition. The message of the article, and of Thomson's engagement with the topic in general, is that Macpherson created a successful and globally appealing phenomenon, a vital part of the Romantic movement, and that it should be discussed, examined and taught, not ignored as an embarrassment. Like the pamphlet *Why Gaelic Matters*, the article on Macpherson reveals Thomson's ability to combine accessibility and revivalist boost without retreating into excessive generalisation and simplification.

Alexander MacDonald

The other research interest that runs through Thomson's academic career is the work of Alexander MacDonald (Alasdair Mac Mhaighstir Alasdair, c. 1695–1770), the most prominent Gaelic poet of the eighteenth century, whose life was marked by political commitment and intertwined with the Jacobite cause. A presumed native of the district of Moidart, MacDonald was an intellectual, studied for some time at Glasgow University, had a command of Latin, and later worked as a schoolmaster at Ardnamurchan. He joined the Jacobites and served as a military officer and Gaelic tutor to Prince Charles Edward Stuart. In a number of poems, he expressed fierce loyalty to the Young Pretender's cause, complemented by equally intense hatred of its enemies. In Whyte's words, MacDonald can be seen as a representative of nationalism in earlier Gaelic tradition, in the sense of 'lively interest in the military conflicts which condition the exercise of political power within and on the confines of a community defined by its use of the Gaelic vernacular'.[28]

It is no surprise that MacDonald, merging Gaelic tradition, the classics and contemporary literary trends, a poet of striking intellectual might and imaginative power, appealed strongly to Thomson's preferences. In 'Reflections After Writing *An Introduction to Gaelic Poetry*', Thomson notes that 'there is a fascinating piece of work to be done on the techniques of political verse before 1750, and I would like to see a full-length literary

---

[27] Thomson devoted a short article, 'Oisean san Iapan' [Ossian in Japan], to this translation in *Gairm* 76 (1971).
[28] Christopher Whyte, 'George Campbell Hay: Nationalism with a Difference', 117.

study of Alasdair Mac Mhaighstir Alasdair'.[29] However, as no one else took the initiative, he proceeded to fill the gap, publishing a pamphlet entitled *Alasdair Mac Mhaighstir Alasdair: His Political Poetry* (1989),[30] and editing a volume of MacDonald's selected poems in 1996 for the Scottish Gaelic Texts Society. The last published result of his involvement with MacDonald is the essay 'Mac Mhaighstir Alasdair's Nature Poetry and its sources' (1990).[31]

In an interview published in 2007, Thomson explained his affinity to MacDonald:

> I'm very strongly attracted to his vivid use of language and, I must say, to his unconventional attitudes, his rather fearless expression of his own views, even at times when they can hardly be popular [...]. And also I think at various times I have been attracted to his political standpoint in a very general sense, looking on him as a Gaelic nationalist, as a very strong defender of Gaelic values, of Gaelic independence. He often has a strength of Gaelic, an independent strength that allows him, for example, to use English words freely without being self-conscious. You can go to another extreme with Gaelic purity, which to my mind may exhibit an insecurity rather than a security.[32]

This is an important indication of Thomson's approach to linguistic purity in Gaelic. In the same interview, he also commented on the eighteenth-century poet's nationalism in relation to his own ideas:

> Mac Mhaighstir Alasdair's nationalism spilled over a little bit. It may have tended a little towards a wider Scottish nationalism, but it would be much more characteristic at the time to have a Gaelic, you might say a narrow Gaelic stance and, taking the thing to a further logical conclusion, I suppose that would sometimes narrow itself down to a very provincial nationalism, an island nationalism, a clan nationalism and so on. One of the things that perhaps attracted me [...] to Mac Mhaighstir Alasdair was that he clearly transcended the narrower aspects of that kind of nationalism.[33]

Thomson here observes in MacDonald, and perhaps to a certain extent also projects onto him, his own stance: a pronounced loyalty to Gaelic Scotland combined with a broader outlook. In the study of his political

---

[29] Thomson, 'Reflections after Writing *An Introduction to Gaelic Poetry*', *Lines Review* 49 (June 1974), 17.

[30] The same treatise also appeared in *The Transactions of the Gaelic Society of Inverness* LVI (1988–90), 185–213.

[31] *Gaelic and Scots in Harmony: Proceedings of the Second International Conference on the Languages of Scotland*, ed. Derick S. Thomson (Glasgow: Department of Celtic, University of Glasgow, 1990).

[32] Whyte, 'Interviews with Ruaraidh MacThòmais', 286.

[33] Whyte, 'Interviews with Ruaraidh MacThòmais', 286.

poetry, he develops a similar point and, interestingly, compares MacDonald to Hugh MacDiarmid:[34]

> There are good reasons for regarding Mac Mhaighstir Alasdair as a symbol of resurgence and renaissance in eighteenth-century Gaelic Scotland, in a fashion similar to the regard for Hugh MacDiarmid in our own century. This is not to say that the symbol will be perfect and flawless, but rather that there is some kind of bigness, heroism, inspiration, vision attached to the man, though he is at the same time a vulnerable human being. It is likely that historical circumstances 'create' such figures to an important extent. In any case, they become landmarks in cultural history.[35]

Another reason for the attraction is MacDonald's activity aimed at the promotion of Gaelic. In 1751, he published the volume entitled *Aiseirigh na Seann Chànain Albannach* (Resurrection of the Ancient Scottish Language). It includes the already-mentioned poem 'Moladh an Ùghdair don t-Seann Chànain Ghàidhlig' (The Author's Praise of the Old Gaelic Language), which wittily and defiantly celebrates the language while the Gaelic culture and way of life were suffering from post-Culloden repercussions. MacDonald appeals to Enlightenment values and expresses surprise that in an age characterised by freedom of thought, love of knowledge and moderation, a nation and its language could be so violently persecuted. However, he calls not for another armed uprising, despite having enough first-hand experience, but for a revival and a deeper study of Gaelic culture. As Thomson notes, the poem is 'concerned to emphasise the larger Scottish relevance of the language and as a humorous bonus to make still larger claims for it', suggesting as it does that Gaelic was the means of communication between Adam and Eve in the Garden of Eden.[36]

In MacDonald's poetry, one may see what Whyte defines as 'the potential of the language and the feasibility of its continued use given the political and national circumstances', according to the coordinates of which 'much subsequent Gaelic poetry could be plotted'.[37] MacDonald also produced the first Gaelic school textbook while he worked as a teacher for the Society in Scotland for the Propagation of Christian Knowledge (SSPCK): the 200-page volume, *Leabhar a Theagasg Ainminnin: No, A Nuadhfhoclair Gaoidheilg & Beurla/A Galick and English Vocabulary*, which appeared in 1741.[38] The dictionary provides evidence of his awareness of the necessity to make Gaelic competitive with English, and to strengthen its use in an

---

[34] MacDiarmid and MacDonald also meet in the poem 'A' Chuimhne' (The Memory) in Thomson's last collection, *Sùil air Fàire*.
[35] Thomson, *Alasdair Mac Mhaighstir Alasdair: His Political Poetry* (Inverness: Bookmag, 1989), 1.
[36] Thomson, *An Introduction*, 158.
[37] Christopher Whyte, 'George Campbell Hay: Nationalism with a Difference', 117.
[38] Derick Thomson, 'Textbooks, Gaelic, for schools', *The Companion to Gaelic Scotland*, 285.

official context and among young people, in many ways foreshadowing Thomson's concerns in the second half of the twentieth century, a fact that surely was not lost on him.

Scholarly engagement with other Celtic languages

As McLeod notes, 'the issue of minority languages also began to receive greater academic attention from the mid-1970s onwards', with activists addressing various aspects of the communities in question and examining the languages in relation to the social, cultural and economic context.[39] He highlights the extensive study *Linguistic Minorities in Western Europe* (1976) by the Welsh author and scholar Meic Stephens as a milestone in the field, and adds that in 1979, a series of international conferences on minority languages was inaugurated and the first of them took place in Glasgow in 1980.[40] Thomson was naturally part of the team, and co-edited the conference proceedings, together with Einar Haugen, an American linguist of Norwegian extraction, and the Scots-language expert and translator J. Derrick McClure. He was also involved in organising the conference *Gaelic and Scots in Harmony* in 1988 and edited the proceedings which appeared two years later.

As discussed in Chapter 2 and Chapter 3, Thomson's sustained interest in developments and policies in Wales and Ireland but also in Brittany and other countries where minoritised languages are present, including Sweden and Finland, is evidenced in his essays, pamphlets and *Gairm* contributions, especially in the travelogues and reviews. Several editorials include references to Thomson's engagement in academic events focused on minority languages. The editorial to *Gairm* 113 (1980) reflects on the aforementioned international conference on minority languages in Glasgow. In the editorial to *Gairm* 124 (1983), he writes about attending a similar conference in Turku, an experience which he also describes in the travelogue 'Sùil air Suòmi', and participating in the International Celtic Studies Conference in Oxford. His awareness of scholarly literature published on the subject of Celtic languages and of minoritised languages in general, including Breton, Cornish and Faroese, is apparent in *Gairm* reviews.

The academic results of these interests are chiefly related to Wales. The most substantial outcome of Thomson's interest in Welsh language and literature was an edition of *Branwen Uerch Lyr* (1961, Dublin Institute for Advanced Studies), the second of the four branches of the Mabinogion. Together with the folklorist and historian John Lorne Campbell, he co-authored the monograph *Edward Lhuyd in the Scottish Highlands* (1963), which traces the travels of the pioneering Welsh nature scholar, linguist

---

[39] McLeod, *Gaelic in Scotland*, 178.
[40] McLeod, *Gaelic in Scotland*, 178.

and antiquary Edward Lhuyd (1660–1709) in Scotland at the end of the seventeenth century.

Editorial and organisational work

Alongside authored academic publications, Thomson was also prolific in the sphere of editorial work. Apart from editing *The Companion to Gaelic Scotland*, his major achievement in this respect, and the two conference proceedings mentioned in the preceding section, he also served as President of the Scottish Gaelic Texts Society (Comunn Litreachas Gàidhlig na h-Alba) and prepared some of its volumes, such as *The MacDiarmid MS Anthology* (1992) and selected poems of Alexander MacDonald (1996).[41] From 1961 to 1976, he edited the journal *Scottish Gaelic Studies*.

In connection with Gaelic revivalist efforts, he edited several volumes that have been referred to already, such as the collection of biographical Gaelic sketches *Ainmeil an Eachdraidh* (1997), and two volumes of articles on the situation of Gaelic and possibilities to revitalise it: *The Future of the Highlands* (1968), in cooperation with Ian Grimble, and *Gàidhlig ann an Albainn/Gaelic in Scotland* (1976). Many of the publications were produced by Gairm Publications. Additionally, Thomson published a number of books at the Celtic Department of Aberdeen and later at the Celtic Department of Glasgow, and founded his own imprint entitled Clò Chailleann.

In terms of organisational work, apart from co-founding and editing *Gairm*, he was also involved in establishing The Gaelic Books Council (Comhairle nan Leabhraichean, originally known as An Comann Leabhraichean), a body which supports publishing in Gaelic and remains one of the most important organisations in the field to this day.[42] It was founded on 20 December 1968 at the Celtic Department of the University of Glasgow in order to administer the Gaelic Books Grant, awarded to the University by the Scottish Education Department to support Gaelic publishing.[43] It received additional funding from the Scottish Arts Council and the Catherine McCaig Trust and later also from the HIDB.[44]

---

[41] The society was founded in April 1934 at the instigation of William Watson (then Professor of Celtic at the University of Edinburgh) and Fred T. Macleod in order to provide proper editions of Gaelic poetry. It published some definitive editions of Gaelic verse with translations and commentaries, reprinted rare editions, and textbook versions of some of the seminal works. Thomson, 'Societies, learned', *The Companion to Gaelic Scotland* (Glasgow: Gairm, 1994), 270. See also the editorial to *Gairm* 131 (1985).

[42] Mairi MacCuish and John Storey, *GBC@50: Sgeul leth-cheud bliadhna* (Glasgow: The Gaelic Books Council, 2018).

[43] Ian MacDonald, 'Gaelic Books Council', *The Companion to Gaelic Scotland*, 108. In 1976, the editorial to *Gairm* 96 mentions that as part of the effort to make Gaelic publications accessible to readers, a dedicated Gaelic Books Council van started to travel through the Highlands and Islands.

[44] MacCuish and Storey, 1.

Thomson served as its chair from 1968 until 1991, when he was succeeded by Donald MacAulay.[45]

Another academic project which Thomson instigated at the Celtic Department of the University of Glasgow, but without seeing it to a successful completion, was the Historical Dictionary of Scottish Gaelic (HDSG). It started in 1966 and Thomson served as the director until 1969.[46] As a summary of the project provided by *DASG: Digital Archive of Scottish Gaelic* puts it, 'the task was a highly ambitious one given the available resources. Despite their having completed an enormous amount of work, it was not possible to sustain a sufficient team to produce the intended published dictionary', and when staff members associated with it retired, it was suspended in 1997, and its aims subsumed into the new project *Faclair na Gàidhlig* based on the collaboration of several universities.[47]

Teaching

Thomson had a long career as a lecturer at a number of Scottish universities and is most closely connected with the University of Glasgow, where he also initiated some changes in the curriculum. As Meek points out,

> his academic hallmark lay pre-eminently in placing Gaelic literature, rather than the minutiae of the language itself, at the centre of his curriculum. The rebalanced programme for Celtic and Gaelic studies was particularly evident at Glasgow where, as Professor, he built a powerful and vibrant department which was at its peak in the 1960s and 1970s, and contributed immensely to the formation of Gaelic teachers, broadcasters, writers, and academics.[48]

In 'Reflections', Thomson notes that at the Celtic Department at the University of Glasgow a number of courses on Gaelic literature are taught in Gaelic, but admits that 'more could be, and should be done', adding the same should apply to schools, and that publishing criticism of Gaelic literature in the language could provide the needed impetus.[49] However, as discussed above, his own contributions in this realm were

---

[45] MacCuish and Storey, 55.
[46] He was succeeded by Donald MacAulay (1991–5) and Cathair Ó Dochartaigh (1995–7). 'Historical Dictionary of Scottish Gaelic', *DASG: Digital Archive of Scottish Gaelic* <https://dasg.ac.uk/about/hdsg/en> Accessed 15 April 2023. Thomson also addressed the topic, in relation to the general question of Gaelic dictionaries, in the editorial to *Gairm* 108 (1979).
[47] 'Historical Dictionary of Scottish Gaelic', *DASG: Digital Archive of Scottish Gaelic* <https://dasg.ac.uk/about/hdsg/en> Accessed 15 April 2023.
[48] Donald Meek, 'Derick Thomson: A Colossus of Twentieth-Century Scotland', *West Highland Free Press* 2086 (20 April 2012), 18.
[49] Thomson, 'Reflections after Writing *An Introduction to Gaelic Poetry*', 18–19.

limited to the relatively short essays and reviews in *Gairm*, and he never published any more extensive scholarly works in Gaelic.

On several occasions, Thomson connected his work at Glasgow University with Gaelic activism. In May 1974, as a period photograph documents, he joined the students for a demonstration at the BBC Scotland headquarters in Glasgow that demanded more space for Gaelic in broadcasting, bringing a placard with the inscription 'Steisean Gaidhlig' [Gaelic station].[50] This proof of personal involvement connects with the importance he accredited to individual action and political engagement in essays such as 'The Role of the Writer' and 'Tìr na Gàidhlig ann a Linn na h-Ola' and in *Gairm* editorials.

A rare glimpse of Thomson's work as a teacher and activist can be gleaned from the article 'Òrdugh Puist an Gàidhlig' [Postal Order in Gaelic], which appeared in *Gairm* 99 (1977). As McLeod notes, 'until the 1980s, for example, almost no government publications were issued in Gaelic; Gaelic was used only in a small number of notices or leaflets relating to public health or law and order, which the authorities were concerned to ensure were understood by all.'[51] In the article, Thomson refers to a class of Higher Gaelic he taught at the Celtic Department in Glasgow. The seminar also explored contemporary Gaelic and the way it was employed in official contexts. Thomson names the five students who attended the course with their places of origin, and mentions they were all convinced 'gun gabhadh mòran a bharrachd de dh'fheum a dhèanamh den Ghàidhlig, 's bha iad glè dheònach an inntinnean a chur an sàs anns an rannsachadh' [that Gaelic could be used much more and were keen to involve their minds in the research].[52]

As part of the seminar, they discussed the usefulness of translating advertisements and official documents into Gaelic, and decided to carry out an experiment and translate the Postal Order into Gaelic. Every participant took a copy of the form, prepared their own translation, and then proposed suggestions of individual sentences and phrases were compared and discussed. Thomson includes some examples in the article and thus illustrates both the challenges of the task and the flexibility of the language, as all the students involved came up with a different solution for the rather technical contents of the document. The students were also encouraged to consult their translations with friends and relatives, thus broadening the discussion to their immediate communities, and Thomson invited the readers of *Gairm* to share their views on the matter. Through this creative piece of teaching, Thomson at the same time managed to prove the ability of the language to cope with the demands of the modern world and engage young users of the language in practical activism.

---

[50] See McLeod, *Gaelic in Scotland*, 224.
[51] McLeod, *Gaelic in Scotland*, 32. For a discussion of the use of Gaelic in official documents and forms in the period between the Second World War and 1974, see McLeod, 155–6.
[52] 'Òrdugh Puist an Gàidhlig', *Gairm* 99 (1977), 245.

Translations

One of the least researched areas of Thomson's work is that of translation, which includes both promoting and facilitating translation into Gaelic from a number of languages and producing his own Gaelic renditions of fiction, non-fiction and poetry. He considered translation a vital method of enriching Gaelic vocabulary, expanding the flexibility of the language, and also broadening the outlook of Gaelic literature and culture, and the main platform he used to put these views into practice was *Gairm*, as discussed in Chapter 3.

Thomson organised and edited the volume *Bàrdachd na Roinn-Eorpa an Gàidhlig/European Poetry in Gaelic*, published by Gairm Publications in 1990. It includes two introductions, a shorter English one and a more substantial Gaelic one, both written by the editor. In them, Thomson mentions that the idea to make a selection of the translations of European poetry that appeared in *Gairm* over the years and add new ones was sparked by the designation of Glasgow as the European City of Culture for 1990. Initially he tried to get support for the volume from the city council, but 'received the mysterious response that it was not sufficiently related to Glasgow'.[53] However, other supporters, including The Gaelic Books Council, stepped in, and the volume appeared the same year.

In the Gaelic introduction, Thomson explains the revivalist motivation behind the volume in much more detail:

> Is fhada bho thòisich *Gairm* a' cur an clò eadar-theangachaidhean Gàidhlig de bhàrdachd à iomadach ceàrn den Roinn Eòrpa. Cha bu chòir saoghal na bàrdachd, no saoghal litreachais, a bhith ro dhùinte, agus bha daoine a riamh a' faighinn ùrachadh bho bhith a' tuigse nan dòighean eadar-dhealaichte a tha aig an co-chreutairean air a bhith beò 's a' smaoineachadh 's a' bruadair.
>
> Is dòcha gu bheil e nas deatamaich buileach do shluagh beag, no do dhùthaich bheag, eòlas a bhith aca air litreachas a tha nas farsainge 'na chomas. Do na Gàidheil, tha e fallain fhios a bhith aca gu bheil daoine eile, is litreachas eile, an seach an fheadhainn Bheurla.
>
> Ann a bhith a' dlùthachadh ris an Roinn Eòrpa a thaobh marsantachd agus poilitigs, tha e feumail is iomchaidh barrachd eòlais a bhith againn air an litreachas, an t-iomadh seòrsa litreachais, a tha aig ar nàbaidhean Eòrpach.[54]
>
> *It has been long since* Gairm *started to publish Gaelic translations of poetry from many a part of Europe. The world of poetry, and the world of literature, should not be too closed, and people have always been finding refreshment from*

---

[53] Derick Thomson, 'Prefatory Note', *Bàrdachd na Roinn-Eòrpa an Gàidhlig/European Poetry in Gaelic* (Glasgow: Gairm, 1990), ii.

[54] 'Facal Toisich', *Bàrdachd na Roinn-Eòrpa an Gàidhlig*, i.

understanding the different ways in which their fellow beings live, think and dream.

Perhaps it is even more necessary for a small nation, or for a small country, to be acquainted with literature that has broader capacity. For the Gaels, it is healthy to be aware that there are other people, and other literatures, apart from that of English.

In getting closer to Europe in terms of trade and politics, it is useful and appropriate for us to have better knowledge of literature, and the many kinds of literature, of our European neighbours.

Thomson highlights the collection includes almost a hundred poems by fifty-five poets, translated into Gaelic from more than twenty languages, and hopes that it will be eye-opening and mind-opening to readers. The annotation on the dust jacket develops a similar point by concluding that 'cha mhisde sinn an sealladh seo timcheall oirnn, agus is dòcha gun toir e oirnn sùil eile a thoirt ornn fhìn' [we wouldn't be worse for looking around us, and perhaps it would make us look differently on ourselves]. Translators involved in the volume include a number of regular *Gairm* collaborators and major Gaelic poets and intellectuals, including George Campbell Hay, Christopher Whyte, Tormod Burns, Anne Frater and others.

The most substantial of Thomson's own translations is, perhaps surprisingly, not a volume of poetry but the complete rendition of Ronald MacLeod's biology textbook in Gaelic as *Bith-eòlas: A' Chealla, Gintinneachd is Mean-fhàs* [Biology: The Cell, Genetics and Evolution] (1976). He explains the motivation behind the decision, which may seem quite unusual for a literary scholar and lecturer, in the following manner:

Nuair a chuir Raghnall MacLeòid na ciad chaibideilean thugam de na sgrìobh e air a' chuspair Bith-eòlas, gu an eadar-theangachadh gu Gàidhlig, is gann gu robh sgrìobhadh sam bith againn nar cànain fhèin air a' chuspair. Ach bha mi riamh gu làidir den bheachd gu bheil a' Ghàidhlig glè chomasach air rudan ùra a thoirt a-steach thuice fhèin, agus gur h-e eachdraidh thruagh nan trì ceud bliadhna chaidh seachad a bha gar bacadh anns an dòigh seo, 's gar stiùireadh cho tric gu beachdan is modhan seann-fhasanta. Mar sin cha bu ruith ach leum gu dhol an sàs anns an obair seo. [. . .] tha mi 'n dòchas gu bheil toiseach fàis againn an seo, agus gum faic sinn iomadh cuspair eile ris nach robh dùil, air a làimhseachadh tre Ghàidhlig. Oir tha làn chòir aig luchd na Gàidhlig air seilbh a bhi aca anns a' bheatha 's anns an eòlas ris a bheil an leabhar seo a' dèiligeadh.[55]

---

[55] 'Roimh-radh', Raghnall MacLeòid, *Bith-eòlas: A' Chealla, Gintinneachd is Mean-fhàs* [Biology: The Cell, Genetics, and Evolution], translated by Derick Thomson (Glasgow: Gairm, 1976), 10.

> When Ronald MacLeod gave to me the first chapters of what he wrote on the subject of biology for translation into Gaelic, there was hardly anything written on the subject in our own language. But I have always been strongly of the opinion that Gaelic is very able to absorb new things into itself, and that it is the miserable history of the last three hundred years that was hindering us in this way, and so often leading us to old-fashioned opinions and approaches. Thus, I jumped at the opportunity to get involved in this work. [. . .] I hope that this is a beginning of growth for us, and that we will see many other unexpected topics discussed through the medium of Gaelic. For the Gaelic people have ample right to take possession of the life and of the knowledge this book deals with.

When commenting on the Czech national revival, Macura highlights the 'strong journalistic and persuasive aspect [. . .] present in the act of using Czech as a language of artistic literature', which was 'working also in the cases when Czech was used as a language of science. Elevation of Czech to the language of science was a proof of the ability of the Czech language to assume its place among the educated languages of Europe.'[56] The same cultural-political aim is evident from Thomson's introduction.

The textbook is Thomson's only book-length translation of non-fiction. Apart from it, he also translated several articles into Gaelic for *Gairm*, including Ian Grimble's essays on travel and politics, 'Na Curdaich' [The Kurds] (*Gairm* 145: 1988–9), 'Khomeini agus an Imam Falaichte' [Khomeini and the Hidden Imam], and likely also 'Bliadhna san Iràin' [A Year in Iran] (*Gairm* 110: 1980), although it was published without credit, and 'An t-Sealg-mhuc Fhàrodhach' [Faroese Whale Hunt] (*Gairm* 152: 1990), and Oliver Friggieri's article on the Maltese national poet Dun Karm (*Gairm* 142: 1988).

In terms of translating fiction, the only published result of Thomson's work in the field seems to be the Welsh short story 'Y Cwilt' by Kate Roberts, one of the most influential Welsh-language writers of the twentieth century, which appeared as 'A' Chuibhrig' in *Gairm* 12 (1955). Given Thomson's lifelong interest in Wales, it is not a surprising choice, as Roberts was a university-educated writer who grew up in a Welsh-speaking family, a prominent nationalist and an advocate of the language. Together with her husband Morris T. Williams, Roberts took over the Welsh-language press Gwasg Gee, which published literature, pamphlets, and also the weekly *Y Faner*, to which she was an important contributor.[57] She thus represents a remarkable fellow figure for Thomson in the Welsh context, and it is intriguing to speculate about whether this translation is a demonstration of a more general interest in her work, but there seem to be no other indications among Thomson's published research or in the *Gairm* reviews.

---

[56] Macura, *Znamení zrodu*, 15.
[57] See, for instance, Katie Gramich, *Kate Roberts* (Cardiff: University of Wales Press, 2011).

Thomson's poetic translations are much more plentiful and diverse, and a number of them appeared in *Bàrdachd na Roinn-Eòrpa an Gàidhlig*. In the introduction, Thomson openly admits that the selection in the volume is by no means balanced and that it reflects the personal tastes of the translators. His own choices, especially when examined side by side with his own poetry and *Gairm* reviews, indeed provide a unique glimpse into his interests. Unlike Sorley MacLean, who discussed his literary influences and reading preferences in personal essays, such as 'My Relationship with the Muse', and in interviews, Thomson, although he published two autobiographical essays and was interviewed by, among others, Christopher Whyte and John Blackburn,[58] rarely spoke about his reading outside the Gaelic canon.

Some of Thomson's translations included in the anthology first appeared in *Gairm* and some only in the volume. From Scots poetry, he translated the sonnet 'Fra Bank to Bank' by the sixteenth-century poet and soldier Mark Alexander Boyd and two poems by Hugh MacDiarmid, 'Lourd on My Hert' and 'Empty Vessel'. Scottish poetry in English is represented by Edwin Muir's 'The Horses'. Translations from Welsh include the anonymous poem 'Hen Benillion' and two pieces by Dafydd ap Gwilym, one of the leading Welsh medieval poets. The only representation of English literature is Shakespeare's Sonnet 18 ('Shall I Compare Thee to a Summer's Day'). Thomson reaches to the Continent by including 'La sera del dì di festa' by Giacomo Leopardi, 'Herbst' by Rainer Maria Rilke, and an extract from Alexander Solzhenitsyn's prose poetry. One of the most striking choices is the poem 'Fil-katakombi' by priest, lexicographer and Maltese national bard Dun Karm (Carmelo Psaila, 1871–1961), which is another manifestation of Thomson's intellectual curiosity and interest in minoritised and lesser-used languages in Europe and in the world, not only the Celtic ones. The poem originally appeared in *Gairm* 142 (1988) alongside the above-mentioned essay on Karm, translated by Thomson into Gaelic, and another of his poems, 'Inti Ma Targax'.

Irish literature is represented most substantially among Thomson's contributions to the anthology, including two anonymous Old Irish poems. More space, however, is given to a representative of Anglo-Irish literature: W. B. Yeats. Thomson translated two of Yeats' iconic poems, 'The Second Coming' and 'Easter 1916', and also 'The Scholars' and 'A Prayer for Old Age'. The astuteness and accuracy of these translations reveals not only a deep engagement with Yeats' work[59] but also Thomson's talent for faithful and fluent translation. As Ronald Black noted, 'the lack of extra lifetime needed to pursue all their talents is the tragedy that has befallen many fine minds caught up in the Gaelic movement of the second half of the

---

[58] Complete references to the interviews and autobiographical essays are included in the bibliography.
[59] I discuss the connection with Yeats in more detail in 'Derick Thomson and Ireland', *Litteraria Pragensia* 33:65 (July 2023).

twentieth century',[60] and, like the small corpus of his short stories, the examples from *Bàrdachd na Roinn-Eòrpa* inspire regret that Thomson did not translate more.

The issue of translation also includes Thomson's English versions of his own poetry, and his attitude to them is illustrative of the development of approaches to self-translation and bilingual Gaelic publishing in general. All publishers and authors working in lesser-used and minoritised languages face a number of decisions. If the books appear in the original only, it makes a bold claim on behalf of the language, showing that not everything published in it is readily available in translation. On the other hand, the inclusion of translations leaves the door open for readers who do not possess the necessary reading competencies, which may apply to second-language users but also to native speakers who had insufficient or no access to education in the language, and has the potential to attract more learners and buyers. At the same time, every such decision reinforces the impression that all content produced in the minoritised language is going to be, as a matter of course, translated for the benefit of the majority.

Thomson's first collection, *An Dealbh Briste* (Serif Books, 1951), brought out with the support of the Catherine McCaig Trust, included a foreword in Gaelic and English, all the poems in Gaelic only, and at the end translations of some of the poems by Thomson himself, some in verse and some in prose. The second collection, *Eadar Samhradh is Foghair* (Gairm, 1967), adhered to the same practice. The original edition of *An Rathad Cian* (Gairm, 1970) is monolingual, but the whole sequence appeared in English in Thomson's own translation in *Lines Review* 39 (December 1971), accompanied by an essay by Donald MacAulay. *Saorsa agus an Iolaire* (Gairm, 1977) was the last Gaelic-only collection. *Creachadh na Clàrsaich/ Plundering the Harp* (MacDonald, 1982) brought together the four previous volumes (with several omissions)[61] and a large section of more recent verse, including such important works as the sequence 'Àirc a' Choimhcheangail' (The Ark of the Covenant), with facing English translations for the vast majority of the poems, apart from several pieces which Thomson himself deemed unsuitable for translation. The dust jacket, in English only, introduces the book as an attempt to bring Thomson's work to a broader audience:

> This volume contains most of the work from the poet's published collections [...] together with much of his more recent work pre-

---

[60] Black, 'Introduction', *An Tuil*, xlii.

[61] 'This book is much closer to being Collected Poems than it is to Selected Poems. There are various omissions, about twenty in all, from previously published collections. Some of the poems omitted seemed too slight to perpetuate, but I have left out a number of poems from my most recent collection, *Saorsa agus an Iolaire* (Freedom and the Eagle), which may not fall into that category, and two translations from Solzhenitsyn.' Thomson, 'Preface', *Creachadh na Clàrsaich* (Edinburgh: Macdonald, 1982), xiii.

sented in the final section. The line-for-line English translations which accompany most of the poems will help a wider public to appreciate that here we have not only a Gaelic poet of very great distinction but also one of the best Scottish poets now writing: and that it is possible to write well and to consider major contemporary issues in a language which, though not so widely spoken or read as English, has still a powerful poetic tradition to which this work makes a rich and variously significant contribution.

In the preface, Thomson also notes that the 'public for poetry by Gaelic poets is no longer co-extensive with the Gaelic-speaking population'.[62] He discusses the question of bilingual publishing in the editorial to *Gairm* 184 (1998), noting both the dangers and positive aspects of the practice for the future development of Gaelic, and reflects on the ongoing debate as to whether bilingual books are beneficial for the language, as they increase the reach of Gaelic literature, or whether they are detrimental and contribute to the bypassing of the original and to the illusion that everything written in Gaelic needs to be automatically accessible in English too.

As Corinna Krause pointed out, 'self-translation has become a firmly established translation practice in connection with contemporary Scottish Gaelic poetry', a development which according to her argument started in the 1950s with authors such as MacLean and Thomson attempting to 'enter into a professional dialogue with others involved with literary writing and appreciation in Scotland and beyond'.[63] The quotes from *Creachadh na Clàrsaich* are evidence of such efforts on Thomson's part. Two collections that followed, *Smeur an Dòchais/Bramble of Hope* (Canongate, 1991) and *Meall Garbh/The Rugged Mountain* (Gairm, 1995), are fully bilingual and the cover information is in English only. The last collection published during Thomson's lifetime, *Sùil air Fàire/Surveying the Horizon* (2008), was produced by the Stornoway publishing house Acair. It is a bilingual publication, but Gaelic is given more prominence, and only about two-thirds of the poems are accompanied by English translations.

Thomson was a skilful translator of his own work, and many of his poems travel across the languages well. Unlike Gaelic poets from later generations, who started to be more wary of the dangers and limitations of automatic self-translation and bilingual editions,[64] may refuse to have their work rendered in English at all, prefer their poems to be translated

---

[62] Thomson, 'Preface', *Creachadh na Clàrsaich*, xiii.
[63] Corinna Krause, *Eadar Dà Chànan: Self-translation, the Bilingual Edition and Modern Scottish Gaelic Poetry* (PhD dissertation, University of Edinburgh, 2009), available at <https://era.ed.ac.uk/handle/1842/3453> Accessed 15 April 2023.
[64] See, for instance, Christopher Whyte's arguments in 'Introduction', Somhairle MacGill-Eain, *An Cuilithionn 1939/ The Cuillin 1939 & Unpublished Poems*, ed. Christopher Whyte (Glasgow: Association for Scottish Literary Studies, 2011), 25; 'Against Self-Translation', *Translation and Literature* 11:1 (Spring 2002).

by other people, or, if they self-translate, play with deliberately misleading translations or simply create two poems on the same topic in the two languages, Thomson's translations of his own poetry are close and reliable, and in some cases of intricate wordplay, they include explanatory notes or admissions that the given passage cannot be reasonably carried over into English. A more mischievous approach to translation can be detected in his essays and introductions, such as in *Gàidhlig ann an Albainn* and *Bàrdachd na Roinn-Eorpa an Gàidhlig*, where the contents of the English and Gaelic texts differ quite substantially, at the expense of readers with no command of Gaelic.

CHAPTER FIVE

Gaelic Revitalisation in Thomson's Poetry and Short Stories

One of the most important decisions in relation to the revitalisation of Gaelic that Thomson ever made was to write in Gaelic, and to write in Gaelic about everything he wanted to. In his own view, it was purportedly not a decision governed by artistic necessity, but a political choice influenced by nationalist motives:[1]

> In my case I had decided by that time fairly firmly to make Gaelic studies my main career. That reinforced tendencies that had been showing up throughout my secondary school, nationalistic tendencies if you like, which I think began to link by my early teens with the language question. That probably had a strong effect in the long run on my choice of Gaelic as a creative writing language. [...] I don't think I've ever written an original English poem since 1948. I've often written translations of my Gaelic poems. Again, there was a strongish political motivation behind that, but it wasn't the only one. I think there was a strong cultural motivation too. I think I felt at that time that whatever I had to say was likely to have stronger relevance if it was against a Gaelic background.[2]

The quiet musicality, rich sensuousness and careful work with sounds in Thomson's poetry may challenge the author's own conviction, and his assured and sensitive command of the language and awareness of its possibilities are also revealed in his translations into Gaelic.

Thomson comments on the choice of language in 'The Role of the Writer', where he notes that 'one often senses, among writers in such a situation, a feeling of communal responsibility and pride in the work they are doing. The role of the writer acquires some extra-literary characteristics.'[3] As Macura points out in relation to the nineteenth-century revival of the Czech language, 'the mere use of Czech as a literary artistic language, as a language of "high" literature, was a polemic against the opponents of literary Czech, it should win and persuade readers, and also refute and

---

[1] In 'My Relationship with the Muse', Sorley MacLean described his own shift from English to Gaelic in a very different manner (9–12).
[2] Thomson, 'Poets in Conversation', *Taking You Home*, 95.
[3] Thomson, 'The Role of the Writer', 267–9.

discredit the arguments of the opponents', and a similar case can be made for Thomson's writing, both creative work and journalism.[4]

The whole body of Thomson's poetry can thus be seen as a revivalist act, a lifelong gesture comprising eight collections of poems. In a number of them, Thomson addresses issues related to the situation of Gaelic openly, from 'Smuaintean an Coire Cheathaich' [Thoughts in the Misty Corrie], included in his first collection, to 'Nuair a Dh'fhalbhas a' Ghàidhlig' (When Gaelic Goes), which appeared in his last volume of verse. When one approaches Thomson's poetry with the Gaelic revitalisation efforts in mind, the topic comes forward in poems where it may be only one among a number of concerns or where the commentary is quite obscure. Both kinds of poems – overt and more oblique – are discussed in this chapter, where a convincing case for a reading that relates to the situation of Gaelic can be made or has already been made by critics.

The chapter is organised according to the collections which came out during the poet's lifetime. Thomson published quite evenly throughout his career, from his thirties to his late eighties, and his collections can be read, as Whyte suggests, 'as a single creation, almost a novel, with a plot-like excitement at discovering what became of its initial premises', offering us 'the privilege of insight into how a single mind responded to half a century of Scottish history'.[5] With regard to the chronological discussion, it is important to keep in mind that the poems included in a certain collection were not necessarily all written around the same time, and the discussion thus relies on the poet's decision to publish them at a particular point and situate them in a particular context.

An Dealbh Briste (1951)[6]

In Thomson's first published book of verse, Gaelic and Gaelic revitalisation are not among the prominent topics. Rather, the collection itself can be seen as a statement concerning the language. In the introduction, Thomson briefly formulates his programme as a poet, claiming:

> If Gaelic is to live, it must be written and read, and the idiom of speech and thought that belongs to our time must find some expression in it. Thus, if both my language and my subject-matter resemble none too closely the language and subject-matter of the old Gaelic

---

[4] Macura, *Znamení zrodu*, 15.
[5] Whyte, 'Review of *Smeur an Dòchais*', *Lines Review* 127 (December 1993), 49.
[6] This chapter is partly based on my doctoral dissertation 'The Political Poetry of Derick Thomson' (Charles University, 2020), which also examines poems engaging with Gaelic and revitalisation efforts. I commented on some of the poems in the essays '"Nuair a Dh'fhalbhas a' Ghàidhlig" (When Gaelic Goes): Gaelic in the Poetry of Derick Thomson' and 'Derick Thomson's *An Rathad Cian* (The Far Road, 1970): Modern Gaelic Poetry of Place Between Introspection and Politics', and in the Scotnote Study Guide *The Gaelic Poetry of Derick Thomson*.

bards, I am not, I think, showing in that any disrespect or lack of humility.[7]

He also acknowledges the encouragement of Sorley MacLean, calling him 'the most notable poet writing in Gaelic to-day', again adding a different perspective to the already-mentioned widespread sense of personal enmity between the two.[8] By openly following in MacLean's footsteps in terms of addressing contemporary concerns, and by writing in free verse, Thomson strives to move Gaelic literature into the present, and thus contribute to the viability of the language.

The collection contains several poems in which Thomson's approach to the revival of Gaelic and of Scottish national consciousness is most straightforward and comes closest to canvassing.[9] In 'Smuaintean an Coire Cheathaich' [Thoughts in Misty Corrie], the speaker revisits a place which has already been firmly embedded in the Gaelic literary tradition, the Misty Corrie which inspired 'Cumha Coire a' Cheathaich' (Lament for the Misty Corrie) by the eighteenth-century poet Duncan Bàn MacIntyre, and works with echoes of the older poem. MacIntyre's own poem is by no means a joyful celebration but a comment on a lamentable change in a place mismanaged by a new bailiff. Thomson's 'Smuaintean an Coire Cheathaich' is thus a *caochladh* poem, meditating on adverse change, also in relation to the situation of Gaelic,[10] employing another *caochladh* poem as its point of departure.

The speaker addresses MacIntyre, complaining that many people would no longer understand his poems and that Gaelic is denigrated and denounced:

Nam bu bheò thu an dràsda, 's tu fuireach san àit seo,
cò a dh'èisdeadh ri'd bhàrdachd, 's cò thuigeadh do cheòl,

---

[7] 'Roimh-radh/Preface', *An Dealbh Briste* (Edinburgh: Serif Books, 1951), page not numbered.
[8] The other person named in the introduction is Hector MacIver. Thomson's relationship to MacIver is discussed in Chapter 3.
[9] Both John MacInnes and Michel Byrne have pointed out the similarities with George Campbell Hay in terms of the open expression of nationalist feeling and rather didactic register: MacInnes, 'Verse, political', *The Companion to Gaelic Scotland*, 298; Byrne, 'Monsters and Goddesses: Culture Re-energised in the Poetry of Ruaraidh MacThòmais and Aonghas MacNeacail', *The Edinburgh History of Scottish Literature*, ed. Ian Brown (Edinburgh: Edinburgh University Press, 2007), 177. According to Whyte, it is 'the comparative stagnation' of the use of Gaelic since the eighteenth century that has 'prompted poets to seek new ways of deploying a basically immobile medium. The fondness for allegorical thinking evident in Campbell Hay's work and in the younger Thomson is not just a matter of personal predisposition but may be primarily a response to a linguistic predicament.' Whyte, 'Derick Thomson: The Recent Poetry', *Aiste* 1 (2007), 25.
[10] See Meek, 'Introduction', *Caran an t-Saoghail/The Wiles of the World: An Anthology of Nineteenth Century Gaelic Verse* (Edinburgh: Birlinn, 2003), xxviii.

cuid a' truailleadh do chainnt 's cuid de d' dhaoine ga h-àicheadh,
is sgread aig a' ghràisg ud nach ceannaich i lòn.[11]

If you were alive now and staying in this place, who would listen to your poetry, who would understand your music, some pollute your language and other people deny it, and that rabble screeching that she will not buy lunch [i.e. that there is no profit in the language].

Despite the dismal present state of affairs, the poem gives voice to remarkable optimism about the revitalisation of Scotland and, more specifically, of the Highlands and Islands and the Gaelic language. In the end, the speaker expresses hope that a change will come over Scotland and that a new day will break over the rugged corrie. Such images of national resurrection, employed in both 'Smuaintean an Coire Cheathaich' and 'Faoisgneadh' [Unhusking], exhibit a link to the Romantic nationalism of the nineteenth century, with the spring of independence and self-awareness arriving after the winter of subjugation, and the poet assuming a priest-like role, assisting the process and reviving the language.[12]

The poem '"Anail a' Ghàidheil am Mullach"' [The Breath of the Gael on the Summit], which takes its title from the Gaelic proverb 'the rest of the Gael is (when they reach) the summit', meditates on national revival in connection with mountain climbing. The idea of Sisyphus still alive in Scotland ('tha Sisyphus beò ann an Albainn')[13] and striving with an immense boulder can be read as a reference to the ongoing laborious struggle for independence. The vision of spring, bringing new hope for the country, recurs. The poem also exhibits features that will become more pronounced in later works, such as the tongue-in-cheek humour revealed in the upside-down alternatives of the mountaineering proverb: 'ghleidheadh na Gàidheil an còmhnard' (the Gaels would keep to the plains) or 'seachnadh nan Gàidheal air beanntan' (the Gaels' avoidance of mountains), commenting on the perceived passivity of Gaelic users and lack of engagement in the revivalist cause.

A poem which can be read as a covert comment on the situation of the Gaelic language and culture is 'An Tobar' (The Well), one of Thomson's most successful and famous early works.[14] The poem opens with the image of an overgrown well in the centre of a village. The speaker mentions hearing about the well from an old woman, who said: 'Tha 'm frith-rathad fo raineach/far am minig a choisich mi le'm chogan,/'s tha 'n cogan fhèin

---

[11] My translation with the kind assistance of Caoimhín Ó Donnaíle and Mòrag NicIlleathain.
[12] Martin Procházka, 'Národ a nacionalismus ve věku globalizace'. In Benedict Anderson, *Představy společenství*, translated by Petr Fantys (Prague: Karolinum, 2008), 252.
[13] *An Dealbh Briste*, 14–15.
[14] Not to be mistaken with the sequence of the same name, 'An Tobar', from the collection *Saorsa agus an Iolaire* (1977).

air dèabhadh' (The path is overgrown with bracken/where I often walked with my cogie,/and the cogie itself is warped).[15]

The abandoned state of the well, which is located in the middle of a township but hidden in grass, together with the fact that the way to it is overgrown with bracken, suggests that the place is no longer inhabited. This may refer to both forced and voluntary abandonment of the former way of life: the village could have been deserted as the inhabitants emigrated, moving to other areas in search of jobs and better services, and the reference may even be to the eighteenth- and nineteenth-century Clearances, as the time is left unspecified. It is only the older people who know about the well and who remember the traditional lifestyle symbolised by 'an cogan' (the cogie), an object of daily use which ceases to be needed in houses with running water.

The old woman also remarks:

> 'Cha tèid duine an diugh don tobar tha sin,'
> thuirt a' chailleach, 'mar a chaidh sinne
> nuair a bha sinn òg,
> ged a tha 'm bùrn ann cho brèagh 's cho geal.'
>
> *'Nobody goes to that well now,'*
> *said the old woman, 'as we once went,*
> *when we were young,*
> *though the water is lovely and white.'*

The old woman's speech serves as a reminder of the wealth of the language, which is disappearing together with the departure of the people. She calls the water 'geal' (white) and the application of the adjective to water is startling, especially to a reader who approaches 'An Tobar' in the English translation. In Gaelic, the word is fitting and aptly captures the freshness and purity of the water.[16] The description implies assured command of the language, and the old woman's short phrase stands for all the phenomena the speaker declares as irretrievably lost at the end.

Throughout the poem, the old woman's face is compared to the overgrown well and her eyes to the water in it, connecting her to whatever the well and its water stands for, and the poem can be thus seen as another take on the personification of the language and culture as a woman:

> 'S nuair sheall mi troimhn raineach 'na sùilean
> chunnaic mi lainnir a' bhùirn ud
> a nì slàn gach ciùrradh
> gu ruig ciùrradh cridhe.
>
> *And when I looked in her eyes through the bracken*
> *I saw the sparkle of that water*

---

[15] *Creachadh na Clàrsaich*, 48–9.
[16] 'Geal', although it denotes white, can also mean 'clear, radiant, bright, glistening'.

that makes whole every hurt
till the hurt of the heart.

Throughout his works, Thomson was interested in the figure of the old woman, and in several cases these strong and independent figures represent the disappearing world of Gaelic-speaking communities. This connection recurs in the collection *Eadar Samhradh is Foghar* and also in the short story 'Tea Feasgair', which is examined below.

When the speaker is asked to bring a drop of that water to the old woman, they comply with her request, manages to find the well and brings her what she has asked for. If the water indeed stands for the Gaelic language and culture, the woman has been living outside the natural and cultural environment of her youth. She still recalls the taste of the water though, so her need is not the greatest – people who are most needful of the refreshing sip are those who lack awareness of the country's Gaelic heritage. Although there is not a single mention of language policy and revival, 'An Tobar', as Whyte suggests, discusses 'the plight of the Gaelic language', for 'a language cannot be conserved, it can only be allowed to live'.[17] A convincing reading along these lines can be proposed, but the poem works even when one misses the political dimension, as a reflection on old age and a disappearing way of life in rural communities, which can easily be the case for readers unacquainted with the context of Gaelic Scotland and Thomson's work.

The poem which precedes 'An Tobar' – and the juxtaposition of individual pieces in Thomson's collections is almost always worth noticing – is entitled 'Làraichean' (Ruins).[18] The translation does not capture the meaning of 'làraichean' fully, for 'làrach' translates as 'site, ruin, (im) print, impression, mark, scar'. Given the frequent occurrence of 'làraichean' in poetry of the Clearances, from William Livingstone (Uilleam MacDhunlèibhe) to Sorley MacLean, the very title of the poem can be read as a reference to the traumatic events that contributed to the break-up of the traditional Gaelic society. The reference may also be to emigration, which was still draining people away from the Gaelic-speaking areas in the 1920s and which could have been the reason of the change of a lively township into a ghost town: apart from the ruins, the poem mentions rotting boats and sleeping empty fields, so both fishing and agriculture are abandoned.

Just like 'An Tobar', 'Làraichean' presents a twilight world. At the beginning of the poem, the sun is warping ('grèidheadh na grèine') and the first stanza ends with the approach of summer ("s tha an samhradh gu bhith againn'). In the second stanza, evening is closing in ('am feasgar am fagas') and the same promise of summer at the end is immediately

[17] Whyte, 'Derick Thomson: Reluctant Symbolist', *Chapman* 38 (1984), 4.
[18] *Creachadh na Clàrsaich*, 46–7.

followed by a shadow of winter ('is an geamhradh gu bhith againn'). The last stanza closes with the prospect of autumn and winter. It is the image of a bygone world, with only old people being able to bear witness to it and its history. The prominent references to the seasons concern the importance of the seasonal cycle for agricultural communities, but also, as the poem replicates the sequence from spring to winter, hint at a more metaphorical winter, one that causes lifestyle, culture and language to wither. Considering the semantic range of 'làrach', it is possible to read it both literally and metaphorically. Apart from the actual traces of buildings, the township as such and the poem become 'làraichean' – ruins, imprints, sites, scars marking a place where a whole world used to exist. The examples of 'An Tobar' and 'Làraichean' vindicate the method of reading Thomson's poems in the collections in sequence – when the two texts are read and examined in immediate proximity, the case for reading them as references to something more general than old women, lazybeds and cogies becomes stronger.

One of the most oblique pieces in the collection is the poem 'A Chionn 's gu Bheil' (Since the Picture is Broken), which also provided the title of the volume. It communicates the feeling of futility in a number of specific images and refuses to be interpreted in relation to any particular disappointment. Words such as 'briste' (broken), 'sgàinte' (cracked), 'sgaoilte' (untied) and 'creachte' (raided), which occur at the end of lines, literally breaking them apart while connecting them semantically and aurally, communicate the prevalent sense of loss and disruption.[19] Although the reference may well be to a frustrated love attachment, for a number of poems in *An Dealbh Briste* deal with romantic disenchantment, it is also possible to read it as another comment on the disruption of the Gaelic world as Thomson knew it in his youth. If the broken picture, the cracked wall, the withered branch and the cleft dream indeed refer to the situation of Gaelic and the cultural and economic state of the Highlands and Islands, then resignation is not the prevailing sentiment one finds in Thomson's subsequent seven books of verse.

Eadar Samradh is Foghar (1967)

As Thomson himself pointed out, political interests, including concern with Gaelic revitalisation efforts, acquire a much harder edge in the second collection than they had in *An Dealbh Briste*.[20] Michel Byrne notes that Thomson develops here a new ironic register which replaces the 'slightly hectoring tone of some earlier political writing',[21] and MacInnes observes

---

[19] *Creachadh na Clàrsaich*, 52–3.
[20] Thomson, 'A Man Reared in Lewis', 139.
[21] Byrne, 'Monsters and Goddesses', 177.

that 'pride and anger – pride in people, anger at what history has done to people, and at what people have allowed to happen – as well as celebration of Gaelic ability to withstand the onslaught of hostile forces, all begin to break surface in *Eadar Samhradh is Foghar*'.[22]

The battle of Culloden and the Clearances, events with a profoundly negative impact on Gaelic-speaking areas, are brought together in the poem 'Cruaidh?' (Steel?). Apart from the disastrous military encounter which crushed Jacobite hopes and the breaking of the tack-farms, it mentions another crucial and, in Thomson's view, damaging event in the history of the region. It is 'Briseadh na h-Eaglaise' (Breaking of the Church), the Great Disruption of 1843 when 450 ministers left the Church of Scotland and established the Free Church, from which the Free Presbyterian Church seceded in 1893, starting a long history of fragmentation and rivalry in the Evangelical churches in the Highlands and Islands. The inclusion of the Great Disruption into the triad of plagues was based on the strong association between these radical churches and hostility to the traditional culture and the Gaelic language.[23]

The second strophe urges the addressee(s) to throw away soft words, otherwise there would soon be no words left, and in the context of the collection, this reference can be read as another appeal on behalf of the Gaelic language. If insufficiently vehement arguments continue to be used in the public debate about the rights of Gaelic Scotland, the language will become extinct.

> Is caith bhuat briathran mìne
> oir chan fhada bhios briathran agad;
> tha Tuatha Dè Danann fon talamh,
> tha Tìr nan Òg anns an Fhraing,
> 's nuair a ruigeas tu Tìr a' Gheallaidh,
> mura bi thu air t' aire,
> coinnichidh Sasannach riut is plìon air,
> a dh'innse dhut gun tug Dia, bràthair athar, còir dha anns an fhearann.[24]

> *And throw away soft words,*
> *for soon you will have no words left;*
> *the Tuatha Dè Danann are underground,*
> *the Land of the Ever-young is in France,*
> *and when you reach the Promised Land,*
> *unless you are on your toes,*

---

[22] MacInnes, 'The World through Scots-Gaelic Eyes' [a review of *Creachadh na Clàrsaich*], *Lines Review* 85 (1983), 13.

[23] I discuss these opinions in the essay 'Eadar Canaan is Garrabost (Between Canaan and Garrabost): Religion in Derick Thomson's Lewis Poetry'.

[24] *Creachadh na Clàrsaich*, 98–9.

> *a bland Englishman will meet you,*
> *and say to you that God, his uncle, has given him a title to the land.*

'Tuatha Dè Danann' is a supernatural race from Irish mythology and 'Tìr nan Òg' (The Land of the Young), visited by Ossian on his famous journey, is the mythological Otherworld and their habitat. Both these elemental concepts of shared Celtic mythology of Scotland and Ireland are dismissed as irrelevant to the present critical situation: this might be a covert reproach to those whose interest in Gaelic topics is limited to the misty charms of a Celtic past and who do not strive to keep Gaelic alive in the present and address the social, cultural and political problems of the region. The Promised Land is likely a reference to religious escapism, which has, especially in the Evangelical context, often been seen as a major factor contributing to the plight of the Gaelic-speaking areas in the nineteenth century, as earthly suffering and injustice were disregarded in favour of divine matters and seen as justified punishment for human sins.

The Gaels are advised to be alert and ready for anything when entering the Promised Land, and the image of a confident Englishman who states that God has entitled him to the land as a favour of kinship serves as a warning about what will, metaphorically, happen to those whose intellect is not sharp enough and who seek false comfort in religion or in the Celtic past and do not stand up for their rights. The connection between the deprivation of land and rights and an English person who moreover presents the situation as the God-approved natural order of things draws both on the history of dispossession in the Highlands and Islands in the nineteenth century and on the continuous neglect of Scottish affairs by the Westminster government in the twentieth century.

The same intersection occurs in the poem 'Rannan air an Sgrìobhadh as dèidh an ath Chogaidh' (Verses Written After the Next War), which appeared for the first time in *Gairm* 30 (1959). Thomson's editorial from the same issue refers to the recent General Election, which marked a third consecutive victory for the Tories, and moves on to education policy, criticising schools in the Highlands and Islands for not acquainting children with their Gaelic heritage and for failing to provide sound instruction in practical skills which would allow more people to stay in the region and make a living, instead of leaving in search of employment. Reading the poem side by side with the editorial gives the former a contemporary edge and the latter a historical dimension.

At the beginning of the poem, the speaker expresses their intention to sing the praise of the Isle of Lewis. They specify that it is not going to be the usual praise of a local sunset or of the heather-covered hills – the people, not the landscape, are the centre of attention:

> oir tha fiamh orm roimh dheireadh an là
> thighinn air eilean ciar-dhearg mo ghràidh,

> 's gum bi Mùirneag 'na tom air an uaigh
> a chladhaich ar rìoghachd do m' shluagh.²⁵

> *for I fear the end of the road*
> *for my dear dark-purple island,*
> *with Mùirneag the mound of the grave*
> *our kingdom has dug for my people.*

Mùirneag, a hillock in the northern part of Lewis which often appears in Thomson's poetry and encapsulates his attachment to the place, here turns into a funeral mound and the speaker fears that 'the end of the road' (in the Gaelic original, literally 'deireadh an là', i.e. the end of the day) will come for his beloved island, and that the government has been digging a grave for its people. This connection is also emphasised by rhyming 'uaigh' (grave) with 'sluagh' (people). The theme of the death of the people is followed up in the next stanza:

> Chan e cliù do dhaoin tha 'nan laighe
> air clachan lìomhte an aigeil,
> no cliù do laochraidh a mharbhadh
> air raointean coimheach nan armailt,
> no cliù an fheadhainn a spadadh
> gu bàs à soithichean-adhair,
> a' gleidheadh onair na rìoghachd
> nach tug air am beatha – fìoguis.²⁶

> *Not praise for your people lying*
> *on the seabed's polished boulders,*
> *nor praise for your heroes killed*
> *on armies' foreign fields,*
> *nor praise for those who were spatchcocked*
> *to death from fighters and bombers,*
> *keeping the country's honour*
> *that gave not a fig for their lives.*

Military commitment has been strongly associated with Gaelic-speaking areas, and as Stroh notes, Thomson in this poem 'writes back to certain colonising tendencies of traditional Romantic Celticism', which included stereotypical discourses that praised 'Scottish Highlanders for their substantial contribution to Britain's military efforts and the sacrifices this entailed', making the region 'more celebrated in (and for) its death than its life'.²⁷ In the context of Lewis, it is impossible not to connect the image of drowned people lying on the seabed with the wreck of HMY *Iolaire*. The connection is also supported by the fact that the ship was bringing

---

²⁵ *Creachadh na Clàrsaich*, 82–3.
²⁶ *Creachadh na Clàrsaich*, 82–3.
²⁷ Stroh, *Uneasy Subjects*, 245.

home veterans of the First World War – as the speaker puts it, defending a kingdom that did not show concern for their lives.

The mention of 'fighters and bombers' moves the poem to the Second World War. Thomson himself served with the RAF in the Outer Hebrides, and references to people who were 'spatchcocked' to their death from aircraft may be a personal remembrance of friends. Still, the speaker proclaims that the focus of their praise lies elsewhere:

> 'S e cliù do bheatha a sheinninn,
> eilein bhig riabhaich, O eilein
> a thoinn do fhraoch mu mo theanga,
> 's a shaill le do shiaban m' anail,
> is dh'iarrainn a seinn an Gàidhlig
> ach am faic na thig is na thàinig
> nach do mharbhadh uile gu lèir sinn
> a dh'aindeoin Airm agus Nèibhi.[28]

> *It's your living praise I would sing,*
> *brown little island, O island*
> *that wound your hearth round my tongue*
> *and salted my breath with your brine,*
> *and I want to sing it in Gaelic*
> *so that people now and later*
> *can see we were not killed entirely*
> *in spite of the Army and Navy.*

In apophasis, the refusal to celebrate the dead is at the same time performed, but the life of Lewis remains the main focus. The decision to express the praise in Gaelic so that future generations will see that the people and their language have not been erased, falls in with Thomson's own decision to write in Gaelic for cultural and political reasons. The last line, which echoes the famous bon mot definition of a language as 'a dialect with an army and a navy',[29] suggests that Gaelic has not been eradicated entirely in spite of lacking these military manifestations of Scottish independence. Stroh points out that in Thomson's view, the union with England forced 'the entirety of colonised Scotland to fight the wars of its coloniser' and that the poem 'expressly refuses to contribute to this fatalistic and fatal discursive tradition and instead asserts the necessity of supporting the present and future survival of the Gaelic world'.[30]

The poem 'Chaidh an Samhradh Thairis' (Summer Passed) takes one step back and attempts to view the history of the Gaels in the context of the

---

[28] *Creachadh na Clàrsaich*, 82–3.
[29] Attributed to various scholars, one of the most likely candidates is the Latvian Yiddish scholar Max Weinreich, the earliest known source being Weinreich's lecture from 5 January 1945.
[30] Stroh, *Uneasy Subjects*, 245–6.

fortunes of other nations, with whom it places them on a par. The speaker proposes a cyclical view of history, with the fortunes of nations rising and falling:

> Tha samhradh mhic-an-duine a' ruighinn ìre
> aig caochladh amannan:
> chinn Babalon tràth, 's a' Ghrèig cuideachd;
> thug an Fhraing na b' fhaide;
> chaidh na Gaidheil a mhùchadh le borbalachd Shasainn
> ach chinn blàth iongantach na bàrdachd sa' Bheurla;
> is dòcha nach dainig dubh-shamhradh na Congo fhathast.[31]

> *Man's summer reaches its peak*
> *at different times:*
> *Babylon flourished early, as did Greece;*
> *France took longer;*
> *the Gaels were obliterated by English barbarity*
> *but the marvellous growth came of English poetry;*
> *perhaps the black-summer of the Congo hasn't come yet.*

The peak of some has not come yet and it may not be through their own fault: the Gaels were deprived of their 'summer' by their southern neighbours.[32] References to the seasons of the year are reminiscent of the poetry from *An Dealbh Briste*, but here the vision is cyclical, rather than the one-time renewal and eternal national summer invoked in the first collection. The acknowledgement of the marvels of English poetry serves both as a counterpoint to colonial barbarity and as a reminder that cultural achievements may go hand in hand with unsavoury politics. Given Thomson's interest in international history and frequent discussions of violence motivated by ethnic and religious hatred in *Gairm* editorials, the mention of Congo is likely a reference to the lasting impact of the atrocities committed during Belgian colonial rule.

The poem 'Uiseag' (Lark) is one of the most effective comments on the situation of Gaelic and a typical representative of one general strategy in Thomson's earlier poetry.[33] The first part describes a seemingly straightforward image or situation, in this case the speaker coming across a wounded bird:

> A' plosgartaich air an fheur an sin,
> air do chliathaich,
> na h-asnaichean beaga ag èirigh 's a' tuiteam,
> is strìochag dhubh-dhearg air an iteig,

---

[31] *Creachadh na Clàrsaich*, 100–1.

[32] As Stroh puts it, 'whereas Anglophone Celticism has often described the Gaels as barbarians, this Gaelic text subverts the tradition by applying the same epithets of "barbarism" to the Anglophone world'. *Uneasy Subjects*, 247.

[33] Whyte discusses Thomson's work with symbols in the essay 'Derick Thomson: Reluctant Symbolist'.

> 's do shùilean a' call an sgèanachd,
> tha do latha dheth seachad,
> is dè math bhith gad iargain?[34]

> *Throbbing there on the grass,*
> *lying on your side,*
> *the little ribs rising and falling,*
> *and a dark-red streak on the wing,*
> *and with the frightened look leaving your eyes,*
> *it's all over with you,*
> *and what's the good of mourning?*

Instead of continuing the story, the second stanza takes one step back and starts to suggest a symbolical meaning to the previously introduced image:

> Ach ged a theireadh mo reusan sin rium,
> 's ged tha 'n fhuil tha mu mo chridhe a' reodhadh
> brag air bhrag, is bliann' air bhlianna,
> cluinnidh mi i ag èigheachd ris a' chuimhne
> 'O! na faiceadh tu i air iteig
> cha sguireadh tu ga h-ionndrain gu sìorraidh.'[35]

> *But though my reason might say that to me,*
> *and though the blood around my heart is freezing –*
> *year upon year I hear its sharp reports –*
> *yet still it shouts to the memory*
> *'O! could you but have seen her on the wing*
> *you would go on longing for her for ever.'*

Whyte notes that the connection between the fate of the lark and that of the speaker is startling indeed, concluding that 'the information demands to be integrated as part of our overall understanding of the poem', and arguing that 'it is the overall context of the other poems in the book, as well as the larger context within which we read the book, that prompts one to attach a meaning such as "Gaelic culture", or "the Gaelic language", to the bird and its imminent demise'.[36] The indication of the revivalist dimension is again mostly contextual, and the poem could be read merely as a memory of a disturbing encounter with a wounded animal, reminding the speaker of the fragility of nature and of their own mortality.

A similar strategy is employed in the poem 'Anns a' Bhalbh Mhadainn' (lit. 'In the dumb morning', translated by the poet himself as 'Sheep'). In this case, the opening image appears to be a memory from the family croft of when sheep got lost on the moor in a sudden snowstorm. It is revealed, however, that the storm did not affect only a region but a whole country,

---

[34] *Creachadh na Clàrsaich*, 104–5.
[35] *Creachadh na Clàrsaich*, 104–5.
[36] Whyte, 'Derick Thomson: The Recent Poetry', 23.

covering it with deadly and smothering snow, and the frozen precipitation is described as deceptive, indicating that a different meaning is going to be introduced. The speaker states that

> dhèanadh mo chridhe iollach
> nam faicinn air a' chlàr bhàn sin ball buidhe
> 's gun tuiginn gu robh anail a' Ghàidheil a' tighinn am mullach.[37]

> *my heart would rejoice*
> *were I to see on that white plain a yellow spot,*
> *and understand that the breath of the Gael was coming to the surface.*

In this situation, the snow therefore must be inevitably interpreted in linguistic and cultural terms. Introducing extensive sheep farms in the Highlands and Islands was one of the chief motives behind the Clearances and thus one of the main impulses which led to the desolation of Gaelic language and culture in the nineteenth century, and the connection between lost sheep and the Gaels is thus loaded with historical resonance and deeply ironic.

Another notable example of indirect commentary on linguistic and cultural matters from the collection is 'Cainnt nan Oghaichean' (Grandchildren's Talk):

> Nuair a thig am feasgar cuiridh sibh làmh anns a' phutan,
> is their sibh gun d' fhuair sibh solas,
> buidheachas do Dhia is do Chalum MacMhaoilein.[38]
> Is dòcha gum bi sgeul eile aig na h-oghaichean
> nuair a bhios iad 'nan cailleachan 's 'nam bodaich:
> iad ag èisdeachd an oghaichean fhèin, na coigrich bheaga,
> a chaill cainnt am màthar, is beus an daoine,
> 's ag ràdh, gach aon 'na aonar,
> 'Chuir sinne an solas às.'[39]

> *When evening comes you will press the switch,*
> *and say that the light has come,*
> *thanks to God and to Malcolm Macmillan.*
> *Perhaps the grandchildren will think otherwise*
> *when they are old men and women:*
> *listening to their own grandchildren, the little strangers,*
> *who have lost their mother tongue, and their people's virtues,*
> *and saying, each one alone,*
> *'We put out the light.'*

---

[37] *Creachadh na Clàrsaich*, 98–9.
[38] Malcolm Macmillan (1913–78) was a Scottish Labour politician and long-serving MP for the Western Isles constituency.
[39] *Creachadh na Clàrsaich*, 92–3.

As Whyte puts it, the poem 'links the arrival of electricity and the demise of Gaelic, so that one light goes on while another is extinguished, and the acuteness of the observation [...] satisfies'.[40] The last line, chilling in its simplicity, lays the blame for the decline of the language on the users themselves and their inability to pass it on, not only on hostile policies.

Thomson himself pointed out that 'the coming of electric light is used as an ironic image of "progress" which has as its accompaniment (factual but not causal) language decline'.[41] The poem is a comment on the paradoxical consequences of technological advancement which leads to distinct improvements in the material aspects of life, but the adoption of modern conveniences contributes to the acceptance of language and culture from which these amenities arise. As Whyte notes, the juxtaposition the poem makes is perilous, in its 'implicit association of Gaelic fluency with a world of candles and peat, almost as if the passage to English were an inevitable consequence of electricity's arrival'.[42] He questioned Thomson about this problem in an interview:

> CW: With the electric light switches, where the desire to modernise, to keep pace, involves the destruction of many of the most valuable things.
> DT: Yes, yes, yes. If that is the result, if that is the way that modernisation is carried out, if it has that effect of, for example, destroying the indigenous, or the traditional language, it isn't altogether a matter for congratulation. But it's not of course as naive as to say one shouldn't have electric light.[43]

Thomson's answer corresponds with his opinions expressed in *Gairm* editorials, where the question of balancing technological and economic advancement in the Highlands and Islands and protection for Gaelic was a frequent topic, as discussed in Chapter 3. The simultaneous withering of the language and improvement in living standards is addressed in the editorial to *Gairm* 148 (Autumn 1989), in which Thomson describes the transformation of Glasgow, recalling how dark and polluted the city used to be at the time when Gaelic was still strongly present in it, and that the cleaned houses, new shops and international restaurants share the space mostly with English. A similar point is touched upon in the short story 'Tea Feasgair', examined later in this chapter.

In contrast to the more or less concealed messages of 'Uiseag', 'Anns a' Bhalbh Mhadainn' and 'Cainnt nan Oghaichean', the discussion of Gaelic and its plight in 'Dùn nan Gall' (Donegal) is much more open:

---

[40] Whyte, 'Derick Thomson: Reluctant Symbolist', 4.
[41] Thomson, 'Tradition and Innovation in Gaelic Verse since 1950', *Transactions of the Gaelic Society of Inverness LIII* (1982–4), 101.
[42] Whyte, 'Derick Thomson: The Recent Poetry', 25.
[43] Whyte, 'Interviews with Ruaraidh MacThòmais', 268.

> Far a bheil a' Ghàidhlig sgrìobht air na creagan
> an sin dh'fhan i,
> is pàisdean luideagach ga caitheamh,
> a stiallan sgaoilte air na rubhachan an iar,
> os cionn na mara
> far a bheil grian na h-Eireann a' dol sìos,
> is grian Ameireagaidh ag èirigh le èigheachd 's caithream.
>
> Cha bheathaich feur a' chànain seo,
> chan fhàs i sultmhor an guirt no 'n iodhlainn;
> fòghnaidh dhi beagan coirce 's eòrna,
> cuirear grad fhuadachadh oirr' leis a' chruithneachd;
> chan iarr i ach, cleas nan gobhar, a bhith sporghail
> os cionn muir gorm, air na bideanan biorach.[44]

> *Where Gaelic is written on the rocks*
> *there it has lived,*
> *and ragged children use it;*
> *its shreds are scattered on the western headlands,*
> *above the sea,*
> *where the sun of Ireland goes down*
> *and the sun of America rises with exultant clamour.*
>
> *Grass does not nourish this language,*
> *it does not grow fat in fields or cornyards;*
> *a little oats and barley suffices it,*
> *wheat quickly frightens it away;*
> *all it asks is to clamber, like the goats,*
> *on sharp rocky pinnacles, above the blue sea.*

The striking personification of the language as an animal and then as a woman is discussed in Chapter 2. Here, as often, one can detect bitter irony on Thomson's part: what have often been presented as intrinsic, fundamental features of the language – its preference for a 'meagre diet' and its strong link with the natural environment – are the preconceptions of the people who deem Irish (and Gaelic) unsuitable for the modern era and who refuse to see it in a different light.

> Gus an tog a' chlann luideagach leoth' i
> air bàta-smùid a Shasainn,
> no a Ghlaschu, far a faigh i bàs,
> an achlais a peathar –
> Gàidhlig rìoghail na h-Albann 's na h-Eireann
> 'na h-ìobairt-rèite air altair beairteis.[45]

---

[44] *Creachadh na Clàrsaich*, 102–3.
[45] *Creachadh na Clàrsaich*, 102–3.

> *Until the ragged children carry it away with them*
> *on the steamer to England,*
> *or to Glasgow, where it dies*
> *in its sister's arms –*
> *the royal language of Scotland and of Ireland*
> *become a sacrifice of atonement on the altar of riches.*

The connection between the plight of the Gaels in Scotland and Ireland echoes William Livingstone's 'Eirinn a' Gul' (Ireland Weeping). The poem implies that speakers of Irish and Gaelic who immigrated to the Lowlands or to England for economic advancement often stopped using the language, so that it would not hinder their prospects. As Whyte notes:

> All languages survive through a process of constant transformation. For Gaelic, this should have meant the evolution of an accepted standard, phonetic and lexical change, even bastardisation, and the creation of a modern vocabulary through borrowing or coining neologisms. Reading 'Dùn nan Gall' hurts so much because we recognize that Gaelic has indeed been this, but that if it continues in the same way, incapable of surviving urbanisation, economic change or the arrival of prosperity, there can truly be no hope.[46]

Eadar Samhradh is Foghar closes with one of Thomson's most famous and critically acclaimed poems: 'Cisteachan-laighe' (Coffins).[47] In Byrne's words, it is both a 'superbly constructed meditation on death, childhood solipsism and adult perception, and a chilling indictment of the education system's corrosion of Gaelic identity'.[48]

According to Thomson's recollections, it was inspired by the death of his maternal grandfather, who lived in Keose and worked as a joiner and coffin maker, but was only written some thirty years after the event: 'What sparked off the writing of the poem was the publication in 1963 of the 1961 census figures for Gaelic speakers, which showed quite a considerable drop from previous census figures in 1951.'[49] The contact with English and earlier with Scots had been affecting Gaelic for centuries, and the language started to recede as early as the twelfth century, yet, as Thomson points out, behind the border contact with English, 'there were the depths of Gaelic country'. In the twentieth century, however, he notices

> a sense in which we can see these contacts taking place at borders which have retreated perceptibly to the west and the north over the centuries, and in such a series we would place the twentieth-century

---

[46] Whyte, 'Derick Thomson: Reluctant Symbolist', 4.
[47] For a discussion and appreciation of 'Cisteachan-laighe', see Iain Crichton Smith, '*Creachadh na Clàrsaich*', *Scottish Gaelic Studies* 14:1 (1983), 137; Whyte, 'Derick Thomson: The Recent Poetry'; and Byrne, 'Monsters and Goddesses'.
[48] Byrne, 'Monsters and Goddesses', 178.
[49] Thomson, 'Poets in Conversation', *Taking You Home*, 100.

contacts in the far west of the country, in the Western Isles. This is much the same as saying that English influence has penetrated to all parts of the Gaelic area. There is now no linguistic hinterland to which the Gaelic writer can retire, except for that hinterland of the imagination which can be summoned up at times; though it too needs its defences.[50]

The poem opens with a childhood memory brought about by a waft of smell:

>gach uair theid mi seachad
>air bùth-shaoirsneachd sa' bhaile,
>'s a thig gu mo chuinnlean fàileadh na min-sàibh,
>thig gu mo chuimhne cuimhne an àit ud,
>le na cisteachan-laighe,
>na h-ùird 's na tairgean,
>na saibh 's na sgeilbean,
>is mo sheanair crom,
>is sliseag bho shliseag ga locradh
>bhon bhòrd thana lom.[51]

>*whenever I pass*
>*a joiner's shop in the city,*
>*and the scent of sawdust comes to my nostrils,*
>*memories return of that place,*
>*with the coffins,*
>*the hammers and nails,*
>*saws and chisels,*
>*and my grandfather, bent,*
>*planing shavings*
>*from a thin, bare plank.*

Out of the usual production of a village joiner, the speaker singles out only one kind of wooden item their grandfather used to make: coffins. This is a subtle introduction of the poem's preoccupation with death on many levels – the passing of a close relative, the spectre of the speaker's own inevitable demise, and also linguistic and cultural death. The notion of baring and shaving does not apply to wood only: it also concerns human life, from which year after year is cut off by the passage of time, and childhood innocence, from which experience removes one shaving after another, and, finally, the diminishing numbers of Gaelic speakers in the concluding stanza:

>Is anns an sgoil eile cuideachd,
>san robh saoir na h-inntinn a' locradh,

---

[50] Thomson, *An Introduction to Gaelic Poetry*, 250.
[51] *Creachadh na Clàrsaich*, 122–3.

cha tug mi 'n aire do na cisteachan-laighe,
ged a bha iad 'nan suidhe mun cuairt orm;
cha do dh'aithnich mi 'm brèid Beurla,
an liomh Gallda bha dol air an fhiodh,
cha do leugh mi na facail air a' phràis,
cha do thuig mi gu robh mo chinneadh a' dol bàs.
Gus an dainig gaoth fhuar an Earraich-sa
a locradh a' chridhe;
gus na dh'fhairich mi na tairgean a' dol tromham,
's cha shlànaich tea no còmhradh an cràdh.[52]

And in the other school also,
where the joiners of the mind were planing,
I never noticed the coffins,
though they were sitting all round me;
I did not recognise the English braid,
the Lowland varnish being applied to the wood,
I did not read the words on the brass,
I did not understand that my race was dying.
Until the cold wind of this Spring came
to plane the heart;
until I felt the nails piercing me,
and neither tea nor talk will heal the pain.

The 'joiners of the mind' in the 'other school' refer to education authorities actively trying to remove Gaelic and replace it with English, and the children's school desks will thus become coffins in which their dying culture and language are going to be buried. The startling image which subverts the traditional association of children with life and hope for the future can also be connected to the 'little strangers' of 'Cainnt nan Oghaichean'. As a child, the speaker did not have the ability to grasp what was happening and only realised the enormity of the loss in adulthood.

These coffins are adorned with English braid, and the varnish applied to the wood is 'Gallda' (Lowland/foreign, alien, non-native). In the English version of the poem, Thomson translates the word 'cinneadh' as 'race', and it is indeed used in that sense in modern Gaelic (the term for racism is 'gràin-chinnidh', lit. 'hatred of race'), but its range of meaning includes also 'clan, tribe, surname, relations, kin, kindred'. The situation in the poem concerns schooling and education, not intermarrying of the Gaels with the English, and what the speaker mourns here is not the disappearance of racial purity – which would anyway be difficult to imagine, given the turbulent history of the region, also in terms of genetic influences – but the death of language and culture. In Thomson's view, these are not a birthright but can be achieved and adopted, as well as lost, as essays and

---

[52] *Creachadh na Clàrsaich*, 122–3.

editorials analysed in Chapter 2 and Chapter 3 indicate. Thomson's indignation at the school system which actively discourages children from using Gaelic or, at best, ignores it, is also the subject of his later poem 'Ceud Bliadhna sa Sgoil' (One Hundred Years in School), discussed below.

An Rathad Cian (1970)

An Rathad Cian (The Far Road), Thomson's third collection, is devoted solely to his native isle of Lewis and addresses the island in various guises, using mostly local imagery. On one level, it is a deeply personal and introspective volume and is usually presented in this manner, also in terms of literary criticism, but as Crichton Smith noted in his review, 'Thomson is generating more sociological comments in this book than in any of his previous ones as he realises more clearly than ever the scale of the attack on island values.'[53] These 'sociological comments' include discussion of issues related to the Gaelic language.

More pronounced than previously, language loss and weakening of culture is related to religion. Although Thomson's relationship to the religious landscape of Lewis was complex and he had great respect for the strength and dignity of some followers of the radical denominations,[54] to an extent, he subscribed to the widespread view that the Evangelical churches had contributed to the suppression of the traditional Gaelic culture and to the endangered state of the language, and that they had helped to sever the strong and profitable cultural links with Catholic Ireland.[55] This point of view is expressed most strongly in the poem 'Am Bodach Ròcais' (The Scarecrow), in which the image of the minister/preacher draws on a tradition of portraying the representatives of Evangelical churches in the Highlands as sinister figures opposed to all things joyful,[56] and the poem makes several ironic correlations between traditional Gaelic folk culture and the imported culture of Evangelical Christianity which superseded it. The same argument underpins the short poem 'Ged a Thàinig Calvin' (Although Calvin Came).

The title of the poem 'Dùsgadh' (Re-Awakening) refers to the great number of religious awakenings which affected Lewis, but the notion of revival is then transferred to other realms. The speaker visits a cemetery and takes stock of the people buried there who in some way attempted to

---

[53] Iain Crichton Smith, 'Review of *An Rathad Cian*', *Lines Review* 36 (March 1971), 44.
[54] Thomson comments on the issue in John Blackburn, 'Interview with Derick Thomson', *Hardy to Heaney: Twentieth Century Poets: Introductions and Explanations*, ed. John Blackburn (Edinburgh: Oliver & Boyd, 1986), 162. I examine the theme of religion in his poetry in 'Eadar Canaan is Garrabost'.
[55] 'Introduction', *The Future of the Highlands*, 12.
[56] For a discussion of this image, see Donald Meek, 'Saints and Scarecrows: The Churches and Gaelic Culture in the Highlands since 1560', *Scottish Bulletin of Evangelical Theology* 14 (1996).

'awaken' Lewis, ranging from a proponent of Calvinism to a socialist from the 'red Clyde'. Faced with these, the speaker asks for a preacher who would find a text in the ancient rocks of Lewis, in its peat and machair, 'nar cainnt fhìn' (in our own tongue).[57] This is not a plea for a new religious movement but for a new sort of civic spirituality which would nurture the local traditions, history and language. In contrast with Thomson's usual resistance to connecting the language with the physical landscape of the traditional Gaelic-speaking regions, expressed also in 'Dùn nan Gall', Gaelic is strongly identified with the natural environment of the Outer Hebrides, including stone, peatbogs and machair, the grass-grown sandy plains covered with flowers.

Several other poems address the withering of Gaelic without references to religion. The poem 'Fàs is Taise' (High Summer, lit. 'Growth and Moistness') starts with the description of a peaceful scene in the countryside, where everything is sprouting. This lush opening image is followed by a startling question: 'Cò chanadh gu bheil am baile seo ri uchd bàis?' (Who could guess this village is at death's door?). Since the place is, as the poem indicates, apparently still inhabited, even by young families, it needs to be the demise of something else than the local people:

> Tha nighean bheag, le sùilean sgèanach,
> a' cluiche air tricycle.
> Dh'fhalbh an liùdhag
> is thàinig an dolla à Hong Kong,
> is falbhaidh tusa cuideachd
> air slighe an fhortain 's an TV
> 's bidh a' chreathail a' breothadh anns an t-sabhal ùr le mullach zinc air.[58]

> *A little girl, with frightened eyes,*
> *plays on a tricycle.*
> *No rag-doll now –*
> *plastic from Hong Kong –*
> *and you in turn will take*
> *the road of fortune and TV,*
> *and the cradle will rot in the new barn with its zinc roof.*

English words, such as 'tricycle' and 'zinc', jut out from the poem. The traditional term for a doll, 'liùdhag', is juxtaposed with the borrowed 'doll', and the contrast is even starker as the doll is made of plastic and imported, not home-made from cloth, as a 'liùdhag' would be. In Thomson's own words, the poem describes 'the break-up of Gaelic tradition on the island, not the break-up of Lewis itself or Lewis society, but certainly of a Gaelic

---

[57] *Creachadh na Clàrsaich*, 150–1.
[58] *Creachadh na Clàrsaich*, 140–1.

one'.⁵⁹ The place may be seemingly fecund, but the cradle, a symbol of continuing human life, is rotting, and fruitful moistness turns to decay.

Similarly to 'Cainnt nan Oghaichean', the criticism here is not directed at technological advancement, such as zinc roofs, but at the suffocating and deadening effect of the rapid changes on the weakened world of Gaelic Scotland. When commenting on *An Rathad Cian*, Thomson remarked:

> I think often my strong preoccupation was of course with the Gaelic society of Lewis, and from that point of view, the move to a different type of linguistic society seemed to me a death. But as you know, looking at it from a different viewpoint, if you like less emotional, a more rational standpoint, I see the place continue with a different kind of society, as it happens in all sorts of places when linguistic change happens.⁶⁰

This ability and willingness to see that the possible death of Gaelic, tragic as it may be to himself and others involved in the revival, is not the end of all life, and the awareness of other languages suffering the same fate, complements Thomson's determination to ensure Gaelic survives as a viable and competitive language.

In several poems that criticise damaging outside influences and hostile policies, Thomson refers to and borrows from the rich repertoire of Gaelic song and satire, using the background of the wealth of eighteenth-century tradition to make his comments on the dismal present state of affairs even more resonant. The first line of the poem 'Cuthag is Gocaman' (Cuckoo and the Look-out Man), 'hileabhag, hoileabhag, ho oro ì' (all nonsense words), establishes, as Thomson explains in a footnote, a link to eighteenth-century songs 'put in the mouth of mavises, etc., in praise of particular districts in the Highlands', and the connection is strengthened also by the pattern of questions and answers.⁶¹ The poem stresses the fact that the Gaelic areas have for long been under assault not only from Westminster but also from the Lowlands and the Scottish capital, and this attack 'from home' is even more insidious and damaging.

'Na Tràlairean' (The Trawlers) continues in the satirical vein and brings together economics and education. It starts with a plain definition of trawlers as boats that pull fishing nets behind them along the seabed, sweeping it clean. This method of fishing is effective but can in consequence be damaging both to the sea environment and to the long-term viability of the economy of the Islands and coastal Highlands, as indeed there would be no successful cultural and linguistic revival without sound business in the

---

⁵⁹ Whyte, 'Interviews with Ruaraidh MacThòmais', 279.
⁶⁰ Whyte, 'Interviews with Ruaraidh MacThòmais', 280.
⁶¹ *Creachadh na Clàrsaich*, 153. One example would be 'Smeòrach Chlann Dhòmhnaill' (The Mavis of Clan Donald) by John McCodrum (Iain MacCodrum, c. 1693–1779), a North Uist poet appointed official bard to Sir James MacDonald; another, Alexander MacDonald's 'Smeòrach Chlann Raghnaill' (The Mavis of Clan Ranald).

region. The speaker then ironically lists a number of local subjects which they would like the Scottish Secretary to consider, such as schools in Uig or a seaweed factory in Keose, but which by implication are highly unlikely to receive attention. The trawler, as a tool of an exploitative, short-sighted economy that drains a place out for a quick profit and leaves it barren, serves as an emblem of the attitude of the Westminster government to Scotland and of the Lowland authorities to the Gaelic-speaking areas. The poem ends on a note of false consolation, imitating the way various bodies address the locals and try to hoodwink them into thinking they are not actually being robbed of their resources: 'Ach, O chlann, na biodh eagal oirbh,/tha na bàtaichean-freiceadain gur dìon,/gheibh sibh adagan gu leòr,/mas e adagan tha dhìth oirbh,/O adagan!' (But, O children, have no fear,/the Fishery Cruisers will protect you,/you will get plenty haddock,/if it is haddock you want,/O haddocks!).[62] The people can get food enough from the trawlers, but other sources of sustenance they may require, such as local schools, are denied to them.

An Rathad Cian also features several poems focusing on the poor of Lewis, such as 'Murdag Mhòr' (Mucka) and 'Bha do Shùilean Ciùin' (Your Eyes Were Gentle, that Day), focusing especially on women. In the latter, the speaker addresses an old 'every-woman' whom they imagine walking the roads of Russia and sitting on the banks of the Ganges.[63] By this address, they commemorate some of the historical injustices committed against Gaelic-speaking areas – land machinations, contemptuous attitudes to the local culture, obliteration of the language, and the destitution during the eighteenth- and nineteenth-century evictions. When commenting on the poem, Thomson mentioned that he employed the figure of the 'archetypal old woman', seen in Tibet, Russia, India or Scotland, to contrast with representatives of imperialism who would seek to obliterate the language of the neighbouring community.[64] Camels which receive the Lord's inheritance while people are dying of consumption are intended as a parallel to sheep in the Highlands at the time of the Clearances.

These politically charged poems are not usually associated with *An Rathad Cian* – the sequence is famous mostly for poems discussing the different shades of internal and external exile, and those in which the spell of the native place is at the same time reinforced and exorcised. However, they form an important layer of Thomson's portrayal of Lewis, one of the islands where Gaelic had remained strongest as the language of everyday communication, but, as the poems suggest, even there its position was no longer secure in the second half of the twentieth century.

---

[62] *Creachadh na Clàrsaich*, 150–1.
[63] Thomson mentions he developed a great interest in Tibet and India, and the challenge of Everest, when at Aberdeen. 'A Man Reared in Lewis', 137.
[64] Whyte, 'Interviews with Ruaraidh MacThòmais', 265.

Saorsa agus an Iolaire (1977)

Saorsa agus an Iolaire, published seven years after *An Rathad Cian*, marks Thomson's move from the past to the present, from the personal to the public, and from the Highlands and Islands to Scotland as a whole, and issues related to the Gaelic revitalisation are not as prominent. The concern for the language is here subsumed under the broader struggle for independence, the only political framework that would provide conditions for the survival of both Gaelic and Scots. It is the most openly political collection Thomson ever published, which has also been noted by contemporary reviewers and later critics. Iain Crichton Smith observed that it contains more 'sustained overtly political poetry' than Thomson had written in the past,[65] and Whyte maintains that in a number of the poems in the collection, 'the political indignation, and a willingness to fight, to search and to hope are even more explicit' than in the previous collections.[66] This is not surprising given the developments in the 1970s: North Sea oil was discovered, the SNP was on the rise – in 1974, eleven candidates of the Scottish National Party were elected to Westminster, an unprecedented success for the party – and Thomson was involved in the campaigns for the General Elections of 1974 as well as for local elections.[67] A growing engagement with Scottish politics and Scottish nationalism is also noticeable in *Gairm* editorials and reviews, as discussed in Chapter 3.

The poem 'Ceud Bliadhna sa Sgoil' (One Hundred Years in School) was first published in *Gairm* 84 (Autumn 1973) under the title '1872–1972'. The dates suggest very clearly that the poem is a comment on the *Education (Scotland) Act 1872*, which introduced state education in Scotland. As McLeod explains, while the Act was undoubtedly a landmark in the history of Scottish education, its usual presentation in the Gaelic context as a disaster for the language is erroneous, partly because it is based on a misunderstanding of its legal nature. Nevertheless, McLeod stresses that clearly the 'state education system as a whole marginalised Gaelic and functioned as a very important motor in the process of language shift in the Gàidhealtachd'.[68] Thomson himself noted in *Gàidhlig ann an Albainn* that it was not the Act as such but its early interpretations that were detrimental.[69]

Thomson's poem follows on from the traditional perception of the Act in the Gaelic context, but it seeks to comment on the overall attitude to the

---

[65] Iain Crichton Smith, 'Review of *Saorsa agus an Iolaire*', *Lines Review* 65 (June 1978), 27.
[66] Whyte, 'Derick Thomson: Reluctant Symbolist', 6.
[67] MacDonald, 'The Poetry of Derick Thomson', 653.
[68] McLeod, *Gaelic in Scotland*, 77. He also stresses that 'neither the 1872 Act nor the Schools Code imposed any kind of ban on the teaching or use of Gaelic in the state schools, or any requirement that only English could be used' (77).
[69] Thomson, 'Gaelic in Scotland: the Background', 6.

language in Scottish education and also on more recent developments. It opens with an ironic expression of wonder:

> Ceud bliadhna sa sgoil
> is sinn nar Gaidheil fhathast!
> Cò shaoileadh gum biodh an fhreumh cho righinn?
> Dhòirt iad eallach leabhraichean oirnn,
> is cànanan, eachdraidh choimheach,
> is saidheans, is chuir iad maidse riutha.
> O abair lasair [. . .]
> Is minig a chunna sinn craobh a chaidh a losgadh –
> A! 'sann le fun tha mi,
> na biodh eagal oirbh, a luchd-stiùiridh an fhoghlaim,
> a chomhairlichean na siorrachd, is a' Bheurla cho math
>   agaibh –
> a' fàs –
> siud sibh, sguabaibh a' chlann a Steòrnabhagh –
> nas braise.[70]

> *A hundred years in school*
> *and we're Gaels still!*
> *Who would have thought the root was so tough?*
> *They poured a load of books on us,*
> *languages, foreign history,*
> *science, and put a match to them.*
> *O what a blaze [. . .]*
> *We have often seen a bush that was burnt –*
> *I'm just joking,*
> *have no fear, directors of education,*
> *county councillors, with your fluent English –*
> *growing –*
> *that's right, centralise education in Stornoway –*
> *faster.*

The last sentence has a more specific implication in the Gaelic original. In literal translation, 'sguabaibh a' chlann a Steòrnabhagh' means 'sweep children to Stornoway', referring to the frequent closures of small local schools in Lewis, and by implication in the remote parts of the Highlands and Islands in general, and centralisation in the main towns, such as Stornoway, which has for long been mostly English-speaking. Such arrangements provide fewer opportunities to keep Gaelic alive in the communities and lead to depopulation, for when schools close, people with young families are naturally prone to move away and less likely to settle in the area.

---

[70] *Creachadh na Clàrsaich*, 198–9.

Very specific references are needed to follow the poem 'Rìomhadh' (Adornment). In *Creachadh na Clàrsaich*, the English translation is accompanied by two footnotes, while in the original edition there are none. One explains the wordplay on ivory ('ibhri'), which refers not only to the material but also to the surname of the Sheriff of Inverness-shire who brought the Glasgow police to Skye to suppress the Battle of the Braes in 1882 and commanded the force of police and marines at Glendale in 1883, while the other acquaints the reader with Donald Munro, the oppressive factor on the Lewis estate and one of the people responsible for provoking the Bernera Riots in 1874. All these events were part of the crofters' resistance in the 1870s and 1880s which contributed to the passing of the groundbreaking *Crofters Holdings (Scotland) Act 1886*, i.e. acts of ordinary and previously oppressed ordinary people who stood up for their rights and thus helped to bring about substantial political change. The poem describes a house adorned with foreign novelties and mementoes, Jean-François Millet's *Gleaners* on the wall next to a picture of the Callanish Stones, and urges the addressees to adorn their mind in a similar manner: not only with a nodding acquaintance with the cornerstones of Western learning, such as Plato, Dante, Shakespeare and Voltaire, but also to know the great Gaelic poets Alexander MacDonald, John MacDonald (Iain Lom) and John Smith of Iarsiadar, all of whom were Thomson's special favourites. The memories of historical events and awareness of the great achievements of Gaelic art should prove a bulwark against complacency.

'Ola' (Oil) is concerned with the discovery of North Sea oil, a turning point in Scottish history with far-reaching consequences for the independence struggle. The SNP launched the campaign 'It's Scotland's Oil' in 1973, realising, as Pittock notes, that the economic case for independence would be immensely strengthened.[71] Thomson's poem starts with a childhood memory of a neighbour, an eccentric old bachelor who buys oil in excessive quantities for fear of running out of it and is compared to the biblical wise virgins. In the second part of the poem, the anecdote is related to the title in a different manner and the political message is introduced:

> Tha iad ag ràdh an diugh gu bheil an saoghal bràth de
>   dh'ol' againn
> anns an dùthaich bheag seo –
> bhig seo, bhog seo? –
> gu bheil sinn air bhog ann a lèig ola.
> Tha mi 'n dòchas gu ruig an t-siobhag oirre.[72]
>
> *They say now that we have an eternity of oil*
> *in this little land –*

---

[71] Pittock, *The Road to Independence?*, 58.
[72] *Creachadh na Clàrsaich*, 186–7.

this toty, flabby land? –
that we are afloat on a lake of oil.
I hope the wick can reach it.

The speaker talks on behalf of a national community which suddenly finds itself afloat on 'an eternity of oil'. However, it is implied that the country may not have enough strength to take advantage of these natural riches. The speaker expresses hope that the wick will reach the oil, combining the images of the overly prudent old man, the biblical parable and North Sea reservoirs. Oil comes to stand for the overall potential of Scotland, including Gaelic and its cultural and economic possibilities, and the wick embodies the determination, active approach and national self-awareness needed to make full use of it.[73]

Smeur an Dòchais (1991)

Thomson's next book of poetry, *Smeur an Dòchais/Bramble of Hope*, is a diverse, contemporary and also a distinctly European collection. It marks a move towards the multicultural world of Glasgow, its inhabitants, and issues such as religion, immigration, poverty and the expansion of popular culture. Glasgow, thanks to its industries, has long been attracting and absorbing newcomers, including Gaelic speakers from the Highlands and Islands, and has become known as 'Baile Mòr na Gàidheal' (City of the Gaels). In the twentieth century, it also became the home of various Gaelic bodies, including the BBC Gaelic Department and, from the 1950s, the *Gairm* offices. As Thomson himself noted, even in the late 1930s there would be streets in Glasgow where children playing in the street habitually spoke Gaelic.[74]

In the sequence 'Air Stràidean Ghlaschu' (On Glasgow Streets), one of the peaks of the collection, the speaker identifies themselves as a Gael, an incomer from the same country and a member of a minority which has had its foot in the place for centuries. Still, they feel as a stranger, someone whose wishes are not fully recognised and whose situation is in a way similar to the new immigrants from overseas. In Poem 7, 'Smuaintean ann an Cafe an Glaschu' (Thoughts in a Glasgow Cafe), the speaker observes young Burmese women and confesses they feel a little kindness towards them ('beagan aoibhneis 'na mo chridhe riutha').[75] This encounter helps the speaker to understand how difficult it is for the authorities to understand a Gael's wishes. As Whyte asks: 'Is the speaker confessing to a limited understanding of the authorities' ethnocentrism or protesting because

---

[73] Iain Crichton Smith perceives a sexual undertone in the poem, such as references to the 'wise virgins' and the 'wick'. In his interpretation, the poem could imply 'the oil on its own is not enough without energy, associated with sex'. 'Review of *Saorsa agus an Iolaire*', 28.
[74] Whyte, 'Interviews with Ruaraidh MacThòmais', 244–5.
[75] *Smeur an Dòchais*, 14–15.

immigrants are accorded greater cultural rights than the Gaels?'[76] Do they inspire a little kindness as fellow outsiders, or would the kindness towards them be more ardent were they from Bernera or Barra, instead of Burma?

Similar issues are raised in Poem 13, 'Stràid Tradestown' (Tradestown Street). The speaker thinks about the nineteenth-century poet and historian William Livingstone, originally from Islay, who spent most of his life working in Glasgow and was also one of the Gaelic-speaking incomers to the city. The speaker recalls Livingstone's hopes for a Scottish reawakening and proceeds to comment on the present situation:

> tha an-diugh againn driop là eile,
> Innseanaich len taighean-badhair,
> turban an àite a' bhonaid Ghaidhealaich,
> eachdraidh air a cur an dìmeas
> 's an là ùr fad air falbh.[77]
>
> *now we have the bustle of another era,*
> *Indians with their emporia,*
> *the turban instead of the Highland bonnet,*
> *history depreciated,*
> *and the new day far distant.*

As Whyte points out in his 1993 review of *Smeur an Dòchais*, there are instances of 'lively human compassion' in the sequence which contrast with 'the more rigid aspects of his [Thomson's] nationalist ethos',[78] suggesting the Indian traders should be seen as successors to Highland immigrants, such as Livingstone himself. In an essay on Thomson's late poetry published in 2007, he proposes a more positive reading of the same poem:

> Thomson cannot help but see them [the Indians] as successors to the Gaels. The joking equation of a turban and a Highland bonnet is unequivocal. While this realisation brings him closer to them, closer perhaps, than to any other inhabitant of the city except the exiled Lewismen (and one wonders to what extent Glasgow has to be seen as a city of exile, of displaced immigrants, without any original or indigenous population to speak of), it also introduces a note of competition.[79]

These two responses from one critic, one of the most perceptive and well-informed readers of Thomson's poetry, illustrate the interpretative challenges involved, especially in comparison with poems and essays in which Thomson seems to be keenly aware of the fact that the Gaelic situation is not unique and that Gaels in their time overcame other cultures and languages, a point put forward in the next collection, *Meall Garbh*.

---

[76] Whyte, 'Review of *Smeur an Dòchais*', *Lines Review* 127 (December 1993), 51.
[77] *Smeur an Dòchais*, 20–1.
[78] Whyte, 'Review of *Smeur an Dòchais*', 50.
[79] Whyte, 'Derick Thomson: The Recent Poetry', 29–30.

Smeur an Dòchais also includes poems that address issues related to Gaelic revitalisation in general. One of the best ones is 'Ceòl' (Music), which constitutes a remarkable reflection on the revitalisation efforts and gives voice to a disappointment with the results of some initiatives.

> Chuala mi ceòl 'na mo latha
> nach cluinnear a chaoidh tuilleadh,
> cha tog inneal-clàraidh e,
> cha lean e ri smùr an dealain-thàirnidh,
> thèid e bàs an taigh-tasgaidh,
> cha cheannaich am BBC e
> 's chan fhaigh iad e 'n asgaidh,
> chan eil e ann am faclair,
> tha gach buaidh
> a bh' air a' sìothladh dhan an uaigh. [. . .]
> tha mi 'n dòchas
> mus tèid sinn a chadal
> gun tilg an ceòl sin faileas fada.[80]

> *I have heard music in my time*
> *that will never be heard again,*
> *no recording instrument will pick it up,*
> *it will not adhere to electro-magnetic particles,*
> *it will expire in a museum,*
> *the BBC won't buy it*
> *and will not get it for nothing,*
> *it isn't to be found in a dictionary,*
> *every excellence it had*
> *is sinking into the grave. [. . .]*
> *I hope*
> *that before we go to sleep*
> *that music will throw a long shadow.*

The poem mentions recordings, museums and dictionaries, and their inability to capture and preserve the living language and culture the speaker experienced. The aspiration is no longer future flourishing, but the prospect that they will survive for another few decades as shadows of their former selves. In the editorial to *Gairm* 167 (1994), written three years after the publication of the collection, Thomson comments on human memory in general, highlights the efforts to preserve Gaelic tradition, and urges universities to become more involved in gathering material from people, so he was clearly preoccupied with the subject at the time. 'Ceòl' prefigures a number of later poems that imagine various possible futures of Gaelic and meditate on the impact and possibilities of the revival.

---

[80] *Smeur an Dòchais*, 96–7.

Meall Garbh (1995)

In its broad mixture of topics, *Meall Garbh/The Rugged Mountain* resembles *Smeur an Dòchais*, and some poems, according to the cover, were actually written before those pieces included in the 1991 volume, which may explain why in some ways *Meall Garbh* feels like a step back, rather than forward. While *Smeur an Dòchais* had a distinct Glaswegian focus, the title of the 1995 collection announces a return to Perthshire, a region which Thomson often visited on family holidays and where he lived, in Aberfeldy, from 1977 to 1984. A number of poems discuss, in various combinations, the position of Scotland and Gaelic in the contemporary world, the loss of cultural awareness, the corruptive influence of the tabloid media and consumerism, and the inscrutable ups and downs of history. These preoccupations also feature significantly in *Gairm* editorials in the 1990s.

'Tursachan' (Standing Stones) comments on the transitory nature of phenomena that are often considered as essentially Scottish, and points out that even seemingly timeless places do not stay the same: once in prehistory, Scotland was a sandy desert south of the equator, there was no St Kilda yet, no eagles and no capercaillies; Lewis was not covered in heather and there were no Callanish Stones, not to mention Edinburgh Castle. In future, some of the places which are considered important in contemporary Scotland, such as the nuclear power stations, may disappear as well. The poem closes with an expression of hope that the breath of the Gaels will not evaporate with the last peat smoke, and that they, the speaker included, will erect standing stones for their own century, i.e. new landmarks, suited to the new era. The poem thus implies that Gaelic identity is not dependent on place or a way of life – burning peat and living in a blackhouse is not imperative – and should not be essentialised in this manner, as it is something far more universal. A willingness to engage with the language, keep it alive and create new culture within it is presented as the decisive marker.

Gaelic identity is also the subject of 'Leisgeul' (Sorry), written as an excuse to a naïve Celtic enthusiast who expects the speaker to be a Gael from the Ossianic ballads:

> Gabh mo leisgeul:
> chan eil mi de chuideachd Fhinn
> no Osgair,
> 's cha mhotha tha gath-bolga agam 'na mo bhaga,
> is ged a bha mo chas rudeigin goirt
> cha b' e sàthadh an tuirc
> a dh'fhàg mar siud i,
> no dearmad dighe Dhiarmaid.[81]

---

[81] *Meall Garbh*, 86–7.

> *Sorry:*
> *I am not one of the company of Finn*
> *or Oscar,*
> *and I don't have a belly-shaft in my bag,*
> *and though my foot is a little painful*
> *it wasn't the boar's thrust*
> *that made it so,*
> *nor forgetting to bring Diarmid something to drink.*

These 'sgeulachdan sgoinneil' (moving stories) lay in the decaying coffin of history and the speaker states their preference for the moor and the hill rather than the graveyard, and finds the primrose sweeter than the White Cockade, one of the symbols of the 1745 rising and the Jacobite cause, the epitome of the romanticised Scotland tourists daydream about. The speaker argues for diversity and moving forward, and would like to see both an eagle and a robin in the Scottish skies, and salmon coming from distant seas, and new songs and tales emerging, again stressing the importance of the continuing creative use of the language.

'Meall Garbh' (Meall Garbh), a sequence which gave the whole collection its name, is framed by the speaker's ascent of the eponymous mountain in Perthshire. In his review of the collection, William Neill finds 'a share of Duncan Bàn MacIntyre's bitterness in "Meall Garbh", where Thomson speaks of more modern usurpations'.[82] This passage is one of the most problematic in Thomson's oeuvre, for the speaker envisages a sort of reverse clearance in the vein of Mary MacPherson's 'Fàistneachd agus Beannachadh do na Gàidheil' (Prophecy and Blessing to the Gaels). The speaker proclaims that had they the divine power to do so, they would banish foreigners to Glasgow, Dundee and Cumbernauld (and to many other dreadful places), thus reversing the Anglophone perspective which often views the Highlands as wilderness, put Gaels in their place, and take stock – with the employment of computers – of all the economic and cultural losses the Gaels had suffered at foreign hands. The lack of self-government in Scotland is put side by side with global consumerist culture. Stroh observes that 'rights of property, justice and injustice are reversed, and it is the "foreign" elites whose hunting and fishing activities are incriminated as theft. The computers imagined to calculate the extent of these thefts thus accomplish not only a mathematical but also a moral reckoning.'[83]

As Whyte notes, 'these lines are problematic both politically and culturally: in their hankering to restore some kind of racial purity to the Perthshire heartland and in their claim that a Scottish parliament might not only have secured better treatment for the Gaels but have saved the country from the ravages of modern consumerism'.[84] The sequence thus

---
[82] William Neill, 'Review of *Meall Garbh*', *Lines Review* 134 (September 1995), 62.
[83] Stroh, *Uneasy Subjects*, 247.
[84] Whyte, 'Derick Thomson: The Recent Poetry', 36.

reveals a more bitter and more defensive vein of the poet's thinking, different from the appreciation of the complexities of migration and cultural change as discussed in *Smeur an Dòchais* and in some poems in *Meall Garbh* itself. Most of the time, though, in both poetry and essays, Thomson managed to avoid narrowly defined anti-English or anti-Lowland sentiment which may be seen in ethnic terms, as expressed for example in some works of MacPherson and Livingstone, who sought to strengthen Gaelic confidence at the time of its acute crisis by defining themselves negatively against Lowlanders and against the English.

In 'Feòrag Ghlas, Tuath air Braco' (Grey Squirrel, North of Braco), Thomson handles the theme of the complex cultural history of Scotland in a different manner. Braco is a village in Perthshire and the speaker recalls travelling there and coming across a grey squirrel – a species originally from North America which is considered invasive in Europe.

> A' siubhal tron an dùthaich bhrèagh sin
> chunna mi feòrag a' teicheadh bhon a rathad:
> tè ghlas a bh' ann, an treubh ùr tha sgaoileadh
> tro dhùthaich nan Cruithneach, [. . .]
> 'S ann á Ameireagaidh a thàinig a sinnsreachd,
> 's thuirt i rium, tha mi 'n dùil,
> ged nach duirt mise guth,
> 'Carson nach tiginn a seo;
> chaidh gu leòr dhe na daoin' agaibhse
> a-null thugainne.'[85]

> *Travelling through that bonny countryside*
> *I saw a squirrel running away from the road:*
> *a grey one, the new tribe colonising*
> *the land of the Picts, [. . .]*
> *Her ancestors came from America,*
> *and I think she said to me –*
> *though I hadn't spoken,*
> *'Why shouldn't I come here;*
> *plenty of your people*
> *went to our country.'*

The idea of the impertinent rodent reminding the speaker of the extensive Scottish emigration to North America adds a humorous touch to the poem and contributes to the central argument. The speaker acknowledges the squirrel has indeed a point, and considers how Gaels in their time overcame the Picts and obliterated their language and culture, which only remain present in carved stones and place names. The poem thus shows a full awareness that the Gaelic situation is not unique – the Gaels also

---

[85] *Meall Garbh*, 14–15.

emigrated abroad and took other people's land, and therefore should not be, as the squirrel asserts, too offended when people from abroad come and settle in their country. Thomson's travelogue from Canada, which he published in *Gairm* in 1979 and which is discussed in Chapter 3, reveals his awareness of the complicity of Scottish and also Gaelic settlers in the dispossession of the First Nations in North America and the suppression of their language and culture. In the end, the speaker suggests that the Picts would have been quite surprised to see the Gaels themselves succumbing to another influence – that of the English.

A similar approach to 'Ceòl' from *Smeur an Dòchais* is adopted in 'Nuair a Thig a' Bhalbhachd' (When Stillness Comes), which imagines the world when Gaelic is gone, but the prospect is not entirely hopeless: there will be traces left in nature, 'ceòl mìn smeòraich/ann an òrgan na coille' (smooth thrush music/in the organ of the wood), fragments of traditional Gaelic songs, and the Gaelic culture will enter the same eternity as Catullus and Sappho. As McLeod observes when commenting on the current prognosis for Gaelic, in some opinions, Gaelic might indeed assume a position similar to Latin, which 'continued as an ecclesiastical and intellectual language long after it went out of popular use'.[86] 'Nuair a Thig a' Bhalbhachd' is an example of a more conciliatory poem dealing with the withering of Gaelic that in a way prepares the ground for the discussion of the language, its situation and its future prospects in the last collection.

Sùil air Fàire (2007)

In the last collection published during Thomson's lifetime, *Sùil air Fàire/ Surveying the Horizon*, all the themes and influences present in the seventy years of the poet's career are represented. Issues concerning Gaelic feature in many poems, often as part of the listing technique where Thomson brings together various phenomena, events and people, and reflects on the changing world he has been witnessing for almost ninety years. It also reflects his interest in the recognition of Scots and its future. In the poem 'Àros nan Sean?' (Old Folks' Home?), Thomson presents a particularly gloomy image of the gradual decay of Gaelic and of the futility of revitalisation efforts: in a care home built with funds from the National Lottery, clients weakened by age and illness will be supported by an apparatus so that they can mumble the slogan of Gaelic activists, 'Suas leis a' Ghàidhlig!' (Up with the Gaelic!), to the accompaniment of harp music, another trope associated with Scotland's Gaelic heritage. The origin of this dismal vision is outlined in connection with place names, as the speaker is surprised that the decline of Gaelic witnessed elsewhere has reached unexpected parts of

---

[86] McLeod, *Gaelic in Scotland*, 335.

Lewis, driving again at the non-existence of a linguistic hinterland where the language still thrives:[87]

> tachdadh sa bhràighe
> is ciorram an ceòs
> liota san teanga [. . .]
> is monbar am mùirneig
> 's na cnàmhan gu bhith ris
> a-nis[88]
>
> *choking at the Bràighe/throat*
> *and maiming in Keose/the hollow*
> *lisping in Tong/the tongue [. . .]*
> *and mumbling at Mùirneag/the loved one,*
> *and the bones just about showing*
> *in Ness/now*

Appreciation of this elaborate wordplay, where the place names oscillate between their toponymic function and their meaning as ordinary nouns, requires advanced competence in the language. Moreover, a reader acquainted with Lewis will be able to associate the images of decay of the language with the specific places and the local communities. This poem about the withering of Gaelic thus becomes a test of what it envisages: when the puns and references can no longer be appreciated, and it is likely many readers will fail to grasp the full complexity of the poem, the loss has actually arrived.

References to place names and the state of Gaelic also inform the poem 'Dà Chànanas' (Bilingualism), in which toponymics serve as a means of demonstrating how different languages have left their imprint on the Western Isles. By examining an amusing instance of place name tautology where the name consists of the same term in different languages, a common occurrence in the Western Isles with layers of Norse and Gaelic influence, the speaker points out how the history of the successive waves of people becomes sedimented in places and their names. It depicts Gaelic as a language in the process of being overcome, incomprehensible to the people who now live in the places where it used to flourish, and suggests the situation repeats cyclically, developing the idea from 'Feòrag Ghlas, Tuath air Braco'.

In 'Àros nan Seann', 'Dà Chànanas' and other poems, such as 'Soidhne nan Tìm' [The Sign of the Times], 'Cridhe an t-Sluaigh' (The Heart of the People) and 'Teagamh' [Doubt], Thomson voices his suspicions of some efforts to promote the language, although he often advocated them in his journalism: putting Gaelic on TV and on road signs, when it

---

[87] Thomson, *An Introduction to Gaelic Poetry*, 250.
[88] *Sùil air Fàire*, 18–19.

is actually dying in the communities and when it loses contact with areas where it was traditionally strong, emerges as hypocritical and specious ('Dh'fhalbh Siud is Thàinig Seo' [That Went and This Came]). It opens up the perspective that these policies become a mere cover-up for a reluctance to use the language in everyday life and asks about the significance of having Gaelic on TV when it is not fluent and correct Gaelic, and when the intended audiences of such programmes keep using English in daily communication. For Thomson, this is not a question of being threatened by non-native users of Gaelic or of the language being moved to new areas of life – the evidence of his support for these innovations is clear in his articles and *Gairm* editorials – but rather, as often, an issue of standards and quality.

'Nuair a Dh'fhalbhas a' Ghàidhlig' (When Gaelic Goes) takes the point of the futility of revivalist efforts further and imagines Scotland without Gaelic: the language becomes a dinosaur, a palaeontological find which will be excavated and examined in the distant future. With the help of the latest technology, people will perhaps manage to hear 'corra òran/a 'strì ri ùrnaigh,/is bloighean bàrdachd/ag èirigh às an t-seann ùir sin' [a song or two/rivalling prayers,/and fragments of poetry/rising from that ancient earth].[89] This chilling vision suggests that various phenomena are only appreciated after they have been irrevocably lost, and that the rush of interest in them comes too late. A slightly more comforting view, similar in tone to that of 'Nuair a Thig a' Bhalbhachd' and 'Ceòl', emerges from 'A' Siubhal nam Blàth' (Reconnoitring the Blossoms), in which the speaker imagines Gaelic as only 'half-dead' on the pages of books and thinks it possible that it will blossom in people's hearts as a language of learning and literature, if not of everyday communication.

The section 'Laoich' (Champions) celebrates some of Thomson's heroes, including people involved in revivalist efforts. The inclusion of Alexander MacDonald is not surprising, and neither is that of MacDiarmid, who is praised for lifting 'fallaing na meirge/bho ulaidhean àrsaidh' (mantle of rust/from age-old treasures), which is a reference to his efforts in the revival of Scots.[90] Scots and Gaelic are brought together again in 'A' Chuimhne' (The Memory), in which the medieval Scots makar William Dunbar meets MacDonald and MacDiarmid. 'Toinneamh is Siubhail' (Twisting and Travelling) contests the popular simplified ideas about the ancient past of Scotland and lists the various languages which have been spoken in the country over the centuries: Latin, Gaelic, Welsh, English and Scots. This engagement with the multilingual reality of Scotland and the importance accredited to promoting both Scots and Gaelic is also reflected in Thomson's scholarship and in *Gairm* editorials from the 1990s and 2000s, as discussed in Chapter 2, Chapter 3 and Chapter 4.

---

[89] *Sùil air Fàire*, 50–1.
[90] *Sùil air Fàire*, 142–3.

Unlike the *Gairm* editorials, where a specific course of action is often strongly recommended, Thomson's poetry addressing the situation of Gaelic does not instruct the reader, and there are no eulogies of the SNP Gaelic Policy or thinly veiled denigrations of ACG's laxity. To be a propagandist poet, Thomson is too playful, ironic and sometimes deliberately obscure. In relation to Thomson's poetry in general, Whyte remarked that he 'set vehicle and tenor oscillating, shimmering in a tension which, as his poetry matures, refuses to let either side preponderate, creating in the process a richness and uncertainty of meaning which are profoundly modern in tone'.[91] Some poems only comment on issues related to Gaelic revitalisation efforts 'by proxy', by being placed in a certain collection or a section. The reading of the poems may also be influenced by the extra-literary context of Thomson's academic, editorial and organisational work.

Thomson decided to write in Gaelic, and the Gaelic world in the second half of the twentieth century was, in terms of the number of speakers, shrinking and expanding at the same time, which also affected the prospective readership of the poems. The target group of his deliberations on the state of Gaelic would be a rather small group of fluent intellectuals with literary leanings, and increasingly also the international community of second-language users of Gaelic. It thus seems Thomson's poetry about the Gaelic revival was primarily not a means of persuading other people to follow a course of action, but rather a private channel to consider the situation of the language and its repercussions, using a different form than an essay, newspaper article or public speech. It is safe to say that the appeal of the *Gairm* editorials, which were often openly persuasive and tried to move the reader to a certain course of action, was much greater.

Thomson's reflective poems which touch on topics related to Gaelic address them, in the space of a collection, from different points of view; Gaelic speakers are victims of injustice and oppression, and at the same time are held responsible for being complicit in their own misfortunes. The decay of Gaelic is mourned and criticised, but in combination with a broader perspective of incessant linguistic and cultural change in human history. The prevailing mode of Thomson's poetry on Gaelic seems to be observation, reflection, and analysis of the current situation, rather than suggesting specific solutions. Thomson may be described as one of the poets who, in Stroh's words, 'employ historical perspectives as a means to encourage present and future resistance and revival'.[92] The poems on Gaelic are characterised by mediated persuasion; the reader of the poems is alerted to certain topics and connections and can therefore start to think about them in a political manner.

When one compares his poetry about Gaelic and his articles and *Gairm* editorials, it seems Thomson moves between the positions of the committed

---

[91] Whyte, 'The Gaelic Renaissance: Sorley MacLean and Derick Thomson', 158.
[92] Stroh, *Uneasy Subjects*, 251.

activist and the cautious, often pessimistic poet. Thomson's opinions naturally developed throughout his life, and so did the situation of Gaelic, yet there seems to be a more general pattern in Thomson's work and thought. It is as if Thomson the poet had the luxury, or the painful duty, of ruminating over dilemmas and questions that Thomson the activist and journalist had to put aside, as his aim was to encourage fellow Gaelic users to action. It seems that in his poetry he afforded himself the space to view these matters from different angles, to explore his doubts and fears, and to point out the weaknesses and shortcomings of the strategies and ideas he was trying to promote. Many of the poems concerned with Gaelic either see it dying, imagine the future without it, envisage its survival as a mere relic or a dead language of learning similar to Latin, or express concern about the directions in which the Gaelic revitalisation efforts are moving and the results they are producing. According to John MacInnes, 'Thomson's political commitment to Nationalism has remained essentially constant for forty years although the tone of his political poetry has become progressively bleaker, more sceptical, more sophisticated',[93] and this observation is also valid for those poems that discuss Gaelic revitalisation and the future of the language.

The commitment to Gaelic did not prevent Thomson from appreciating other traditions in Scotland, and Gaelic is not presented as being superior to them. In 'Dà Chànan' (Two Languages), Gaelic and English are compared to two encroaching but separate trees in one garden that exist in harmony, despite their vast differences. When he writes about the multicultural environment of Glasgow from the 1990s onwards, he is not appalled by the presence of people of different ethnic origin and by the multitude of languages that may be heard on Glasgow's streets, but rather attracted to them. Sometimes he is curious as to what will become of the world he will not see, sometimes he is wary of the cultural melange, especially as he thinks his own nation is losing its self-awareness: through its own lack of confidence and effort, not under the pressure of incomers. The poetry and *Gairm* contributions provide ample proof of how much Thomson valued the diversity of languages and cultures, in Scotland and globally, and his preference is clearly for them to retain their distinctiveness, to enrich one another and to coexist peacefully, resisting both colonising tendencies and the unifying pressures of global consumerism.

As Whyte observed when *Creachadh na Clàrsaich* emerged, 'the publication of Derick Thomson's collected poems makes it clear yet again that the material for the creation of a Scottish consciousness is there in great richness and abundance'.[94] Thomson's poetry certainly provides ample material for developing an open, outward and forward-looking vision of the Highlands and Islands and of Scotland in general, where lesser-used and previously minoritised languages are supported and where there is

---

[93] MacInnes, 'The World through Scots-Gaelic Eyes', 18.
[94] Whyte, 'Derick Thomson: Reluctant Symbolist', 6.

space for both traditional culture and innovative cosmopolitan impulses. The poems contribute to the Gaelic revitalisation efforts on several levels: as ambiguous and courageous explorations of its various aspects, as proof of the flexibility and creative potential of the language; and, through their richness of meaning and aural beauty, as persuasive advocates of Gaelic whose appeal will draw new users to the language in the years to come.

Gaelic in Thomson's short stories

The other form of creative writing Thomson explored, though to a very limited extent, is fiction, namely the short story. Eight of his ten known stories appeared in *Gairm*, one in the short-lived magazine *Alba*, and one was recorded for the BBC.[95] Two of them, 'Foghar, 1976' [Autumn, 1976] very openly and 'Tea Fesgair' [Evening Tea] more covertly, reflect his concern with the Gaelic revival.

'Foghar 1976' is chronologically the first of Thomson's stories that appeared in *Gairm*, in the seventeenth issue of the magazine in autumn 1956,[96] and it presents a scathing satire of the Gaelic movement twenty years hence in an original revivalist dystopia. It is, as MacLeod points out, one of the few successful humorous short stories in Gaelic from the period, 'a satiric reversal of the Gaelic–English culture conflict, and one of the few examples of the use of the short story form for satire in Gaelic',[97] and it reveals Thomson's skills as a satirist that are also documented in his other contributions to *Gairm*.

The unnamed protagonist and narrator of the story has lived abroad for twenty years and upon his recent return to Scotland finds accommodation in a Lowland village hotel. To his astonishment, he realises that during his absence a revival of Gaelic has been accomplished, directed from England, and that the London variety of Gaelic is now considered preferable (as it has the distinct advantage of involving seven ways in which the consonant 'l' can be pronounced). A protracted singing competition is held, presided over by an English-speaking chairperson, during which the participants choose the same song, and their performance is evaluated by a machine on the basis of their pronunciation. The absurd nature of the revival is gradually revealed, with a measured mixture of hyperbole and phenomena based on existing tendencies. The stringent criticism of ACG and the Mòd in *Gairm* editorials, in terms of failing to introduce efficient policies that would strengthen the language, come to mind, but, as discussed in Chapter 3, even these comments do not denounce the organisation and the festival as such, they merely point out their unfulfilled potential.

[95] The following discussion is partly based on points raised in my essay 'Old Women, Dreams, and Reversed Revivals: Derick Thomson's Gaelic Short Stories'. 'Mòd Thorgaboil', although relevant as a satirical account of the Mòd, is not discussed here, as it was only discovered after this monograph first appeared.
[96] *Gairm* 17 (1956), 21–4.
[97] MacLeod, *Twentieth-Century Gaelic Literature*, 100.

To surmise that Thomson dismissed music, singing and folklore culture from Gaelic revitalisation would be both unjust and incorrect, as proved by his research into traditional song[98] and his collecting activities. Also, the biting ridicule of the London Gaelic Society should not be read as a critique of Gaelic learners and users coming from outside the traditional Gaelic-speaking areas – as discussed in Chapter 2 and Chapter 3, Thomson was ready to welcome anyone with a genuine interest in the language, irrespective of their origin, and realised these new speakers were going to play a vital part in the language's future. What is taken to task here is a revival where obsessive interest in traditional music subsumes present-day subjects, pronunciation becomes more important than the ability to communicate, and where Gaelic is reduced to a medium of greetings and unsubstantial polite conversation, while more challenging subjects remain reserved for English.

'Tea Feasgair' [Evening Tea], a story which appeared in *Gairm* in 1961, captures a moment when a young man comes to visit two old Gaelic-speaking sisters who live by themselves in a house they stubbornly refuse to modernise, and ends up discussing progress and cultural domination with them. The story is likely at least partly autobiographical, for the two women in the story are called Cotrìona and Murdag, i. e. the same as neighbours from Bayble whom Thomson recalled in several interviews and essays and whom he celebrates in *An Rathad Cian*.[99] In the poems, they are portrayed as the personification of strength and courage and as living repositories of the Gaelic tradition. The visitor, returning to the area after spending an unspecified amount of time away, could be modelled on Thomson himself.

The visitor mentions the presence of English people in the village, and when the sisters inquire after them, he explains that they were sent by the King and the Parliament to protect the local people should enemies attack. With regard to topics covered in the *Gairm* editorials in the years preceding the publication of the story, i.e. the 1950s, this could be a reference to the military presence and army projects in the Western Isles, especially in South Uist and Lewis.[100] Towards the end of the visit, one of the sisters declares that ''s e galair gabhailteach a th' anns an adhartas' (progress is a catching disease),[101] acknowledging at the same time that while people without

---

[98] See, for instance, Derick Thomson, 'Scottish Gaelic Traditional Songs from the 16th to the 18th Century', *Proceedings of the British Academy* 105 (2000), being a published version of the Sir John Rhys Memorial Lecture, read at the Academy on 9 December 1999.

[99] As Thomson recalls in an autobiographical essay, 'She [Cotrìona] and her sister Murdag lived together, with a frightened cat; they were a devoted couple, and had entertaining domestic quarrels.' 'A Man Reared in Lewis', 135. A cat makes an appearance in the short story. Cotrìona is also likely the inspiration for the short story 'Aig a' Phump'.

[100] I discuss the issue at length in the chapter on *Gairm* in the upcoming monograph *Scottish Magazines and Political Culture, 1968–99: From Scottish International to the Scottish Parliament*, ed. Eleanor Bell, Scott Hames and Malcolm Petrie (Edinburgh: Edinburgh University Press, 2024).

[101] 'Tea Fessgair', *Gairm* 35 (1961), 227.

children can resist progress more easily, keeping up with modern trends is much more important for families, which can also be read as a comment on the implications of this trend for the Gaelic revitalisation efforts. The old women do not claim that their hearth with a peat fire is superior to an electric cooker, and even acknowledge its disadvantages, but express the hope that retaining cultural distinctiveness is possible in spite of the substantial changes in living conditions and material environment. Although their lifestyle, opinions and concerns may seem like an anachronism – and they themselves realise that – the women retain their dignity, and the young visitor leaves puzzled and perhaps uncertain whether the modern world outside the house truly offers a better alternative.

On one level, the story is a covert comment on the situation of Gaelic and works with the idea of putting side by side language decline and technological progress, though not necessarily arguing for a causal relationship, as do the poems discussed earlier in this chapter, especially 'Cainnt nan Oghaichean' from *Eadar Samhradh is Foghar* and 'Fàs is Taise' from *An Rathad Cian*. The hinted-at presence of the army in the region extends the comment on the distorted relationship between Gaelic and English in the Highlands and Islands to the political and military domination of England in Scotland.

CHAPTER SIX

Thomson's Legacy

As Donald Meek noted in 2013, Thomson took the opportunity 'to stamp his own vision on Gaelic and on Scotland', arguing that 'it is not too much to say that that vision made Gaelic what it is today, with its numerous means of enlightened support, but it also went some way to making Scotland what it is today', and adding that those engaged in Gaelic revitalisation efforts nowadays are 'by and large, doing no more than finessing the templates which Derick Thomson and his team created all those years ago'.[1] In 1966, Thomson himself made a list of the most important tasks a writer working in a minoritised language should carry out: 'to increase the range of writing in that language, to provide a minimum bulk of such writing, to express the ethos of his society but also to interpret the outside world to it, and to satirise it periodically'.[2]

He exerted himself to fulfil these assignments (and many more) and to provide opportunities and encouragement for others to do likewise, and, as this book has tried to illustrate, he succeeded in carrying out much of what he attempted, although some of the initiatives did not always achieve immediate resonance or inspire followers. The tendency of being ahead of his time had the effect that what he proposed during the most active periods of his career was only accomplished decades later, and he did not play an active role in the major developments regarding the provisions for Gaelic in Scotland in the period 1985 to 2012, including the passing of the *Gaelic Language (Scotland) Act 2005* and the launch of BBC Alba in 2008.

Had Thomson lived to be a hundred, he would have witnessed some satisfying events and tendencies, in the Gaelic world and in Scotland, and others that would have likely merited some sharp commentary. This short concluding chapter touches on selected developments in the last decade, i.e. the ten years between Thomson's death and the completion of this study, discusses Thomson's legacy and suggests possible directions for future work.

---

[1] 'Appreciation of Professor Derick S. Thomson: funeral oration, as delivered', <http://meekwrite.blogspot.cz/2013/04/appreciation-of-professor-derick-s.html>. Meek himself followed on Thomson's work by preparing the 2002 report *A Fresh Start for Gaelic*, which advocated for the establishment of new development board, substantial increase in educational funding, and the introduction of a Gaelic language act.
[2] Thomson, 'The Role of the Writer', 271.

Gaelic and Scottish nationalism

A major disappointment, given the hopes Thomson was putting into the SNP as the only political force likely to take substantial steps on behalf of Gaelic, would be the party's continuing lack of decisive action on behalf of the language.[3] As McLeod notes:

> Although the SNP's coming to power in 2007 was a landmark in Scottish political history, in relation to Gaelic there has been ongoing broad continuity in policy from the late 1980s onwards. The SNP government has not introduced any major new policy initiatives concerning Gaelic. Instead, the previous pattern of path-dependent, incremental development of existing policies, originating in the 1980s, has continued, with successive improvements to existing programmes and structures building upon each other.[4]

McLeod also observes the SNP's lukewarm attitude to Gaelic and that its provision for both Scots and Gaelic leaves much to be desired, a tendency illustrated for instance by the fact that the government refused to produce a Gaelic version of the ballot paper for the 2014 independence referendum.[5] One can only imagine what sort of commentary in a *Gairm* editorial this decision would have provoked, had the magazine still existed and had Thomson been alive to write it. The new Gaelic plan for the period 2023–28 is being consulted, and the Scottish parliament, through its bilingual website, offers various ways in which Gaelic can be used in contact with the body or within its operations,[6] but substantial steps, like establishing a dedicated ministerial position for Scotland's languages, similar to the Gaelic Secretariat proposed in the 1978 SNP Gaelic Policy, still remain to be taken. Thomson's vision that Gaelic culture should be presented to the wider world through cultural institutes similar to the British Council may be yet achieved, depending on the future political status of Scotland, but even within the current legislative framework initiatives in the realm of cultural diplomacy could be more substantial and creative.

The results of the two referenda, on Scottish independence in 2014 and on EU membership in 2016, would have come as a severe blow to Thomson due to his nationalist stance and also his pro-European orientation,

---

[3] An example of a promising but rather isolated development within the SNP regarding Gaelic is the activities of Kate Forbes, who has since 2016 been an MSP for Skye, Lochalsh and Badenoch, and the first woman to hold the post of Finance Secretary. Given her constituency, she has also been Convener of the Scottish Parliament's Cross-Party Group on Gaelic, and has called for Gaelic to be given UNESCO status.

[4] McLeod, *Gaelic in Scotland*, 275.

[5] McLeod, *Gaelic in Scotland*, 275–8.

[6] 'Get Involved | Gaelic', *The Scottish Parliament/Pàrlamaid na h-Alba* <https://www.parliament.scot/get-involved/gaelic> Accessed 15 April 2023.

mitigated by continuing support of the SNP in Scotland, the ongoing discussion of a second independence referendum (tuned down temporarily due to the Covid-19 pandemic in 2020–21), and the party's progressive social and environmental agenda, support of human rights, and efforts to model Scotland on the example of Scandinavian countries and steer it away from Westminster Tory policies.

Gaelic periodicals and media after *Gairm*

When *Gairm* ceased publication in 2002, it had transformed into a mostly literary periodical, but Thomson's editorials still commented on current issues in Scotland and beyond, be it immoderate salaries in professional football, war crimes motivated by religious hate, or global warming. The obvious motive for discontinuing the magazine was Thomson's advanced age – he was eighty-one – and the fiftieth anniversary probably seemed like a suitable occasion to end the venture while it was still retaining its high standards. As Ronald Black notes, *Gairm* had an impressive readership of about eight hundred when it stopped appearing.[7] In the editorial to the last issue, *Gairm* 200 (2002), Thomson expresses the conviction that researchers in the upcoming century will conduct detailed examinations of *Gairm*'s contents, hoping the quarterly will live on and provide more encouragement to Gaelic writers. This examination is now facilitated by the database *Gairm Air-loidhne* and the ongoing digitisation of the quarterly's contents.

The decision to discontinue *Gairm* and not to look for another editor, apart from the unenviable prospect of stepping into Thomson's shoes after fifty years and having to live up to the expectations, was also influenced by the changed Gaelic media scene. As McLeod points out, 'following the closure of *Gairm*, two literary/cultural journals, *Gath* and *STEALL*, have appeared, but only about a dozen issues have been published between them'.[8] In Ronald Black's summary, *Gath*, edited by Donald Meek and Jo MacDonald (Jo NicDhòmhnaill), was a decided attempt to follow up on *Gairm* and was in many ways similar to its predecessor.[9] It chose the same size and format, the same frequency, attracted a number of the same writers, and featured a similar mixture of fiction, poetry, essays, stories, reviews and photographs. It also opted for a piercing name beginning with the letter 'g', as the noun means a dart, a beam, or the sting of an insect or a plant. The annual anthology *An Guth* [The Voice], edited by the poet Rody Gorman, was designed as a platform for the publication of new poetry

---

[7] Raghnall MacilleDhuibh, 'Bho Ghairm a' Choilich gu Gath an t-Seillein', *The Scotsman*, 3 October 2003 <https://www.scotsman.com/whats-on/arts-and-entertainment/bho-ghairm-choilich-gu-gath-t-seillein-2461335> Accessed 15 April 2023.
[8] McLeod, *Gaelic in Scotland*, 54.
[9] Raghnall MacilleDhuibh, 'Bho Ghairm a' Choilich gu Gath an t-Seillein'.

and translations in Scottish Gaelic and Irish by a wide variety of writers. However, neither publication shared *Gairm*'s punctuality and longevity.

STEALL [Splash] was founded in 2016 by the publishing house CLÀR, still keeping the same format as *Gairm* and with the ambition to sustain the same periodicity, but with a striking modern minimalist design and typesetting and a distinctly literary and cultural agenda. It started to publish new Gaelic writing, criticism, interviews and translations connecting Gaelic directly to other languages, avoiding English as the bridge. With direct translations from Irish, Hungarian and Russian, among other languages, and a diverse pool of contributors, *STEALL* seems to come closest to Thomson's vision of a forward-looking and cosmopolitan Gaelic literary magazine with high standards, with the other functions of *Gairm* being fulfilled by other media, both online and in print. *STEALL* has so far produced eight issues, the latest appearing in 2023.

It might be easy to attribute the hesitation and irregularity in the realm of printed Gaelic periodicals to the absence of an editor of Thomson's determination, stamina and all-round competence, but they also arrived at a time when, gradually, the Gaelic media scene is becoming much more diversified, the era of long-running printed periodicals seems to be coming to an end, and magazines that combine print and an online presence are showing more viability and resilience.

The dedicated TV channel BBC Alba and Radio nan Gàidheal provide news coverage and various kinds of content, aimed at both entertainment and instruction, and are accompanied by a number of affiliated online resources. In *Why Gaelic Matters*, Thomson argued for funding and promoting Gaelic films, and a number of initiatives, including the annual short-film festival FilmG, founded in 2008, have emerged in recent years. The publishing house Stòrlann issues and distributes educational materials, textbooks, simplified versions of literary classics and other amenities for Gaelic learners of all ages. The scene has become even more diverse with the widespread accessibility of the internet: the Gaelic mutation of Wikipedia, founded in 2003, offers information on a growing number of subjects, and numerous websites and social media outlets cater for the creation and sharing of content and facilitate connections between the increasingly international and dispersed body of Gaelic users.

Scholarship, translations, organisational work

After Thomson's death, no comparable figure with an equally broad range of activities and a comparably successful long-term career in so many realms emerged, and perhaps this is also a symptom of a structural change. The time of the polymath activists like Thomson seems to have passed and been gradually replaced with a more diverse and fragmented landscape, with more institutional checks and braces and official support but less space for the implementation of a distinct individual vision and far-reaching initiatives. Returning to Donald John MacLeod's observation that at three periods, the cosmopolitan and experimentally inclined Gaelic revival was centred around one distinct personality, it may be said that Thomson was perhaps the last one, and he was already commenting on the growing diversification of revitalisation efforts and commending them in *Gairm* editorials, as examined in Chapter 3.

In the realm of Gaelic scholarship, the situation has changed markedly when it comes to research presented and published in Gaelic itself. The bi-annual conference Rannsachadh na Gàidhlig [Researching Gaelic], with a growing number of contributions delivered through the medium of Gaelic itself, is one example of this trend. However, the substantial focused studies devoted to the major personalities and topics in Gaelic literature that Thomson called for in 'After Writing *An Introduction to Gaelic Poetry*', including a monograph on Alexander MacDonald,[10] have not yet materialised, and the historical dictionary has not been completed. Thomson also called for a modern comprehensive volume that would cover Scottish Gaelic literature as a whole, and such a general companion volume, is currently being prepared for publication by the Association for Scottish Literature, in the form of a collective monograph addressing the chronological development of Gaelic literature across the centuries, with chapters on main genres and selected topics. Another realm whose importance Thomson stressed was the application of the latest theoretical approaches to Gaelic writing. This trend has been growing too but is arguably still not as established in either Gaelic or even Scottish literary studies as it has been for decades in other academic contexts.[11]

When it comes to Scottish literature in general, Thomson would likely have welcomed the emergence of the International Association for the Study of Scottish Literatures, which was founded in 2014 and has since been engaged in promoting research of Scottish literature, including Gaelic, worldwide, and has organised major international congresses similar to those events Thomson enjoyed attending and drew inspiration and encouragement from.

In the realm of producing new literature, poetry, fiction and translation, Gaelic literature continues to grow, and the publishing scene continues to diversify, reflecting the growing needs of schools, pupils/students and parents, and taking advantage of possibilities for publishing connected with self-publishing and online marketing. In 1981, Thomson described the focus of *Gairm* as a general publisher whose purview included dictionaries, language books, poetry, fiction, biography, school texts and music, and

---

[10] Thomson, 'Reflections after Writing *An Introduction to Gaelic Poetry*', 17. Thomson also reproaches Ian Grimble for not fulfilling his promise to write a monograph on Rob Donn Mackay. However, Grimble's *The World of Rob Donn* did appear in 1979, i.e. five years later.

[11] In 'Reflections after Writing *An Introduction to Gaelic Poetry*', Thomson specifically calls for a 'comprehensive Marxist criticism' (17).

Acair as mostly focusing on schoolbooks and books related to the Western Isles.[12] Over the past two decades, the Stornoway-based publishing house has taken over much of what *Gairm* was producing, has diversified its production, and is currently the largest Gaelic publisher.[13] The Gaelic Books Council has recently celebrated its fiftieth anniversary and successfully continues to expand its activities, especially online.

Most of the content published is either Gaelic original production or re-editions of older works. Translations from other languages into Gaelic appear mostly in the form of individual poems or extracts in magazines, while the potential for systematically supporting translations from Gaelic remains so far overlooked. With the growing activity of various bodies, including Literature Scotland, that promote Scottish literature internationally through awarding publishing grants and arranging author visits, more direct translations from Gaelic into languages other than English may start to emerge.

Directions for future work

Given Thomson's habit of making lists of practical suggestions of what he felt needed to be done in the Gaelic world (and then readily taking on some of the tasks), it seems fitting to outline some possible future directions for the examination of his work. At the time when this book is being finished, two projects aiming to make Thomson's prose more readily available again are under way: an anthology of his English essays and another of his Gaelic prose writings. A major step towards the appreciation of *Gairm* and Thomson's role in the quarterly has been taken in the form of the already-mentioned project *Gairm Air-loidhne*, which involves the gradual digitisation of all the issues, including Thomson's numerous contributions.

A detailed contextual biography which would consider archival material and correspondence would provide not only a much-needed background for further analysis of Thomson's oeuvre but no doubt also a fascinating account of a long life rich in activity and achievement, contact with artists, intellectuals and politicians, and international travel, against the background of a momentous period of Scottish history of almost a hundred years, together with a more nuanced appreciation of Thomson's personality, which this book does not attempt to present, apart from what can be gleaned from the material discussed.[14]

A bilingual volume of complete poems with commentary and annotations, including previously uncollected pieces which appeared in magazines,

---

[12] Thomson, *Why Gaelic Matters*, 28.
[13] Mairi MacCuish and John Storey, *GBC@50: Sgeul leth-cheud bliadhna*, 3.
[14] For the time being, accounts of Thomson's personal traits can be found in works of Donald Meek, Ian MacDonald and Christopher Whyte.

similar to the editions of MacLean's work prepared by Christopher Whyte, would provide readers, both those with a command of Gaelic and without it, with ready access to Thomson's verse, and inspire critics to explore it from different angles and with the employment of productive theoretical frameworks. A certain amount of comparative work on Thomson the poet has already been done, as the introduction to this study summarises, but a number of possibilities still present themselves, be it Scottish poets of the same generation writing in Scots or English, or poets who worked in other lesser-used languages around the same time and from similar positions.

The comparative perspective might also yield new insights into Thomson's work in the Gaelic movement by bringing him together with other figures engaged in the revival of minoritised languages who combined revivalist agenda with a cosmopolitan and progressive outlook and were active in several fields; this volume has suggested some possibilities, such as the links to Micheál Mac Liammóir and Máirtín Ó Cadhain in Ireland or Kate Roberts in Wales. In fighting for recognition of a then non-official language in the UK and combining the 'role of the traditional academic scholar and the more engaged stance of a public intellectual determined to achieve cultural change', as Paul O'Leary puts it, Thomson was not dissimilar to Douglas Hyde, although unlike the first president of the Republic of Ireland he never carried out a political function.[15] Other productive parallels could be sought in minoritised languages and cultures within the Celtic sphere, in Europe and across the globe.

More engagement with Thomson's legacy within the contemporary and future Gaelic world would also promote values he was himself keen to foster, such as intellectual rigour, high standards, international cooperation, progressiveness and a cosmopolitan outlook, and a readiness to explore new possibilities, be they technological developments or literary forms. Apart from contributing to a more nuanced appreciation of his achievement, such explorations could ultimately enrich the current and future efforts to strengthen Gaelic in Scotland and inspire those involved in them. Perhaps sometime soon, a memorial cairn will appear near Hòl, to mark the not-so-great a hill near Thomson's childhood home, about which he wrote two memorable and vastly different poems,[16] and remind visitors of the necessity to erect 'tursachan dhar linn fhìn' (standing stones for our own century).[17]

When outlining the blank spaces of research into Gaelic writing in 'Reflections after Writing *An Introduction to Gaelic Poetry*', Thomson

---

[15] Paul O' Leary, 'Public Intellectuals, Language Revival and Cultural Nationalism in Ireland and Wales: A Comparison of Douglas Hyde and Saunders Lewis', *Irish Studies Review* 17:1 (2009), 12 February 2009 <http://dx.doi.org/10.1080/09670880802658109> Accessed 15 April 2023.

[16] 'Mu Chrìochan Hòil' (In the Vicinity of Hòl) from *Eadar Samhradh is Foghar* and 'Hòl, air Atharrachadh' (Hòl, Changed) from *Smeur an Dòchais*.

[17] Thomson, 'Tursachan (Standing Stones)', *Meall Garbh*, 22–3.

expresses his conviction that 'once Scotland is standing on its own feet again', such projects will 'suddenly seem more natural and more attractive, and the scholars will appear to undertake more work of this kind', and notes that Scottish scholars may find themselves racing with American academics working in Scottish and Gaelic studies.[18] Perhaps it would have amused and gratified him that a focused study of his own work and role in the twentieth-century Gaelic world in a way proves his point, although it emerged not from the USA, but from Central Europe, thus confirming the international reach and relevance of his work.

[18] Thomson, 'Reflections after Writing *An Introduction to Gaelic Poetry*', 17.

Bibliography

WORKS BY DERICK THOMSON

Note on available bibliographical resources: A bibliography of Thomson's publications up to 1993 is included in *Feill-Sgrìbhinn do Ruaraidh MacThòmais – Scottish Gaelic Studies* XVII (1996). A complete overview of Thomson's contributions to *Gairm* in all genres is available via *Gairm Air-loidhne* (Search for: last name: MacThòmais, first name: Ruaraidh, origin: Bayble, Lewis). This bibliography only lists items quoted or referred to in this study.

Poetry collections
An Dealbh Briste. Edinburgh: Serif Books, 1951.
Eadar Samhradh is Foghar. Glasgow: Gairm Publications, 1967.
An Rathad Cian. Glasgow: Gairm Publications, 1970.
Saorsa agus an Iolaire. Glasgow: Gairm Publications, 1977.
Creachadh na Clàrsaich/Plundering the Harp. Edinburgh: Macdonald, 1982.
Smeur an Dòchais/Bramble of Hope. Edinburgh: Canongate, 1991.
Meall Garbh/The Rugged Mountain. Glasgow: Gairm Publications, 1995.
Sùil air Fàire/Surveying the Horizon. Stornoway: Acair, 2007.

Prose edition
An Staran: Rosg Gàidhlig le Ruaraidh MacThòmais. Ed. Petra Johana Poncarová. Stornoway: Acair, 2025.

Short stories
'Dubhsgeir.' Recorded for the BBC on 9 August 1945.
'Ri Taobh an Teine.' *Alba* (1948).
'Foghar, 1976.' *Gairm* 17 (1956).
'Bean a' Mhinisteir.' *Gairm* 22 (1957).
'Mar Chuimhneachan.' *Gairm* 31 (1960).
'Tea Feasgair.' *Gairm* 35 (1961).
'Mòd Thorgaboil.' *Gairm* 36 (1961).
'An Staran.' *Gairm* 38 (1961).
'Aig a' Phump.' *Gairm* 173 (1995).
'Seann Iain.' *Gairm* 186 (1999).

Autobiographical essays

'A Man Reared in Lewis.' *As I Remember: Ten Scottish Authors Recall How Writing Began for Them*. Ed. Maurice Lindsay. London: Robert Hale, 1979. 123–40.

'Some Recollections.' *Spirits of the Age: Scottish Self Portraits*. Ed. Paul Henderson Scott. Edinburgh: The Saltire Society, 2005. 55–67.

Academic publications

Monographs and pamphlets

Alasdair Mac Mhaighstir Alasdair: His Political Poetry. Inverness: Bookmag, 1989.

An Introduction to Gaelic Poetry. Edinburgh: Edinburgh University Press, 1989.

The Gaelic Sources of Macpherson's 'Ossian'. Edinburgh and London: Oliver & Boyd, 1952.

Why Gaelic Matters. Edinburgh: The Saltire Society, 1983.

(Co-)edited publications

Ainmeil an Eachdraidh. Iomradh air dusan a bha ainmeil ann an caochladh sheòrsachan eachdraidh, gu h-àraid an Albainn. Glasgow: Gairm, 1997.

Bàrdachd na Roinn-Eorpa an Gàidhlig/European Poetry in Gaelic. Glasgow: Gairm, 1990.

Gaelic and Scots in Harmony: Proceedings of the Second International Conference on the Languages of Scotland. Glasgow: Department of Celtic, University of Glasgow, 1990.

Gàidhlig ann an Albainn/Gaelic in Scotland: A blueprint for official and private initiatives. Glasgow: Gairm, 1976.

The Companion to Gaelic Scotland. Glasgow: Gairm, 1983, 1994.

The Future of the Highlands. Ed. Derick S. Thomson and Ian Grimble. London: Routledge & Kegan Paul, 1968.

Academic essays and book chapters

'Gaelic in Scotland: Assessment and Prognosis.' *Minority Languages Today*. Ed. E. Haugen, D. J. McClure and D. Thomson. Edinburgh: Edinburgh University Press, 1981. 10–20.

'Literature and the Arts.' *The Future of the Highlands*. Ed. Derick S. Thomson and Ian Grimble. London: Routledge & Kegan Paul, 1968. 205–37.

'Reflections after Writing *An Introduction to Gaelic Poetry*.' *Lines Review* 49 (June 1974): 15–19.

'Scottish Gaelic Traditional Songs from the 16th to the 18th Century.' *Proceedings of the British Academy* 105 (2000). Published version of Sir John Rhys Memorial Lecture, read at the Academy on 9 December 1999.

'The Role of the Writer in a Minority Culture.' *Transactions of the Gaelic Society of Inverness* XLIV (1964–6): 256–71.

BIBLIOGRAPHY: SELECTED SOURCES ON THOMSON

Note: Every effort has been made to provide a comprehensive overview of available sources on Thomson, but it is possible there may be yet more theses, articles and other materials, especially reviews of Thomson's poetry collections.

Interviews

Blackburn, John. 'Interview with Derick Thomson.' *Hardy to Heaney: Twentieth Century Poets: Introductions and Explanations.* Ed. John Blackburn. Edinburgh: Oliver & Boyd, 1986.

Mitchell, Andrew, Derick Thomson and Iain Crichton Smith. *Taking You Home: Poems and Conversations.* Glendaruel: Argyll Publishing, 2006.

Whyte, Christopher. 'Interviews with Ruaraidh MacThòmais.' *Glasgow: Baile Mòr nan Gàidheal/City of the Gaels.* Ed. Sheila M. Kidd. Glasgow: Roinn na Ceiltis, Oilthigh Ghlaschu, 2007. 239–94.

Reviews and introductions

Hay, George Campbell. 'Review of *Creachadh na Clàrsaich*.' *Gairm* 122 (Spring 1982): 183–6.

Killick, John. 'Plundering the Harp: The Poetry of Derick Thomson.' *PN Review* 10:2 (January 1983): 38.

MacAulay, Donald. 'Introduction.' *Derick Thomson: The Far Road and Other Poems. Lines Review* 39 (December 1971): 3–12.

MacDhùghaill, Iain. '*An Dealbh Briste*: Ath-sgrùdadh.' *Gairm* 97 (Winter 1976–7): 55–61.

MacInnes, John. '*An Rathad Cian.*' *Scottish International* (January 1972): 36–7.

—— 'Review of *Saorsa agus an Iolaire*.' *Gairm* 105 (Winter 1977): 89–92.

—— 'The Poetry of Derick Thomson: An Introduction by John MacInnes.' *Bàrdachd le Ruaraidh MacThòmais* [Audio CD]. Perth: Scotsoun and Artistes, 2002.

—— 'The World through Gaelic-Scots Eyes.' [Review of *Creachadh na Clàrsaich*.] *Lines Review* 85 (1983): 11–20.

Neill, William. 'Review of *Meall Garbh*.' *Lines Review* 134 (September 1995): 62–3.

Ó Drisceoil, Proinsias. 'Fruitful Intersections. Review of *Smeur an Dòchais/Bramble of Hope* by Ruaraidh MacThòmais/Derick Thomson; *Oráistí* by Gabriel Rosenstock.' *The Poetry Ireland Review* 36 (Autumn 1992): 120–2.

Smith, Iain Crichton. 'Review of *Creachadh na Clàrsaich*.' *Scottish Gaelic Studies* 14:1 (1983): 136–8.

—— 'Review of *An Rathad Cian*.' *Lines Review* 36 (March 1971): 44.

—— 'Review of *Saorsa agus an Iolaire*.' *Lines Review* 65 (June 1978): 27–30.

Whyte, Christopher. '*Smeur an Dòchais*.' *Lines Review* 127 (December 1993): 48–51.

Appreciations, festschrifts, obituaries

Hayes, David. 'Derick Thomson at 90: Gaelic Poet in the World.' *Open Democracy*. 5 August 2011. <https://www.opendemocracy.net/david-hayes/derick-thomson-at-90-gaelic-poet-in-world> Accessed 15 April 2023.

MacAulay, Donald, James Gleasure and Colm Ó Baoill, eds. *Fèill-sgrìbhinn do Ruaraidh MacThòmais = Festschrift for Professor Derick S. Thomson, Scottish Gaelic Studies XVII*. Aberdeen: University of Aberdeen, 1996.

Meek, Donald. 'Appreciation of Professor Derick S. Thomson: funeral oration, as delivered.' *Passages from Tiree* [Donald Meek's personal blog], 5 April 2013. <http://meekwrite.blogspot.cz/2013/04/appreciation-of-professor-derick-s.html> Accessed 15 November 2014.

—— 'Derick Thomson: A Colossus of Twentieth-Century Scotland.' *West Highland Free Press* 2086 (20 April 2012): 18.

Williamson, Marcus. 'Derick Thomson: Poet and Champion of the Gaelic Language.' *The Independent*. 9 April 2012. <http://www.independent.co.uk/news/obituaries/derick-thomson-poet-and-champion-of-the-gaelic-language-7627275.html> Accessed 15 April 2023.

MA and doctoral theses

Macleod, Michelle. *Cianalas Redefined*. Doctoral dissertation, University of Aberdeen, 1999.

Poncarová, Petra Johana. *From the Woods of Raasay to Glasgow Streets: Poetry of Place in the Works of Sorley MacLean and Derick Thomson*. MA dissertation, Charles University, 2014.

Poncarová, Petra Johana. *The Political Poetry of Derick Thomson*. Doctoral dissertation, Charles University, 2020.

Study guides

Poncarová, Petra Johana. *The Gaelic Poetry of Derick Thomson*. Scotnote Study Guide. Glasgow: Association for Scottish Literary Studies, 2020.

Essays and book chapters

Black, Ronald. '*Gairm*: An Aois Òir.' *Aiste* 2 (2008): 94–119.

—— 'Sorley MacLean, Derick Thomson, and the Women Most Dangerous to Men.' *The Bottle Imp* 21 (July 2017): 1–7.

—— 'Thunder, Renaissance and Flowers.' *The History of Scottish Literature. Volume 4: Twentieth Century*. Ed. Cairns Craig. Aberdeen: Aberdeen University Press, 1989.

Byrne, Michel. 'Monsters and Goddesses: Culture Re-energised in the Poetry of Ruaraidh MacThòmais and Aonghas MacNeacail.' *The Edinburgh History of Scottish Literature, Vol. 3. Modern Transformations: New Identities*. Ed. Ian Brown. Edinburgh: Edinburgh University Press, 2007. 176–84.

Grimble, Ian. 'The Poet and Scholar as Journalist.' *Scottish Gaelic Studies* XVII (1996): 159–71.

MacDonald, Ian. 'Derick Thomson: Poet and Scholar.' *Scottish Language* 37: 2018.

—— 'The Poetry of Derick Thomson.' *Alba Litteraria: A History of Scottish Literature*. Ed. Marco Fazzini. Venezie Maestre: Amos Edizioni, 2005. 641–60.

Macleod, Michelle and Moray Watson. 'Ruaraidh MacThòmais: the Glasgow Verse.' *Glasgow: Baile Mòr nan Gàidheal/City of the Gaels*. Ed. Sheila M. Kidd. Glasgow: Roinn na Ceiltis, Oilthigh Ghlaschu, 2007. 216–27.

Macleod, Michelle and Mícheál Mac Craith. 'Home and Exile: A Comparison of the Poetry of Máirtín Ó Direáin and Ruaraidh MacThòmais.' *New Hibernia Review* 5:2 (Summer 2001).

O'Gallagher, Niall. 'Sùil eile air bàrdachd 'Ghlaschu-ach' Ruaraidh MhicThòmais.' *Aiste* 3 (2009–10).

Poncarová, Petra Johana. 'Derick Thomson and Ireland.' *Litteraria Pragensia* 33:65 (July 2023).

—— 'Derick Thomson and the Ossian Controversy.' *Anglica* 29:3 (2020).

—— 'Derick Thomson's *An Rathad Cian* (The Far Road, 1970): Modern Gaelic Poetry of Place Between Introspection and Politics.' Ed. Monika Szuba and Julian Wolfreys. *The Poetics of Place and Space in Scottish Literature*. Palgrave Macmillan, 2019.

—— '"Eadar Canaan is Garrabost" (Between Canaan and Garrabost: Religion in Derick Thomson's Lewis Poetry.' *Studies in Scottish Literature* 46:1 (2020). Also included in the collection *The Ghost at the Feast: Religion in Scottish Literary Criticism* (ed. Patrick Scott, 2020).

—— '"Nuair a Dh'fhalbhas a' Ghàidhlig" (When Gaelic Goes): Gaelic in the Poetry of Derick Thomson.' Ed. Aniela Korzeniowska and Izabela Szymańska. *Scottish Culture: Dialogue and Self-Expression*. Warsaw: Semper, 2016.

—— 'Old Women, Dreams, and Reversed Revivals: Derick Thomson's Gaelic Short Stories.' *Scottish Literary Review* 13: 2 (2021).

—— 'Ruaraidh MacThòmais is *Gairm*.' *Rannsachadh na Gàidhlig 9: Cànan is Cultar*. Deas. le Meg Bateman agus Riseard Cox. Slèite: Clò Ostaig, 2019.

Smith, Iain Crichton. 'A Sensuous Perception: An Aspect of Derick Thomson's Poetry.' *Feill-Sgrìbhinn do Ruaraidh MacThòmais – Scottish Gaelic Studies* XVII (1996). 356–60.

—— 'The Poetry of Derick Thomson.' *Towards the Human*. Edinburgh: Macdonald Publishers, 1986. 140–3.

Whyte, Christopher. 'Derick Thomson: Reluctant Symbolist.' *Chapman* 38 (1984): 1–6.

—— 'Derick Thomson: the Recent Poetry.' *Aiste* 1 (2007): 22–37.

—— 'The Gaelic Renaissance: Sorley MacLean and Derick Thomson.' *British Poetry from the 1950s to the 1990s*. Ed. Gary Day and Brian Docherty. London: Macmillan, 1997. 143–69.

Recordings of Thomson's poetry
Bàrdachd le Ruaraidh MacThòmais (Audio CD). Perth: Scotsoun and Artistes, 2002.

Films about Thomson
Creachadh na Clàrsaich. Produced by Anna Mhoireasdan. Interviews by Fionnlagh MacLeòid. BBC Alba, 2000.

Online resources
Derick Thomson: *Scottish Poetry Library*, https://www.scottishpoetrylibrary.org.uk/poet/derick-thomson/
Gairm Air-loidhne, https://dasg.ac.uk/gairm/
Ruaraidh MacThòmais: *Làrach nam Bàrd*, https://www.bbc.co.uk/alba/foghlam/larachnambard/poets/ruaraidh_macthomais/am_bard
Ruaraidh MacThòmais: *Kist o Riches/Tobar an Dualchais* https://www.tobarandualchais.co.uk/person/1092
Ruaraidh MacThòmais/Derick S. Thomson website https://ruaraidhmacthomais.wordpress.com/

GENERAL BIBLIOGRAPHY

Alston, David. *Slaves and Highlanders: Silenced Histories of Scotland and the Caribbean.* Edinburgh: Edinburgh University Press, 2021.
An Teachdaire Gaelach, 1829–1830. W. R. McPhun, Glasgow/W. Blackwood, and Maclachlan & Steward, Edinburgh: 1830.
Ascherson, Neal. *Stone Voices: The Search for Scotland.* London: Granta Books, 2003.
—— 'When Was Britain?' *Litteraria Pragensia: Scotland in Europe*, Vol. 19:38 (December 2009): 3–18.
Bazin, Fenella. 'Douglas, (Constance) Mona (1898–1987), folklorist.' *Oxford Dictionary of National Biography.*
Black, Ronald. 'Introduction.' *An Tuil: Anthology of Twentieth-Century Scottish Gaelic Verse.* Edinburgh: Polygon, 1999.
Brown, Ian. *Scottish Theatre: Diversity, Language, Continuity.* Amsterdam: Rodopi, 2013.
Cairns, Gerard. *No Language! No Nation! The Life and Times of the Honourable Ruaraidh Erskine of Marr.* Perth: Rymour Books, 2021.
Campbell, John Francis. *Popular Tales of the West Highlands*, Vol. 4. Middlesex: Wildwood House Ltd, 1984.
Devine, Tom M. (ed.). *Recovering Scotland's Slavery Past: The Caribbean Connection.* Edinburgh: Edinburgh University Press, 2015.
Finlay, Richard. 'Changing Cultures: The History of Scotland since 1918.' *The Edinburgh History of Scottish Literature, Vol. 3. Modern Transformations: New Identities*, edited by Ian Brown, 1–10. Edinburgh: Edinburgh University Press, 2007.

Ferriter, Diarmaid. 'Greene, David William.' *Dictionary of Irish Biography.* October 2009. <https://doi.org/10.3318/dib.003606.v1> Accessed 15 April 2023.

Gramich, Katie. *Kate Roberts.* Cardiff: University of Wales Press, 2011.

Hart, F. R. and J. B. Pick. 'Politics and Society between the Wars.' In *Neil M. Gunn: A Highland Life,* 108–24. London: John Murray, 1981.

'Historical Dictionary of Scottish Gaelic.' *DASG: Digital Archive of Scottish Gaelic.* https://dasg.ac.uk/about/hdsg/en Accessed 15 April 2023.

'Hugh MacDiarmid, 1892–1978.' *The Poetry Foundation.* <https://www.poetryfoundation.org/poems-and-poets/poets/detail/hugh-macdiarmid> Accessed 15 April 2023.

Krause, Corinna. *Eadar Dà Chànan: Self-translation, the Bilingual Edition and Modern Scottish Gaelic Poetry.* Doctoral dissertation, University of Edinburgh, 2009. <https://era.ed.ac.uk/handle/1842/3453> Accessed 15 April 2023.

Leerssen, Joep. *National Thought in Europe.* Amsterdam: Amsterdam University Press, 2010.

Lyall, Scott. 'Hugh MacDiarmid and the British State.' *The Bottle Imp* 18 (June 2015): 1–4.

Longley, Edna. 'Phoenix or dead crow? Irish and Scottish Poetry Magazines, 1945–2000.' *Modern Irish and Scottish Poetry*, edited by Peter Mackay, Edna Longley and Fran Brearton. Cambridge: Cambridge University Press, 2011.

Loughran, Anne. 'Bibliography of the Non-Traditional Creative Gaelic Skye Prose: *An Cabairneach.' Gaelic Literature of the Isle of Skye: an Annotated Bibliography*, 2018. <http://www.skyelit.co.uk/prose/creat2.html> Accessed 15 April 2023.

Lynch, Peter. *SNP: The History of the Scottish National Party.* Cardiff: Welsh Academic Press, 2002.

MacAulay, Donald, ed. *Nua-bhàrdachd Ghàidhlig/Modern Scottish Gaelic Poems.* Edinburgh: Canongate Books, 1995.

—— *The Celtic Languages.* Cambridge: Cambridge University Press, 1992.

MacCuish, Màiri and John Storey, eds. *GBC@50: A Unique Insight into Fifty Years of The Gaelic Books Council.* Glasgow: The Gaelic Books Council, 2018.

MacDonald, Murdo. *Patrick Geddes's Intellectual Origins.* Edinburgh: Edinburgh University Press, 2020.

MacilleDhuibh, Raghnall. 'Bho Ghairm a' Choilich gu Gath an t-Seillein.' *The Scotsman*, 3 October 2003. <https://www.scotsman.com/whats-on/arts-and-entertainment/bho-ghairm-choilich-gu-gath-t-seillein-2461335> Accessed 15 April 2023.

Mackay, Peter. *Sorley MacLean.* Aberdeen: AHRC Centre for Irish and Scottish Studies, 2010.

MacKinnon, Kenneth. 'A Century on the Census: Gaelic in Twentieth-Century Focus', *Gaelic and Scots in Harmony: Proceedings of the Second*

International Conference on the Languages of Scotland, edited by Derick Thomson. Glasgow: Department of Celtic, University of Glasgow, 1990.

—— *Gaelic: A Past & Future Prospect*. Edinburgh: Saltire Society, 1991.

—— *Language, Education and Social Processes in a Gaelic Community*. London: Routledge & Kegan Paul, 1977.

MacLean, Sorley. *Caoir Gheal Leumraich/White Leaping Flame. Sorley MacLean/Somhairle MacGill-Eain: Collected Poems*, edited by Emma Dymock and Christopher Whyte. Edinburgh: Polygon, 2011.

—— *Ris A' Bhruthaich: The Criticism and Prose Writings of Sorley MacLean*, edited by William Gillies. Stornoway: Acair, 1997.

MacLeod, John Donald. *Dualchas an Aghaidh nan Creag: The Gaelic Revival 1890–2020*. Inverness: Clò Bheag, 2011.

—— 'Gaelic Prose.' *Transactions of the Gaelic Society of Inverness* XLIX (1976): 198–230.

—— *Twentieth Century Gaelic literature: a description, comprising critical study and a comprehensive bibliography*. Doctoral dissertation. University of Glasgow, 1969.

Macleod, Michelle and Moray Watson, eds. *The Edinburgh Companion to the Gaelic Language*. Edinburgh: Edinburgh University Press, 2010.

McLeod, Wilson. *Gaelic in Scotland: Policies, Movements, Ideologies*. Edinburgh: Edinburgh University Press, 2020.

Macura, Vladimír. *Znamení zrodu*. Prague: H+H, 1995.

Márkus, Gilbert. *Conceiving a Nation: Scotland to AD 900*. Edinburgh: Edinburgh University Press, 2017.

Markus, Radvan. 'Micheál mac Liammóir, the Irish Language, and the Idea of Freedom.' *A Stage of Emancipation: Change and Progress at the Dublin Gate Theatre*, edited by Marguérite Corporaal and Ruud van den Beuken. Liverpool: Liverpool University Press, 2021.

—— 'Máirtín Ó Cadhain and Scotland.' *Litteraria Pragensia* 33:65 (July 2023).

Meek, Donald. 'Introduction.' *Caran An-t-Saoghail/The Wiles of the World: An Anthology of Nineteenth Century Gaelic Verse*. Edinburgh: Birlinn, 2003.

—— 'Saints and Scarecrows: The Churches and Gaelic Culture in the Highlands since 1560.' *Scottish Bulletin of Evangelical Theology* 14 (1996): 3–22.

O'Leary, Paul. 'Public Intellectuals, Language Revival and Cultural Nationalism in Ireland and Wales: A Comparison of Douglas Hyde and Saunders Lewis.' *Irish Studies Review* 17:1 (2009), 12 February 2009. <http://dx.doi.org/10.1080/09670880802658109> Accessed 15 April 2023.

Phillips, Kate. *Bought and Sold: Slavery, Scotland and Jamaica*. Edinburgh: Luath Press, 2022.

Piette, Gwenno. 'Breton Literature During the German Occupation

(1940–1944): Reflections of Collaboration?' Conference paper, 'Celtic Literature in the 20th Century', University of Ulster, 2000. <https://www.aber.ac.uk/mercator/images/breton_literature_during_German_Occupation.pdf.> Accessed 15 April 2023.
Pittock, Murray. *The Invention of Scotland: The Stuart Myth and the Scottish Identity.* London: Routledge, 2014.
—— *The Road to Independence? Scotland since the Sixties.* London: Reaktion Books, 2008.
—— 'What is a National Culture?' *Litteraria Pragensia: Scotland in Europe* 19:38 (December 2009): 30–47.
Procházka, Martin. 'Národ a nacionalismus ve věku globalizace.' In Benedict Anderson, *Představy společenství,* translated by Petr Fantys. Prague: Karolinum, 2008.
Richards, Eric. *The Highland Clearances.* Edinburgh: Birlinn, 2008.
Ross, Susan. *The Standardisation of Scottish Gaelic Orthography 1750–2007: A Corpus Approach.* Doctoral dissertation, University of Glasgow, 2016.
Shaw, Michael. *The Fin-de-Siècle Scottish Revival: Romance, Decadence and Celtic Identity.* Edinburgh: Edinburgh University Press, 2020.
Sher, Richard B. 'Percy, Shaw and the Ferguson "Cheat": National Prejudice in the Ossian Wars.' *Ossian Revisited,* edited by Howard Gaskill. Edinburgh: Edinburgh University Press, 1991.
Smith, Anthony D. *Nationalism and Modernism.* London: Routledge, 1998.
—— *The Nation in History: Historiographical Debates about Ethnicity and Nationalism.* UPNE, 2000.
Smith, Iain. 'A Hebridean Bohemian in Rose Street.' *Scottish Review.* Originally published 2014. Republished online 8 August 2018. <https://www.scottishreview.net//IainSmithannals441a.html> Accessed 15 April 2023.
Stafford, Fiona. *The Sublime Savage: A Study of James Macpherson and the Poems of Ossian.* Edinburgh: Edinburgh University Press, 1988.
Stroh, Silke. *Uneasy Subjects: Postcolonialism and Scottish Gaelic Poetry.* Amsterdam: Rodopi, 2009.
Titley, Alan. 'The Ravelling of Narratives: Irish and Scottish Gaelic Life Stories Compared.' *Nailing Theses: Selected Essays.* Belfast: Lagan Press, 2011.
Wall, Ian. *Twelve Poets at Edinburgh Park.* Edinburgh: Scottish National Galleries, 2005.
Watson, Moray. *An Introduction to Gaelic Fiction.* Edinburgh: Edinburgh University Press, 2011.
Williams, Gwyn. *When Was Wales?: A History of the Welsh.* London: Penguin Books, 1985.
Witt, Patrick. 'Connections Across the North Channel: Ruaraidh Erskine and Irish Influence in Scottish Discontent 1906–1920.' *The Irish Story* 2013. <http://www.theirishstory.com/2013/04/17/connections-

across-the-north-channel-ruaraidh-erskine-and-irish-influence-in-scottish-discontent-1906-1920/> Accessed 15 April 2023.

Whyte, Christopher. 'Against Self-Translation.' *Translation and Literature* 11:1 (Spring 2002).

—— 'George Campbell Hay: Nationalism with a Difference.' *Gaelic and Scots in Harmony: Proceedings of the Second International Conference on the Languages of Scotland*, edited by Derick Thomson, 117–54. Glasgow: Department of Celtic, University of Glasgow, 1990.

—— 'Introduction.' *Somhairle MacGill-Eain: An Cuilithionn 1939/The Cuillin 1939 & Unpublished Poems*, edited by Christopher Whyte. Glasgow: Association for Scottish Literary Studies, 2011.

—— *Modern Scottish Poetry.* Edinburgh: Edinburgh University Press, 2004.

—— *William Livingston/Uilleam Macdhunleibhe (1808–70): A Survey of His Poetry and Prose.* Doctoral dissertation, University of Glasgow, 1991.

Websites

Am Faclair Beag <www.faclair.com>
Bliadhna nan Òran, BBC Alba <http://www.bbc.co.uk/alba/oran>

Index

Aberdeen, 10, 13, 81, 98
Aberfeldy, 160
Acair, 105, 129, 176
Aeschylus, 81
Alba (magazine, 1948), 65, 80, 95, 168
Alba (newspaper, 1908–9), 64
Alba Mater, 66
Akhmatova, Anna, 93
America, 146, 162, 163
Andersson, Otto, 97
Anglo-Celt, 50
Anglo-Irish, 50
Anglo-Irish Treaty, 21
Anglo-Irish literature, 127
Anglo-Scottish, 50
Aran Islands, 37, 60
Arvor, 62
Ascherson, Neal, 24, 26, 31, 56

Badenoch, 111, 112, 115
Bhaldraithe de, Tomás, 57
Bangor, 12, 55
Bannockburn, Battle of, 22
Am Bàrd, 64
Basque Country, 3
Bateman, Meg, 92, 93
Bayble, 9, 10, 11, 41, 65, 95, 169
Bayble Herald, 65
BBC ALBA, 21, 80, 171, 174
Bernera Riots, 156
Black, Ronald (Raghnall MacilleDhuibh), 2, 5, 69, 73, 110, 127, 173
Blackburn, John, 127
Blackwell, Thomas, 115
Book of the Dean of Lismore, 110, 111
Books of Clanranald, 111
Bòrd na Gàidhlig, 21
Borges, Jorge Luis, 69
Boyd, Mark Alexander, 127

Braes, 6, 156
Bradford, 12
Brahms, Johannes, 116
Breton language, 16, 94, 120
Breton literature, 62
British Academy, 14
British Army, 12, 19, 169
Burns, Norman (Tormod Burns), 93, 125
Burns, Robert, 53, 93
Byrne, Michel, 133, 137
Byron, George Gordon, 116

An Cabairneach, 69
Caesar, Julius, 114
Callanish Stones, 156, 160
Cameron, Morven (Morven Chamshron), 90
Campbell, John Francis (Iain Frangan Caimbeul), 112
Campbell, John Lorne (Iain Latharna Chaimbeul), 66, 81, 109, 120
Campbell, Norman (Tormod Caimbeul), 103, 111
Canada, 96, 97, 109, 163
Cape Breton, 19, 96
Cardiff, 49
Carloway, 101
Carmichael, Alexander (Alasdair MacGilleMhìcheil), 48
Catherine McCaig Trust, 121, 128
Catullus, 163
Cavafy, Constantine, 93
Celtic languages, 16, 47, 76, 98, 104, 120
Chadwick, Hector Munro, 12
Chadwick, Nora Kershaw, 12
Chinese minority in Scotland, 30
Church of Scotland, 10, 11, 50, 63, 138
CLÀR, 105, 174

Clearances, 19, 103, 135, 136, 138, 144, 153
Clò Chailleann, 121
Comhairle nan Eilean (Siar), 67, 75
Comhar, 57, 61
Comann an Luchd-Ionnsachaidh (CLÌ), 74
An Comunn Gàidhealach (ACG), 10, 20, 44, 45, 51, 64, 67, 68, 74, 78, 80, 81, 83–6, 100, 101, 168
Comunn na Gàidhlig (CNAG), 74
Communist Party of Great Britain, 52
Conan Doyle, Arthur, 93
Congo, 142
Cornwall and Cornish language, 16, 54, 94, 104, 120
Cotrìona Mhòr, 65, 95, 169
Cranwell, 12
Crofters' Commission, 82
Crofters Holdings (Scotland) Act 1886, 156
Cuairtear nan Gleann, 63
Culloden, battle of, 18, 79, 111, 115, 119, 138
Cumbernauld, 161
Cunninghame Graham, Robert Bontine, 22

Dante Alighieri, 156
Davey, John, 109
Declaration of Arbroath, 21
An Deò-Ghréine, 64, 66
Derick Thomson Award (Duais Ruaraidh MhicThòmais), 6
devolution, 24, 50
Dick, Chrissie (Criosaidh Dick), 70, 92
Disruption (1843), 138
Diverrès, Paul, 65
Douglas, Mona, 62
drama (Gaelic), 39, 42, 43, 51, 58, 59, 65, 79, 80–2, 84, 86, 99
Dublin Institute for Advanced Studies, 13, 61, 120
Ua Duinnín, Padraig, 65
Dunbar, William, 165
Dundee, 161

Easter Rising, 52
Edinburgh, 6, 12, 13, 28, 29, 71, 99
Edinburgh Castle, 160
Edinburgh Park, 6
Education (Scotland) Act 1872, 20, 154
Education (Scotland) Act 1908, 20
Education (Scotland) Act 1918, 20
Egypt, 59
England, 12, 18, 25, 51, 52, 109, 141, 147, 168, 170
Erskine of Mar, Ruaraidh, 8, 22, 27, 49–52, 53, 64, 65, 66, 67, 69, 80, 83, 88, 90, 110
European Charter for Regional or Minority Languages, 21
Ewing, Winnie, 13, 23

Y Faner, 55, 62, 126
Faraday, Michael, 114
Faroe Islands and Faroese language, 104, 120, 126
Fay Shaw, Margaret, 103
Fèis Dràma Ghlaschu, 81
Ferguson, Calum (Calum MacFhearghuis), 83
Finland, 97, 98, 120
Finlay, Richard, 23
Fir Chlis, 81
First Nations (America and Canada), 96, 97, 163
First World War, 10, 20, 21, 141
Flower, Robin, 41
folklore, 12, 32, 33, 65, 89, 103, 169
football, 73, 102, 173
Forbes, Kate, 172
France, 36, 51, 59, 93, 98, 138, 142
Fraser, Ian (Iain Friseal), 98–9
Frater, Anne, 92, 125
Free Church, 138
Free Presbyterian Church, 138
Friggieri, Oliver, 126
Fulton, Robin, 107

Gaelic Books Council (Comhairle nan Leabhraichean), 6, 9, 15, 78, 121, 124, 176
Gaelic Language (Scotland) Act 2005, 21
Gaelic Society of Inverness, 35
An Gàidheal (bilingual monthly), 63
An Gàidheal (ACG magazine), 10, 64, 66, 71, 85, 110

Gairm Air-loidhne (Gairm Online), 72, 100, 102, 103, 173, 176
Gairm, 4–5, 7–10, 13–15, 30, 32–3, 35–6, 39–42, 47, 48, 50, 52–60, 62–105, 106, 110, 120, 121, 123–7, 139, 142, 145, 154, 157, 159, 160, 163, 165–9, 172, 173–6
Galbraith, Carol (Carol Nic a' Bhreatannaich), 13
Ganges, 153
Garrabost, 101
Gath, 173
Geddes, Arthur, 10
Geddes, Patrick, 48, 110
Germany, 59, 62, 75
Gershon, Karen, 104
Glasgow, 4, 6, 13–14, 20, 24, 34, 36, 70, 76, 79, 81, 95, 120, 123, 124, 145, 147, 156, 157, 158, 161
Glasgow Gaelic Drama Association, 81
Glasgow University Scottish Nationalist Association, 22
Goethe, Johann Wolfgang, 116
The Golden Treasury of Scottish Poetry, 52
Goodsir Smith, Sydney, 99
Gorman, Rody, 173
Govan, 20, 24
Gray, Thomas, 116
Greene, David, 61
Grimble, Ian, 76, 109, 121, 126, 175
Gunn M., Neil, 21, 22, 41
Gustavus Adolphus, 96
An Guth, 173
Guth na Bliadhna, 51, 64, 65, 66, 80
Gwalarn, 62
Gwasg Gee, 55, 62, 126
ap Gwilym, Dafydd, 127

Halifax, 96, 97
Hallaig, 6, 88
Hamilton, 23
Hanham, J. H., 104
Haugen, Einar, 97, 120
Hay, George Campbell (Deòrsa Mac Iain Dheòrsa), 88, 110, 125, 133
Hebrides, 6, 9, 17, 59, 96, 141, 151
Hemon, Roparz, 62
Henderson, Angus (Aonghas Mac Eanruig), 65

Herder, Johann Gottfried, 25, 116
Highlands and Islands Development Board (HIDB), 35, 67, 73
Historical Dictionary of Scottish Gaelic (HDSG), 122
Hogg, James, 64
Hòl, 177
Holyrood, 24
Home Rule, 21, 22, 73
Homer, 115, 116
Hong Kong, 71, 151
Hopkins, Gerard Manley, 41
Humboldt von, William, 25
Hyde, Douglas, 35, 177

Independent Labour Party, 52
India, 153
Indian minority in Scotland, 30, 158
International Association for the Study of Scottish Literatures, 175
International Celtic Studies Conference, 120
Inverness, 10, 20, 77
Iolaire, 20, 140
Iona, 40
Iran, 126
Ireland, 3, 5, 8, 16, 17, 18, 21, 27, 35, 37, 39, 49, 50, 51, 52, 54, 56–61, 62, 68, 80, 104, 120, 139, 146, 147, 150, 177
Irish language, 16, 17, 27, 35, 37, 41, 48, 57–61, 79, 94, 146, 147, 174
Irish literature, 57–61, 127
Italy, 75, 93

Jacobitism, 18, 21, 115, 117, 138
James VI and I, King, 18
James VII and II, King, 18
Jewish minority in Scotland, 30
Johnson, Boris, 25

Karm, Dun (Carmelo Psaila), 126, 127
Kay, Billy, 104
Kellas, James G., 26, 104
Keose, 10, 147, 153, 164
King, Dennis, 93
Kinsella, Thomas, 58
Krause, Corinna, 129
Kurds, 126

Lallans (magazine), 54
Lallans, 52; *see also* Scots language
Latin, 17, 52, 117, 163, 165, 167
Leerssen, Joep, 25
Leopardi, Giacomo, 127
Levenson, Christopher, 104
Lewis, Isle of, 4, 9, 10, 11, 12, 20, 32, 34, 69, 73, 96, 97, 98, 99, 101, 109, 139, 140, 141, 150, 151, 152, 153, 155, 156, 158, 160, 164, 169
Lewis, Saunders, 23, 35
Lhuyd, Edward, 120–1
Lines Review, 107, 128
Linklater, Eric, 22
Livingstone, Duncan (Donnchadh MacDhunlèibhe), 98
Livingstone, William (Uilleam MacDhunlèibhe), 5, 136, 158, 162
Loch Erisort, 10
Lochs, 10
London, 41, 59, 71, 100, 101, 168
Longley, Edna, 68, 87
Lordship of the Isles, 17
Lowlands, 18, 19, 20, 29, 54, 74, 75, 147, 152
Lynch, Peter, 50

Mac Liammóir, Micheál, 58–60, 177
MacAskill, Alexander John (Alasdair Iain MacAsgaill), 73
MacAulay, Donald (Dòmhnall MacAmhlaigh), 43, 67, 88, 96, 105, 106, 110, 122, 128
McClure, J. Derrick, 45, 53, 97, 120
MacCodrum, Margaret (Mairead NicCodruim), 90
MacColla, Fionn, 49, 103
MacCormick, John (Iain MacCormaig, author), 65
MacCormick, John (politician), 22
MacCormick, Neil, 104
MacDiarmid, Hugh (Christopher Murray Grieve), 8, 21, 41, 49, 52–4, 99, 104, 108, 119, 127, 165
MacDonald, Allan (Maighstir Ailean), 81
MacDonald, Alexander (Alasdair mac Mhaighstir Alasdair), 8, 46, 53, 109, 110, 111, 117–21, 152, 156, 165, 175
MacDonald, Finlay J. (Fionnlagh Iain MacDhòmhnaill), 13, 32, 59, 66, 69, 94
MacDonald, Ian (Iain MacDhòmhnaill), 5, 12, 176
MacDonald, Jo (Jo NicDhòmhnaill), 173
MacDonald, John (Iain Lom), 156
MacDonald, Margo, 24, 29
MacDonald, Martin (Màrtainn Dòmhnallach), 43
MacDonald, Murdo, 48
MacEwen, Alexander, 11
MacInnes, John (Iain MacAonghuis), 2, 5, 63, 94, 133, 137, 167
MacInnes, Paul (Pòl MacAonghais), 88
Macintyre, Duncan Bàn (Donnchadh Bàn Mac an t-Saoir), 10, 109, 110, 133, 161
McIntyre, Robert, 15, 22
MacIver, Donald John (Dòmhnall Iain MacÌomhair), 89
MacIver, Hector (Eachann MacÌomhair), 65, 80, 88, 98, 99, 133
Mackay, Christine (Cairistìona NicAoidh), 90, 91
McKay, Girvan (Garbhan MacAoidh), 93
Mackay, Mary Jane (Màiri Sìne NicAoidh), 92
Mackenzie, Anna (Anna NicCoinnich), 90
MacKenzie, Colin (Cailean T. MacCoinnich), 88, 101
Mackenzie, Compton, 49, 66
Mackenzie, Murdina (Murdag NicCoinnich), 90
MacKinlay, Fergus (Fearghas MacFhionnlaigh), 30, 93
MacKinnon, Jonathan G., 63
MacKinnon, Kenneth, 16, 31, 103
Mackintosh, Charles Rennie, 110
MacLean, Donnie (Donnchadh MacGillEathain), 43
MacLean, John (Iain MacGill-Eain), 66, 81

MacLean, Malcolm (Calum MacGill-Eain), 65
Maclean, Sorley (Somhairle MacGill-Eain), 4, 5, 34, 53, 66, 69, 87, 96, 103, 110, 127, 131, 133, 136
MacLennan, Dolina (Dolina NicIllFhinnein), 85
MacLeod, Calum (Calum MacLeòid), 85
MacLeod, Donald John (Dòmhnall Iain MacLeòid), 43, 51, 63, 64, 67, 73, 88, 89, 94, 105, 175
Macleod, Michelle (Michelle NicLeòid), 5, 16
MacLeod, Murdo (Murchadh MacLeòid), 43
MacLeod, Norman, Rev. (Tormod MacLeòid), 63, 69, 90
MacLeod, Ronald (Raghnall MacLeòid), 125–6
McLeod, Wilson, 2, 3, 11, 14, 17, 18, 20, 26, 27, 31, 33, 35, 40, 45, 47, 49, 51, 52, 54, 56, 63, 66, 68, 75, 76, 80, 83, 83, 106, 120, 123, 154, 163, 172, 173, 174
MacMhuirich bards, 111
MacMhuirich, Niall Mòr, 111
Macmillan, Malcolm, 144
MacNeacail, Aonghas, 4
MacNeice, Louis, 99
MacNicol, Donald, Rev. (Dòmhnall MacNeacaill), 110
Macpherson, James (Seumas Mac a' Phearsain), 8, 110, 111–17
MacPherson, Mary (Màiri Nic a' Phearsain, 'Màiri Mhòr nan Òran'), 91, 114, 161
Mac-Talla, 63
Macura, Vladimír, 26, 126, 131
Mairead Nighean Lachlainn, 91
Màiri Nighean Alasdair Ruaidh, 91
Maltese literature, 126–7
Man, Isle of, 17, 54, 62, 104
Mann, Thomas, 44
Manninagh, 62
Manx language, 16, 94
The Manxman, 62
Markus, Radvan, 59, 60, 61
Márkus, Gilbert, 16, 17

Matheson, Angus (Aonghas MacMhathain), 13, 76
Maupassant, Guy de, 93
Meek, Donald E. (Dòmhnall Eachann Meek), 2, 12, 28, 29, 122, 171, 173
Mendelssohn, Felix, 116
Millet, Jean-François, 156
Mocaër, Pierre, 65
Mòd, 9, 10, 13, 79, 80, 83, 84, 85, 101, 102, 168
Moidart, 117
Montgomery, Catriona (Catrìona NicGumaraid), 92
Montgomery, Mary (Màiri NicGumaraid), 92
Mount Everest, 153
Muir, Edwin, 53, 103, 104
Mùirneag, 140, 164
Munro, Donald, 156
Murchison, T. M. (Tòmas MacCalmain), 65, 110
Murdag Mhòr, 95, 153, 169
Murison, David, 11
Murray, John (Iain Moireach), 81, 89
music, traditional, 20, 33, 37, 38, 46, 53, 79, 83, 97, 169

Nakamura, Tokusaburo, 94
Napoleon Bonaparte, 115
National Party of Scotland, 22, 50, 52
Neill, William (Uilleam Nèill), 93, 104, 161
Neruda, Pablo, 93
Ness, 81, 101, 164
Nic a' Bhruthainn, Dìorbhail, 91
Nicolson Institute, 9, 11
Nicolson, Angus (Aonghas MacNeacail), 63
North Sea oil, 23, 29, 154, 156, 157
Norway, 36, 93, 96, 98, 114
Nova Scotia, 19, 63, 67, 97

Ó Cadhain, Máirtín, 61, 177
Ó Conaire, Pádraig, 93
Ó Direáin, Máirtín, 4, 57, 60
Ó Dochartaigh, Cathair, 122
Ó Faoláin, Seán, 57
Ó Huallacháin, Colmán

Oban, 29
Oftedal, Magne, 94, 97, 109
Oliver Brown Award, 14
Orwell, George, 87
Ossian Prize, 14, 60
Ossian, 5, 48, 110, 111–17, 139

Pakistani minority in Scotland, 30, 36
Pearse, Patrick, 21, 22, 49, 65
Perthshire, 160, 161, 162
Picture Post, 69
Pittock, Murray, 21, 24, 156
Plaid Cymru, 22
Plato, 156
Plockton, 6
Point (Lewis), 9, 12
Polish minority in Scotland, 30
Pope John XXII, 21
Portree, 69, 81
Pound, Ezra, 93
Prebble, John, 103

Radio nan Gàidheal, 174
Rannsachadh na Gàidhlig, 175
Raasay, 6
Raetoromans in Switzerland, 36
referendum 1979 (establishing Scottish Assembly), 15, 24, 30, 31, 45
referendum 1997 (establishing Scottish Parliament), 15, 24
referendum 2014 (Scottish independence), 15, 24, 172
referendum 2016 (Brexit), 25
Reformation, 18, 49
Rilke, Rainer Maria, 103, 127
Robert the Bruce, 22
Roberts, Kate, 55, 93, 126, 177
Robertson, Angus (Aonghas MacDhonnchaidh), 65
Rodel, 12
Romanticism, 19
An Ròsarnach, 64
Ross, William (Uilleam Ros), 10, 109, 110
Royal Air Force, 12, 141
Royal Society in Edinburgh, 14
Runciman, Alexander, 116
Russia, 51, 98, 153
Ruthven, 111, 115

Sáirséal agus Dill, 57, 59
Salmond, Alex, 24
Saltire Society, 45
Sámi people and their language, 98
Sappho, 164
Scandinavia, 61, 96, 97, 173
School of Scottish Studies, 12, 33
Scotland Act 1998, 24
Scots Independent, 21
Scots language, 11, 13, 17, 21, 26, 27, 28, 30, 45, 52–4, 76, 94, 104, 120, 127, 147, 154, 163, 165, 172, 177
Scots Language Society, 54
Scots National League, 22, 50
Scottish Arts Council, 67, 81, 121
Scottish Chapbook, 53
Scottish Education Department, 121
Scottish Gaelic Studies, 121
Scottish Gaelic Texts Society, 20, 118, 121
Scottish National Party (SNP), 11, 22–5, 28–31, 50, 84, 154, 156, 166, 172–3
Scottish National Portrait Gallery, 6
Scottish Office, 21
Scottish Parliament, 15, 21–4, 44, 76, 161, 172
Scottish Poetry Library, 6
Second World War, 11, 23, 37, 50, 75, 141
Secretary for Scotland (Scottish Secretary), 21, 81, 153
An Sgeulaiche, 64, 67
Shawbost, 99
Shakespeare, William, 93, 127, 156
Sikh minority in Scotland, 30
Sìleas na Ceapaich, 91
Sinclair, Donald (Dòmhnall Mac na Ceàrdaich), 65
Skye, Isle of, 6, 32, 156
Smith, Anthony D., 27, 32
Smith, Christina (Tìneag Aonghais Alasdair), 10
Smith, Iain Crichton (Iain Mac a' Ghobhainn), 5, 28, 41, 88, 89, 94, 96, 103, 104, 110, 150, 154, 157
Smith, John, of Iarsiadar (Iain Mac a' Ghobhainn), 109, 156
SNP Gaelic policy (1978), 43, 54, 74, 84, 166, 172

Society in Scotland for the Propagation of Christian Knowledge, 119
Solzhenitsyn, Alexander, 103, 127, 128
South Africa, 99
South America, 93
South Uist, Isle of, 32, 169
Spain, 92
St Kilda, 69, 160
Statutes of Iona, 18
STEALL, 173
Stephens, Meic, 104, 120
Sterenn, 62
Stevenson, Robert Louis, 64
Stirling, 22, 23
Stockholm, 95
Stòrlann Nàiseanta na Gàidhlig, 174
Stornoway, 9, 10, 11, 29, 98, 99, 129, 155, 176
Stornoway Gazette, 83, 99, 100, 101
Stroh, Silke, 19, 140, 141, 142, 161, 166
Stuart, Charles Edward, Prince (Young Pretender), 18, 117
Sturgeon, Nicola, 25
Sweden, 96, 98, 120

An Teachdaire Gaidhealach, 63
Thatcher, Margaret, 24
Theatre Gu Leòr, 82
Thomas, Ned, 56
Thomas, Dylan, 41, 99
Thomson, Derick (Ruaraidh MacThòmais)
  biography, 9–15
  books, authored and (co-)edited
    Ainmeil an Eachdraidh (Famous in History, 1997), 114, 121
    An Introduction to Gaelic Poetry (1974), 9, 14, 14, 56, 107–9
    Bàrdachd na Roinn-Eòrpa an Gàidhlig/European Poetry in Gaelic (1990), 14, 53, 93, 124–5, 127, 130
    Branwen Uerch Lyr (1961), 13, 120
    Edward Lhuyd in the Scottish Highlands (1963), 120
    Gaelic and Scots in Harmony (1990), 14, 53, 120
    Gàidhlig ann an Albainn/Gaelic in Scotland (1976), 8, 29, 33, 42–5, 46, 55, 74, 121, 130, 154
    Minority Languages Today (1981), 97
    The Companion to Gaelic Scotland (1983), 9, 14, 15, 48, 107, 109–10, 111, 113
    The Future of the Highlands (1968), 87, 121
    The Gaelic Sources of Macpherson's 'Ossian' (1952), 12, 112, 113
  essays and pamphlets
    'After Writing *An Introduction to Gaelic Poetry*' (1974), 107, 117, 175
    Alasdair Mac Mhaighstir Alasdair: His Political Poetry (1989), 118
    'Gaelic in Scotland: Assessment and Prognosis' (1981), 6, 30, 32
    'Mac Mhaighstir Alasdair's Nature Poetry and its sources' (1990), 118
    'The Role of the Writer in a Minority Culture' (1966), 1, 8, 35–42, 47, 54, 60, 61, 123, 131
    Why Gaelic Matters (1984), 8, 16, 45–6, 51, 53, 63, 81, 82, 114, 117, 174
  poetry
    An Dealbh Briste (The Broken Picture, 1951), 9, 13, 15, 99, 128, 132–7, 142
    'A Chionn 's gu Bheil' (Since the Picture is Broken), 137
    '"Anail a' Ghàidheil am Mullach"' (The Breath of the Gael on the Summit), 134
    'Faoisgneadh' (Unhusking), 134
    'Làraichean' (Ruins), 136–7
    'An Loch a Tuath' (The North Loch), 65
    'Smuaintean an Coire Cheathaich' (Thoughts in the Misty Corrie), 132–4
    'An Tobar' (The Well), 134–6

Thomson, Derick (Ruaraidh
    MacThòmais) (*cont.*)
  poetry (*cont.*)
    Eadar Samhradh is Foghar (Between
      Summer and Autumn, 1967),
      14, 15, 128, 136, 137–50, 170,
      177
      'Anns a' Bhalbh Mhadainn'
        (Sheep), 143–5
      'Cainnt nan Oghaichean'
        (Grandchildren's Talk), 144–5
      'Cisteachan-laighe' (Coffins),
        147–50
      'Cruaidh?' (Steel?), 138–9
      'Chaidh an Samhradh Thairis'
        (Summer Passed), 141–2
      'Dùn nan Gall' (Donegal), 48,
        145–7
      'Mu Chrìochan Hòil' (In the
        Vicinity of Hòl), 177
      'Rannan air an Sgrìobhadh
        as dèidh an ath Chogaidh'
        (Verses Written After the Next
        War), 139–41
      'Uiseag' (Lark), 48, 142–3, 145
    An Rathad Cian (The Far Road,
      1970), 150–3
      'A' Cluich air Football le Fàidh'
        (Playing Football with a
        Prophet), 73
      'Am Bodach Ròcais' (The
        Scarecrow), 150
      'Bha do Shùilean Ciùin' (Your
        Eyes Were Gentle, that Day),
        153
      'Cuthag is Gocaman' (Cuckoo
        and the Look-out Man), 152
      'Ged a Thàinig Calvin'
        (Although Calvin Came), 150
      'Dùsgadh' (Re-Awakening),
        150–1
      'Fàs is Taise' (High Summer),
        151–2
      'Murdag Mhòr' (Mucka), 153
      'Na Tràlairean' (The Trawlers),
        152–3
    Saorsa agus an Iolaire (Freedom
      and the Eagle, 1977), 14, 15,
      154–7
      'Ceud Bliadhna sa Sgoil' (One
        Hundred Years in School),
        154–5
      'Ola' (Oil), 156–7
      'Rìomadh' (Adornment), 156
    *Creachadh na Clàrsaich / Plundering
      the Harp* (1982), 15, 53, 60, 73,
      97, 128–9
      'Adhlacadh Ùisdein
        MhicDhiarmaid, 13. 9. 78'
        (Hugh MacDiarmid's Burial,
        13. 9. 78), 53
      'Àirc a' Choimhcheangail' (The
        Ark of the Covenant), 128
      'Alba v. Argentina 2/6/79', 73
      'Aodannan' (Faces), 97
      'Do Mháirtín Ó Direáin' (To
        Máirtín Ó Direáin), 60
    Smeur an Dòchais / Bramble of Hope
      (1991), 14, 15, 47, 61, 129,
      157–9
      'Air Stràidean Ghlaschu' (On
        Glasgow Streets), 157
      'Ceòl' (Music), 159
      'Cuimhne' (Memory), 33
      'An Cuimhne Dháithi Ó
        hUaithne' (In Memory of
        David Greene), 61
      'Hòl, air Atharrachadh' (Hòl,
        Changed), 177
      'Smuaintean ann an Cafe an
        Glaschu' (Thoughts in a
        Glasgow Cafe), 157–8
      'Stràid Tradestown' (Tradestown
        Street), 158
    Meall Garbh / The Rugged Mountain
      (1995), 14, 15, 33, 129, 160–3
      'Feòrag Ghlas, Tuath air Braco'
        (Grey Squirrel, North of
        Braco), 162–3
      'Leisgeul' (Sorry), 160–1
      'Meall Garbh', 33, 161–2
      'Nuair a Thig a' Bhalbhachd'
        (When Stillness Comes), 163
      'Tursachan' (Standing Stones),
        160
    Sùil air Fàire / Surveying the Horizon
      (2007), 14, 15, 47, 53, 129,
      163–5

'Àros nan Sean?' (Old Folks' Home?), 163–4
'Dà Chànanas' (Bilingualism), 164
'Dh'fhalbh Siud is Thàinig Seo' (That Went and This Came), 165
'Nuair a Dh'fhalbhas a' Ghàidhlig' (When Gaelic Goes), 165
'A' Siubhal nam Blàth' (Reconnoitring the Blossoms), 165
'Soidhne nan Tìm' (The Sign of the Times), 164
'Cridhe an t-Sluaigh' (The Heart of the People), 164
'Teagamh' (Doubt), 164
'A' Chuimhne' (The Memory), 165
'Toinneamh is Siubhail' (Twisting and Travelling), 165

short stories
'Aig a' Phump' (At the Pump), 95
'Bean a' Mhinisteir' (The Minister's Wife), 95
'Foghar, 1976' (Autumn, 1976), 95, 168–9
'Mar Chuimhneachan' (As a Keepsake), 96
'Ri Taobh an Teine' (By the Fireside), 65, 95
'Seann Iain' (Old John), 95
'An Staran' (The Stepping Stone Path), 95
'Tea Feasgair' ('Evening Tea'), 95, 145, 169–70

Thomson, James (Seumas MacThòmais), 9–10, 11, 64
Tibet, 153
Titley, Alan, 27
Tolkien, J. R. R., 93
Tong, 9, 164
Trinity College Dublin, 61
Turku, 97, 98, 120

Union of the Parliaments, 18, 21
Union of the Crowns, 18, 21

University College of North Wales, 12, 55
University of Aberdeen, 2, 9, 11, 12, 13, 14, 66, 121, 153
University of Cambridge, 2, 12, 112
University of Edinburgh, 12, 20, 121
University of Glasgow, 2, 10, 12, 13, 14, 15, 53, 55, 61, 76, 78, 97, 117, 121, 122, 123
University of Oxford, 98, 120
University of St Francis Xavier in Antigonish, 96
University of Wales, 14
United States of America, 36, 59, 67, 109, 178

Verne, Jules, 87
Voltaire (François Marie Arouet), 156

Wales, 8, 12, 22, 24, 31, 35–7, 54–6, 61, 62, 80, 98, 104, 120, 126, 177
Wallace, William, 23
Wars of Scottish Independence, 21
Watson, Bruce, 11
Watson, Moray, 90
Watson, William. J., 20, 121
Watt, Eilidh, 89, 92, 103
Watt, James, 114
Welsh language, 12, 13, 16, 23, 35, 37, 41, 54–6, 62, 79, 94, 98, 165
Welsh literature, 13, 36, 55–6, 126–7
Western Isles, 11, 15, 23, 50, 75, 79, 148, 164, 169, 176
Whyte, Christopher, 5, 6, 53, 88, 93, 119, 125, 127, 132, 133, 136, 142, 143, 145, 147, 154, 157, 158, 161, 166, 167, 176, 177
Wikipedia, 174
William of Orange, 18
Williams, Gwyn, 31, 56
Williams, Morris T., 126
Witt, Patrick, 49
Wolfe, Billy, 13

Yeats, William Butler, 41, 103, 116, 127
Young, Douglas, 11

EU representative:
Easy Access System Europe
Mustamäe tee 50, 10621 Tallinn, Estonia
Gpsr.requests@easproject.com

www.ingramcontent.com/pod-product-compliance
Lightning Source LLC
Chambersburg PA
CBHW051125160426
43195CB00014B/2346